PRAISE FOR *The Meaning of Sports*

"*The Meaning of Sports* is not only fascinating but enormously entertaining. A knowledgeable sports fan will learn more than a thing or two. I'm one and I did. The non-sports fan will discover just why sports are woven so tightly into the fabric of American life." —Fred Barnes, *The Wall Street Journal*

"[Mr. Mandelbaum writes] with clarity, in prose mercifully free of academic jargon. He explains why Americans are usually absorbed by all three sports, almost always rooting for the home teams. He examines the crucial power of our nostalgias, the ways sports help erase ethnic and religious differences, the corruptions of money and the use of performance-enhancing drugs, which form a hidden script in our scriptless dramas. In its way, Mr. Mandelbaum's book can help explain America to Americans, but it is also a subtle extension of his own expertise in foreign policy. It can help explain the United States to the rest of the often-baffled world." —Pete Hamill, *The New York Times*

"Why do we care about spoiled millionaires who happen to be good at throwing, kicking, hitting or catching balls? It is the underlying question in this fascinating, anthropological look at the three dominant American team sports: baseball, basketball and football. Known largely for his foreign-policy expertise, Mandelbaum argues that these games are, in fact, extensions of 20th-century America. Baseball conveys a nostalgic relationship to a lost agrarian past; football embodies the post World War II admiration for a force battling for turf, and basketball is the tech-era competition in which players can use quick thinking and agility to defeat bigger opponents. These games are us—an idea compelling to sports lovers and haters alike." —*Newsweek International*

"The most fun I had reading a book was with Michael Mandelbaum's *The Meaning of Sports*, which gave me a chance to understand something mysterious but all around me." —Daniel Pipes, *The New York Sun*

"Colloquial and readable...when Mandelbaum is explaining how the games men play reflect the society we live in, he is at his best." —*Washington Post Book World*

"A great book for educated non-fans and recent initiates to American sports to kick off with." —*The Economist*

"Sports fans will find this fascinating; others (you know who you are) will find a deeper appreciation and understanding of the dynamics of sports." —*Dallas Morning News*

"Insightful explanations for why we care so much about sweaty men (and women) playing games." —Sportsillustrated.com

"A sports fan who also happens to be a pre-eminent foreign policy thinker, Mandelbaum goes deep into the American psyche." —*Atlanta Journal Constitution*

"This is a rich and immensely subtle work of historical sociology." —*The Telegraph* (Calcutta)

"A . . . readable study of why Americans watch so much baseball, football, and basketball." —*USA Today*

"Recommended reading: *The Meaning of Sports* . . . has confirmed what Southerners have known innately since the single-wing: Sports is a religious experience." —*Arkansas Democrat Gazette*

"Whether riffing on baseball's nostalgic evocations, football's warrior ethos, or the way basketball—with its always unfolding innovations and 'network' play—mirrors post industrial worklife, Mandelbaum reveals the subconscious reasons we're drawn, moth-to-lightbulb-style, to stadiums and TV sets." —*Men's Journal*

"[A]n intellectual tour de force. . . It is a dizzying but worthwhile experience to read a book so information-rich." —*St. Louis Post-Dispatch*

"So *that's* why we sports fans are so devoted. Thank you, Michael Mandelbaum, for your dazzling and witty insight into this addictive American wonder—for giving new meaning to the games we play. I will watch my next jump shot with renewed awe." —Lynn Sherr, ABC News *20/20*, author of *America the Beautiful: The Stirring True Story Behind Our Nation's Favorite Song*

"A marvelous piece of work. This will be of interest to the entire spectrum of our society. A true history of sport." —Bill Walsh, former coach of the San Francisco 49ers, member of the Pro Football Hall of Fame

"Michael Mandelbaum has turned his fine eye and keen intellect toward sports—and shown us why they matter." —Michael Shapiro, author of *The Last Good Season: Brooklyn, the Dodgers, and Their Final Pennant Race Together*

"This is a great account of how and why sports have become so popular and important in America." —Robert Kraft, owner of the New England Patriots, Super Bowl XXXVI, XXXVIII, and XXXIX Champions

THE MEANING OF SPORTS

ALSO BY MICHAEL MANDELBAUM

*The Nuclear Question: The United States and
Nuclear Weapons, 1946–1976* (1979)

*The Nuclear Revolution: International Politics Before
and After Hiroshima* (1981)

The Nuclear Future (1983)

Reagan and Gorbachev (Co-author, 1987)

*The Fate of Nations: The Search for National Security
in the Nineteenth and Twentieth Centuries* (1988)

The Global Rivals (Co-author, 1988)

The Dawn of Peace in Europe (1996)

*The Ideas That Conquered the World: Peace, Democracy
and Free Markets in the Twenty-first Century* (2002)

THE MEANING
OF SPORTS

Why Americans Watch Baseball, Football,

and Basketball and

What They See When They Do

Michael Mandelbaum

PublicAffairs

New York

No part of this book may be reproduced in any manner whatsoever without written permission except in the case of brief quotations embodied in critical articles
and reviews. For information, address PublicAffairs, 250 West 57th Street, Suite
1321, New York NY 10107. PublicAffairs books are available at special discounts
for bulk purchases in the U.S. by corporations, institutions, and other organizations. For more information, please contact the Special Markets Department at
the Perseus Books Group, 11 Cambridge Center, Cambridge MA 02142, call
(617) 252-5298, or email special.markets@perseusbooks.com.

Book design by Mark McGarry
Set in Janson

Library of Congress Cataloging-in-Publication data
Mandelbaum, Michael.
The meaning of sports : why Americans watch baseball, football, and basketball,
and what they see when they do / Michael Mandelbaum.
p. cm.
Includes bibliographical references and index.
ISBN-13 978-1-58648-330-2 (pbk)
ISBN-10 1-58648-330-7 (pbk)
1. Professional sports—Social aspects—United States. 2. Baseball—Social
aspects—United States. 3. Football—Social aspects—United States.
4. Basketball—Social aspects—United States. 5. National characteristics,
America. I. Title.
GV706.5.M345 2004
2003070696

To Thomas L. Friedman, James Klurfeld,
Peter C. Kostant, Eugene A. Matthews, Alan Platt, and
Mark L. Wolf—sports fans;
and to Anne Mandelbaum, wife of a sports fan.

I have to admit it: I feel better when the Raiders win.

JONATHAN EDWARD MANDELBAUM, M.D., 1949–1976

CONTENTS

ACKNOWLEDGMENTS

MY GREATEST DEBT is to my wife, Anne Mandelbaum, for enthusiastically encouraging me to write a book about a subject of lifelong interest, and for applying her matchless editorial skills to what I wrote, thereby making this book clearer and more graceful than it would otherwise have been.

I am indebted as well to my agent, the peerless Morton L. Janklow, for placing the book, and to my publisher, Peter Osnos, and his superb team at PublicAffairs, Robert Kimzey, Gene Taft, Clive Priddle, and especially David Patterson, for bringing it expertly to publication.

David C. Speedie III gave me the benefit of his considerable knowledge of both American and British sports.

David Ortiz, editorial coordinator of *ESPN The Magazine*, and Sheryl Spain, associate director of communications of

Sports Illustrated, were kind enough to help track down references to articles in those two estimable publications.

After completing this book I discovered that several of the concepts developed in *The Meaning of Sports* have been applied by professor Robert Keidel to the world of business and management, notably in his 1985 book *Game Plans: Sports Strategies for Success*.

The Meaning of Sports reflects the influence on me of two social scientists. From one of them, my late father, David G. Mandelbaum, a professor of anthropology at the University of California at Berkeley, I absorbed an interest in the customs and rituals of different cultures, including my own. The other, David Riesman, a professor of sociology at Harvard University, taught a wonderful course for undergraduates on "Character and Social Structure in America" in which I served as a teaching assistant. That course, and many conversations and exchanges of correspondence with him, introduced me to the study of American society and culture. David Riesman died before this book was completed, so I cannot know what he would have thought of it; but I am certain that he would have been glad that I have written it.

INTRODUCTION

THIS BOOK has its origins in two incidents separated by three decades. One summer afternoon in 1966 my brother and I were making plans to attend a baseball game in San Francisco, to see the San Francisco Giants and their star players, Willie Mays and Willie McCovey. Also present was our maternal grandfather, who had emigrated to the United States from Eastern Europe fifty years earlier and had never to our knowledge displayed any interest in the game. We asked him, half-jokingly, "Would you like to see a ball game, Grandpa?" "No thanks," he replied, "I've already seen one."

One Monday night in 1996, I was watching a football game on television. My wife entered the room and stopped to look at the screen. Puzzled by something she saw, she asked me: "Didn't they just show that?" "Yes, they did," I responded. "They always show the play when it happens and then show it again, sometimes in slow motion. It's called instant replay." She thought for a moment and then asked, "Isn't once enough?"

These episodes illustrate two features of contemporary American society. One is that competitive team games play a significant role in the life of the nation. Millions of Americans devote considerable time, money, and emotional energy to following baseball, football, and basketball. The other is that, for many of their fellow citizens, their interest in sports defies rational explanation. Their intense preoccupation with men performing odd, combative group exercises all centered on a mere ball seems unaccountable.

The passion for sports can strike those who do not share it as distinctly eccentric, and even downright sinister. According to the writer Fran Lebowitz, "What is truly chilling is that there are a lot of smart people interested in sports. That just gives you no hope at all for the human race."[1]

The author Richard Reeves once observed that when American men gather, two topics of conversation tend to predominate: real estate and sports. The reason for the first is obvious—everyone has to live somewhere—but why sports? The answer to that question is the subject of this book.

The book's intended audience includes both those who, like my grandfather and my wife, find the question utterly baffling, and those, like my brother and me, for whom sports are so much a part of their lives that they would never think to ask it.* For the mystified, *The Meaning of Sports* is an exer-

---

* This is not to say that those preoccupied with sports are unaware of the gulf that separates them from people who do not share it. The journalist Simon Bourgin was once in a city where the World Series was being played and found himself in a hotel elevator with a well-known sportswriter. One of the other passengers

cise in anthropological explanation, which makes strange customs, in which they cannot imagine themselves taking part, intelligible by connecting these three games to more widely shared social patterns and human needs. For the committed, the book is like a family history. It traces the origins, the development, and the social functions of a world that, like the home into which they were born, is so familiar that they take it for granted and are unable to explain its profound appeal to them.

Why is America so interested in sports? What do these games mean to Americans? The answer that follows in the pages of this book has four parts. The first part—the first chapter—divides that large question into three closely related smaller ones. First, what human purposes are served by organized athletic competitions, which date at least from the time of the ancient Greeks? Second, what accounts for the rise, in the last decades of the nineteenth century, of organized *team* sports, matching two cooperating groups of players against each other, to a place of cultural prominence alongside long-established individual competitions such as boxing, wrestling, and racing? Third, why did the United States develop its own distinctive set of team sports? Baseball, football, and basketball all have roots, or parallels, in the major British team games of cricket, rugby, and soccer. When transplanted to, or reinvented in, North America these British sports took different forms. What is the significance of these differences?

continued

recognized the sportswriter and asked him which team he thought would win the baseball championship, but got no answer. When they got off the elevator Bourgin asked his colleague why he had not responded to the question. He replied, "I never discuss baseball with civilians."

The answers to these three questions apply to all three major American team sports. But these sports also differ from one another, and the next three parts of *The Meaning of Sports* explore and explain the differences. The questions that Chapters 2, 3, and 4 of the book address are, respectively, why baseball? why football? and why basketball?

Each of the three sports is a cultural practice, and like other cultural practices each has a social function. Each expresses part of the experience and some of the values of the wider society in which it is embedded. In particular, as the chapters describe, baseball, football, and basketball each reflects a particular era, with distinctive social and economic arrangements, through which the United States, and other Western countries, have passed: the agrarian, the industrial, and the post-industrial.

Baseball, football, and basketball are also American social institutions and, like other institutions, they have histories. Chapters 2, 3 and 4 therefore also deal with the origins and development of each sport. They chart the evolution of the rules of each game and the birth and growth of the associations—the leagues and conferences—within which competition at the highest levels takes place. These three chapters cover, as well, the most successful teams, the most important games, and the outstanding players and coaches in the history of each game. An historical overview of baseball, football, and basketball could no more exclude the New York Yankees, the Green Bay Packers, and the Boston Celtics, or Babe Ruth, Red Grange, and Michael Jordan, than a history of Hollywood could omit Charlie Chaplin, Marilyn Monroe, and Marlon Brando.

A few years after Elvis Presley died someone observed that the accumulation of memorabilia, legend, and rumor about him—the Elvis industry—was like the universe itself: vast, unknowable, and expanding. So it is with the literature of team sports. Where does *The Meaning of Sports* fit into this literature? Most of the immense outpouring of writing about sports, much of it printed in the pages of daily newspapers, concerns the teams, the players, and the games. For these voluminous accounts this book provides a cultural and historical context.

A smaller part of the literature of sports is polemical in purpose, with two subjects in particular commanding special attention. One stems from the uniquely American relationship between major team sports and institutions of higher education. Universities in the United States, although not in other countries, play host to teams that perform at a high level of skill and attract huge audiences for their games. To qualify to play on one of these teams an athlete must enroll in the university. Whether this is a match made in heaven, enlivening campus life and providing otherwise unavailable opportunities for education to poor, deserving, athletically gifted youngsters, or, on the other hand, an unholy alliance that, because the ethos and the commercial orientation of major sports are at odds with the purposes of the university, has a corrupting effect on institutions of higher education, is a fiercely contested issue. *The Meaning of Sports* embraces neither position wholeheartedly but does explain the circumstances—especially the national popularity of collegiate sports—that give rise to the issue.

The second of the regularly debated topics concerns the comparative merits of teams and individual players. Sports are inherently comparative. The purpose of a game is, after all, to compare the performances of the opposing teams. So it is natural to make comparisons between individual players and between teams across time. It is natural to ask whether Barry Bonds, a star of the early twenty-first century, is the equal as a baseball player to the great Babe Ruth, the prime of whose career came in the 1920s, or whether the Green Bay Packers football teams of the 1960s could have defeated the San Francisco 49ers of the 1980s.

Because there are no agreed-upon standards for judgment there can be no final answer to such questions, which means that discussions of this kind are destined to be what the Dutch historian Pieter Geyl said the writing of history necessarily is: "an argument without end."[2] *The Meaning of Sports* does not concentrate on these ongoing controversies, the subjects of innumerable conversations over the years, although the book does explain why individual comparisons are more common and more important for baseball than for football or basketball.

One other set of contributions to the literature of sports sees them through the eyes of the athletes themselves, telling what it is like to play the game. This book, by contrast, concerns what it is like to witness the game being played. The chapters that follow adopt the perspective that the military historian brings to war, surveying the broad patterns and investigating the origins and consequences of the clashes that are his or her subject.

This book's concerns are less the experience of the man in the arena than those of the person in the seats, the person who regularly travels long distances, pays substantial sums of money, and endures inclement weather to watch a game of baseball, football, and basketball in person, and who also devotes hundreds of hours each year to sitting in his or her home watching broadcasts of such games on television. *The Meaning of Sports* tells why so many Americans watch these games, and what they see when they do.

CHAPTER I

A Variety of Religious Experience

We sell fun. We sell the answer to "What do you want
to do tonight?"

MARK CUBAN, *Owner, Dallas Mavericks basketball team*[1]

A MODERN CREATION

Baseball, football, and basketball loom large in American life.
The annual professional football championship game, the
Super Bowl, regularly attracts the largest television audience
of the year: As many as half of all Americans tune in to watch
it.[2] The attention that team sports command is not only
broad, it is also intense. A Web site for loyal supporters of
the perennially unsuccessful Chicago Cubs baseball team
called CubsAnonymous offers a 12-step program for curing
an addiction to the team.[3] Why are these sports so important? Why do people invest so much of their time, money,[4]
and emotional energy in following them? Why do team
sports mean so much to Americans, and what is it that they
mean?

One way to begin to answer these questions is to note

that baseball, basketball, and football are distinctly modern creations. It is the modern era of world history, the era created by the vast political changes inspired by the French Revolution and the even more sweeping alterations triggered by the industrial revolution, that made them possible.

An essential feature of modern life, and a prerequisite for the rise of team sports, is longer childhoods. For almost all of human history, children joined the workforce as soon as they were physically able to do so. Only in the nineteenth century did the period between birth and work stretch beyond a few years. In the time that became available to them, children learned, among many other things, to play baseball, football, and basketball. Often they associated childhood—for many people the happiest, most carefree years of their lives—with the games they played then. This nostalgia for childhood often sustained their interest in these games into their adult lives. Watching others play these games became a way of recapturing their own past.

Beginning in the nineteenth century, a great part of American childhoods came to be spent in another modern innovation—public school. The industrial revolution created a world in which the skills needed for productive work could no longer all be acquired within the family or in guilds. School provided the setting not only in which skills were learned but also in which games were organized. The majority of the spaces for baseball, football, and basketball, including many of the largest ones, belong to institutions of education. The association between sports and school began in the private English academies that trained the leaders of English society and the British empire. From them sports spread to institutions open to all children, first in Britain and then in North America.[5]

One of the most striking nineteenth-century developments in America was the growth of cities, which were also crucial to the rise of team sports. By bringing large numbers of people together in one place, cities created the pools from which both players and spectators could be drawn. In the twentieth century baseball, football, and basketball became commercially viable enterprises that filled large arenas with paying spectators. These spectators live mainly in cities and their suburbs.

The industrial revolution brought to the United States and to the world modern methods of transportation, and on these, too, the emergence of team sports depended. Beginning with the railroad, the revolution in transportation had the same effect on sports as on American business: It provided both with the means to become national in scope. Teams from one section of the country could travel to compete in other regions. Local rail transport, including urban subways, also made it easier for spectators to travel to games in their home areas. Baseball teams in the early part of the century built their arenas on street car lines. In Brooklyn, the need to avoid these cars while walking to the games gave the local team its name: the Dodgers.

Dramatically increased mobility led to the need for uniform standards. Just as customers in New York expected the same quality of automobile as those in Texas or California, so baseball games played in New York had to have the same format as baseball in Texas.

While team sports could not have come into existence without the sweeping changes that the modern age produced, the meaning of sports, the source of their powerful grip on the imaginations of Americans, has deeper roots. These games respond to human needs that can be traced back to the earliest human communities, needs to which the dominant responses for most of human history came from organized religion.[6] Sports and organized religion share several important features. Both address the needs of the spirit[7] and the psyche rather than those of the flesh. Neither bears directly on what is necessary for physical survival: food and shelter. Both stand outside the working world.[8] And team sports provide three satisfactions of life to twenty-first-century Americans that, before the modern age, only religion offered: a welcome diversion from the routines of daily life; a model of coherence and clarity; and heroic examples to admire and emulate.

DIVERSION AND CLARITY

The word sport is related to "disport"—to divert oneself. Baseball, football, and basketball divert spectators from the burdens of normal existence. They are modern forms of entertainment. Once virtually all of the diversion available to human beings came from organized religion. The writings that people read were religious, painting and sculpture had religious themes, and it was from religion that music drew its inspiration. The great buildings were churches, the great spectacles religious ceremonies. The days set aside for temporary escape from the daily routine had religious origins and religious significance.

The need for diversion became, if anything, more acute in the modern era. More people came to have more time to fill and in the confusions and traumas of a world of large cities and world wars they encountered new and different troubles from which to be diverted. Along with religion (and sometimes as part of religion), human beings have sought diversion in staged drama. Baseball, football, and basketball possess the defining property of drama, which is tension and release—that is, uncertainty ultimately relieved by a definitive conclusion. The prominence of the word "play" in team sports reveals their affinity with drama, the oldest form of which is, in English, the play, and the participants in which—the actors—are by tradition, like participants in games, called players.

Team sports offer a particularly compelling form of drama. The outcome of a game, unlike that of a scripted drama, is unknown. Few people watch the same play or motion picture repeatedly because after they have seen it once they know the ending. The tension is gone. But tension suffuses each and every game of baseball, football, and basketball. Moreover, in organized sports the tension carries beyond each individual game and tends to increase over time. Each game is part of a designated sequence—a season—the goal of which is to produce a champion. Both individual games and the season as a whole attract interest and attention. Spectators follow the first to find out which of the two contesting teams will win, and the second to learn which one will emerge as the ultimate champion. Suspense mounts because, as the end of the season approaches, games tend to become more important to the determination of the champion.

In this way baseball, football, and basketball resemble the oldest of literary forms, the epic. Like the greatest of them, the Odyssey, the protagonist—in the case of sports, the team—encounters a series of challenges that it must meet to achieve its ultimate goal.

Baseball, football, and basketball are powerfully attractive forms of entertainment because of another feature: coherence. It is easy to underestimate the importance in human affairs of coherence, which is the property of making sense, of hanging together. Coherence is not necessary to sustain life, as are food and shelter. It is not a cause for which people have fought and died, like liberty. But it is evidently a basic human need. All cultures have methods for making life intelligible to those who are living it.* For most of history this was a manageable task. In the premodern—traditional— world, life was, for most people, simple and predictable. It closely resembled the one their forbears had led. It contained little variety. A person lived his or her entire life in the same place, interacted with the same narrow circle, worked in an easily learned way—almost invariably in agriculture—and died at what by modern standards qualifies as an early age. The answers to the questions to which this simple pattern gave rise—what comes before and after life, and how should it be lived?—were supplied by religious teachings.

The industrial revolution changed all that. Human existence became far less routinized and predictable. People began to move about, change jobs, encounter others with whom they had not grown up, and find themselves in unfamiliar circumstances. Life for the average person became much more confusing. Indeed, almost the only thing about which a person could be certain was that his or her life would *not* duplicate the one his or her parents had led.

---

* "The strange opacity of certain empirical events, the dumb senselessness of intense or inexorable pain, and the enigmatic unaccountability of gross iniquity all raise the uncomfortable suspicion that perhaps the world, and hence man's life in the world, has no genuine order at all—no empirical regularity, no emotional form, no moral coherence. And the religious response to this suspicion is in each case the same: the formulation, by means of symbols, of an image of such a genuine order of the world which will account for, and even celebrate, the perceived ambiguities, puzzles, and paradoxes in human experience." Clifford Geertz, "Religion as a Cultural System," in Geertz, *The Interpretation of Cultures* (New York: Basic Books, 1973), pp. 108–109.

At the same time, powerful forces such as wars, revolutions, and convulsive swings in economic activity affected people's lives even more than they had in the past. Human beings found themselves at the mercy of social and political hurricanes that had not been predicted and that they could not understand, control, or escape. The modern era has been a time of disorientation, in which religion could not account for the vicissitudes of life as it once had.

Nor did art, traditionally an alternative, or at least supplementary, source of coherence, offer what was needed. The modern age brought incoherence to the traditional forms of artistic expression. The twentieth century was the era of free verse in poetry, stream-of-consciousness writing in literature, atonal music in place of traditional harmony and melody, and abstract rather than figurative art. James Joyce succeeded Charles Dickens, Jackson Pollack filled the place Rembrandt had occupied. The highest value of a work of art came to be regarded as originality; but what was original was also often obscure. For most people modernity in art served to mirror, even to compound, rather than to clarify, the confusion rampant in the world.

Indeed, the twentieth century intensified the informal division of the arts into high and low or "mass" forms, the second distinguished from the first by its accessibility not only to an elite but to the majority of society. It is to the second category that team sports belong. They offer entertainment to the masses, and a principal reason for this is that they are supremely coherent.

They do not, of course, explain the mysteries or clarify the uncertainties that pervade modern life. Instead, baseball, football, and basketball provide a haven from them. While they do not furnish a coherent picture of the world as a whole, they do at least offer a coherent picture of *something*. Each game is a model of coherence for two reasons. Each is transparent: spectators can see for themselves what is happening and why. And each is definitive. At the end of each game, the spectators and the participants know which side has won. While the news section of the daily newspaper may report the baffling and the unintelligible, the sports section features succinct histories that everyone can understand, with a clear-cut beginning, middle, and end.

In this way team sports resemble a literary genre that first appeared at roughly the same time that baseball began to be organized, in the 1840s: the detective novel.[9] Both place the audience in a familiar setting: Each game of baseball, football, and basketball resembles all the others in fundamental ways, as does every detective novel. Each novel has a stock central character for the reader to admire and with whom to identify: the detective. The experience of reading a detective novel and watching a game follow the same pattern: initial uncertainty yielding to a definite conclusion. At the end of each it is clear, as it frequently is not in life, what has happened and why. The world has become, if not necessarily a happier, then at least a more intelligible, place.

Detective novels are often turned into dramas and in the twentieth century technological innovation produced a new medium for drama. Films can reach more people more quickly than the most enduring of pre-modern dramas—the plays of the ancient Greeks and of Shakespeare—did in their own time. The history of movies runs parallel to, and occasionally intersects with, that of baseball, football, and baseball.

Both forms of entertainment reach very large audiences and are staples of mass culture. The same conditions provided the audiences for motion pictures and sports: the growth of cities filled with people with sufficient time and money to pay to attend movies and games on a regular basis. Both had a particular appeal to people who had come to American cities from other countries. No special cultural background was required to understand either. In fact, it was not even necessary to understand English to appreciate and enjoy what was happening on the screen, especially in the era of silent films, or on the field.

As industries, the two evolved in similar fashion. In both, power shifted, over the course of the twentieth century, from management to labor, a shift epitomized by the rise in the importance of the person representing the performer, whether actor or player, in contract negotiations—the agent. In Hollywood, at first the heads of the major production companies wielded enormous authority. They decided which films would be made and who would act in them. By the end of the century, however, it was the actors who had greater control over these decisions and they received enormous sums for their performances. Similarly, in professional team sports the players were at first at the mercy of the all-powerful team owners but ultimately came to command high salaries and have the right to decide for which team they would play. The shift had a common basis. Unlike most industries, the labor in movies and sports, at least the most talented actors and players, could not readily be replaced. The best performers acquired enormous leverage over the terms of their employment for this reason and another, related one: It was they whom the public paid to watch. Team sports and Hollywood achieved widespread popularity in the United States in the twentieth century because they offered the public something for which there turned out to be a large demand: stars.

Shining Examples

Astronomical stars, the ones visible in the sky at night and scattered across the universe, produce their own light and heat rather than, as with the planet Earth, relying on other bodies for illumination and warmth. So it is, metaphorically, with the stars of motion pictures and team sports. They attract attention by themselves. People will pay to attend movies or games in which they appear *because* they are appearing. When Michael Jordan, the dominant basketball player of the last decade of the twentieth century, ended his second retirement from the sport, the team for which he played, the Washington Wizards, attracted sellout audiences everywhere it played. The previous year, when Jordan was not playing for the Wizards, far fewer spectators had attended the team's games. This pattern resumed after he retired again.

Interest in movie and sports stars goes beyond their performances on the screen and in the arena. Newspaper columns, specialized magazines, television programs, and Web sites record the personal lives of celebrated Hollywood actors, sometimes accurately. The doings of skilled baseball, football, and basketball players out of uniform similarly attract public attention. Both industries actively promote such attention, which expands audiences and thus increases revenues. But a fundamental difference divides them: What sports stars do for a living is authentic in a way that what movie stars do is not.

Actors give scripted performances, which are designed by others and in which all cooperate to follow a preestablished course with a predetermined outcome. The tension inherent in movies, and all forms of drama, affects the audience but not, ordinarily, the participants. Players in games, by contrast, give spontaneous, unscripted performances in which two sides compete, with each trying to produce a different—indeed the opposite—outcome. Actors who appear to do dangerous, difficult things on the screen almost never actually do them. Stunt men and women take their places, and the feats are usually made to appear more dangerous than they actually are. By contrast, baseball, football, and basketball players really do what spectators see them do. And while the purpose of acting is to produce an effect on the audience, the purpose of playing the game is to produce a particular outcome in the arena.

The star baseball player Sandy Koufax expressed this difference clearly: "Though the game of baseball itself is an entertainment, I don't think ballplayers are really entertainers. An entertainer works directly with his audience, adjusting his performance to its reactions. The audience is the second party. We are in a contest—every one guaranteed to be a bit different—and we adjust ourselves not to the reactions of the spectators but to the actions and reactions of the opposing team.... The customers come to hear the entertainer perform; they come to watch us live a part of our lives."[10]

Because what sports stars do is real and spontaneous rather than contrived and predetermined, because the outcome of their efforts is unknown in advance to both audience and participants, the sports figure fills a role that responds to yet another need that religion once monopolized. Sports, like religion, supplies heroes.

Heroes serve two purposes. They are objects of both admiration and emulation. The two purposes originated in different eras of the long history of Western civilization.

From the classical period, the time of ancient Greece and Rome, comes the exceptional figure, the individual who towers above all others. He is the man who changes the course of history, such as the Macedonian conqueror Alexander the Great, or who accomplishes what many have tried to do but no one else has done, such as the most successful competitors in the ancient Greek Olympic games.

From the post-classical, Christian era comes the exemplary figure who embodies the virtues to which everyone can aspire and that everyone can practice. (Hollywood has offered the public both types: Charlton Heston as Moses in *The Ten Commandments*, James Stewart as the bank clerk George Bailey in *It's a Wonderful Life*.) Both types of hero, but especially the second, provide, like religion, answers to the eternal, basic question of how life should be lived.

Sports stars fill both heroic roles. They do great deeds. Team sports, especially baseball, are saturated with statistics, the quantitative measure of accomplishment, and the statistics of the games and the seasons of years past are the records that make it possible to identify the individual players with the greatest achievements to their credit. A player can also attain heroic status by a single decisive feat at a crucial moment. The Pittsburgh Pirates' second basemen Bill Mazeroski was one of the most adroit fielders at his position in baseball history, but is best known not for his career-long defensive skills but rather for a single home run he hit in the ninth inning of the final game of the 1960 World Series that won the championship for his team.

Outstanding baseball, football, and basketball players at their best also exemplify, at least when they are playing, universally desirable traits of character. In the second half of the twentieth century a term borrowed from social science came to be applied to them: role models.

Superior athletes seem appropriate role models, relevant to the tasks of everyday life, for two reasons. First, they train diligently to achieve the level of skill they display in their games. The universally applicable lesson of their example is that hard work brings success. Second, the star player performs under pressure. As he goes about the business of helping his team to win the game, other, almost equally skilled players are striving to prevent him from doing so. Baseball, football, and basketball therefore offer an example of success in one of life's ubiquitous tasks: overcoming obstacles. A typical letter to the editor of a sports magazine about a profile of a college basketball player illustrates the point: "It's great to see an athlete who has worked so hard and been so dedicated to basketball lead a Big Ten team in scoring and rebounding. He is a small-town boy whom all kids can look up to and emulate."[11]

English private schools adopted organized team games as part of their curricula in the nineteenth century because the games were thought to inculcate the qualities of character necessary for leading the country and managing the empire, a conviction expressed in the nineteenth-century saying that attributed a celebrated British military victory to the habits formed at its most famous school: "The battle of Waterloo was won on the playing fields of Eton."

An institution common to all three team sports, the hall of fame, honors the most accomplished baseball, football, and basketball players in both the classical and the Christian style. Each of the three professional sports has one of its own. Dozens of smaller halls of fame, celebrating the achievements of local athletes, are scattered throughout the country.

These museums honor exceptional players in the Roman manner, with their likenesses engraved in metal. The Roman likenesses were early coins, and their equivalents in team sports are the plaques with likenesses of star players exhibited in halls of fame and the cardboard cards, each with a photograph of a particular player on one side and information about his athletic accomplishments on the other, that are sold in packages of bubble gum.[12] Christianity honored saints by venerating relics of their lives—ordinarily a shred of clothing displayed in a church.[13] Similarly, halls of fame display the uniforms worn by celebrated players, balls used in important games, and other memorabilia.[14]

The parallel between sports stars and classical heroes and Christian saints is, of course, a partial one. Baseball, football, and basketball players do not change history, nor do they exhibit the full range of virtues that the roster of saints embodies. Some of those virtues—chastity, poverty, and humility, for example—are notable for their absence in many of those who achieve success in the athletic arena.

Sports stars possess a narrow range of skills but those skills have a potent appeal because in twenty-first-century America they have come to be rare. The United States is a country in which ever more people work at desks and ever fewer earn their living through physical labor. War, the ultimate test of physical qualities, is increasingly waged by computer-operated machines, with success depending almost as much on the sophistication of the engineer who designed them as on the bravery of the personnel who operate them. In such a world the largely physical accomplishments of baseball, football, and basketball payers stand out, and perhaps evoke an appreciation embedded in the human genetic structure for the skills necessary for survival in the wild.

The fact that, unlike movie stars, sports stars actually do what they appear to do also helps to account for their heroic appeal in the twenty-first-century United States. In contemporary America, appearances count for a great deal. The twentieth century saw the birth of a new profession, public relations, the purpose of which is to influence not what happens but rather how the public perceives and understands what has happened. New words entered the American vocabulary: *ballyhoo*, *hype*, *spin*. All refer to the deliberate and increasingly widespread effort to persuade people that public officials and corporate moguls are more trustworthy and effective, dramas more entertaining, and consumer products more useful than they actually are.[15]

Often it is not outright deception that public relations and its adjunct, advertising, practice but rather exaggeration. As the twentieth-century songwriter Johnny Mercer put it in one of his lyrics:

> *Hooray for Hollywood,*
> *Where you're terrific if you're even good . . .*

Because the achievements of baseball, football, and basketball players are, by and large, public, transparent, and measurable, the spectator can confidently judge for him- or herself which among them are terrific, which merely good, and which entirely worthless. Where these sports are concerned, the fog of promotional excess that has come to envelop so much of American life can be penetrated.

Along with star players' superior achievements in the arena, it was this quality of authenticity that, beginning early in the twentieth century, commended them to the advertising industry as spokesmen for consumer products. They carried conviction in touting packaged wheat flakes as "the breakfast of champions" because they themselves had earned championships. They could also effectively promote soup, automobiles, and laser eye surgery because their testimonials would attract less of the skepticism that advertising customarily provoked. Because the spectator could be confident of the authenticity of their deeds, the consumer could believe in the sincerity of their words.

But this is also true of the other, older category of sports that Americans watch, the sports, such as boxing, tennis, golf, and racing, in which the contestants are individuals, not teams. Like team sports, these individual sports offer diversion, providing entertainment for millions of people. Individual sports, like team sports, provide islands of coherence, with transparent plots and clear conclusions. Individual sports, like team sports, supply heroes, some of whom have graced the outsides of cereal boxes and promoted other commercial products. In the 1960s and 1970s the boxer Muhammad Ali was the most celebrated athlete in the world. At the outset of the twenty-first century that distinction belonged to the golfer Eldrick (Tiger) Woods.

Why did the older, longer-established individual sports not suffice to supplement, in the modern world, what religion had provided in the traditional era? Why, for the purposes of providing diversion, coherence, and heroes—and for what other purposes—do baseball, football, and basketball exist?

A helpful way to answer that question is to turn to the methods of the anthropologist.

THE RISE OF TEAM SPORTS

The anthropologist is a well-educated, specially trained observer whose purpose it is to visit societies different from his or her own—alien and unfamiliar ones—to try to make sense of them. Anthropologists customarily adopt one of two approaches to the societies they study. The functional approach treats the society as if it were a kind of machine and seeks to discover how the different parts fit together to make it work. The alternative, interpretive approach, sees the society as a kind of text and tries to decipher the meaning of its institutions and practices by connecting them to its dominant social patterns, of which the interpretive anthropologist considers them reflections.[16] An interpretive anthropologist, seeking to understand the social role of team sports, would ask which features of the modern world baseball, football, and basketball express.

One major feature of the modern Western world that team sports reflect is what the Frenchman Alexis de Tocqueville called "democracy in America."[17] By democracy he did not mean the now familiar but then rare political system of free elections and constitutionally protected rights. Rather, he meant social equality. In America he found a society that lacked the kind of hereditary aristocracy that had exercised social, political, and economic dominance in Europe for centuries.

While once the distribution of power and wealth was decided by the accident of birth, by the end of the twentieth century, in the United States, in Europe, and in much of the rest of the world as well, this was less and less the case. Baseball, football, and basketball reflect this overriding feature of modern society in three ways: in their origins; in the way the participants dress; and in the principle at the heart of all three games.

Officially recognized, formally organized, systematically recorded competition certainly dates back twenty-five centuries to the time of ancient Greece. During all but the last of these centuries, however, such competitions involved individuals, not teams, because individual sports were everywhere associated with society's upper classes, who had the resources and the authority to confer recognition, provide organization, and keep records. Horse racing, for example, came to be known as "the sport of kings" because of the monarchical patronage it enjoyed from ancient times. The association between horses and those atop the social pyramid, an association embodied not only in the ownership of race horses but in ancient chariot racing and modern polo as well, rested on the vital contribution the ownership of swift, strong horses made for much of human history to what the aristocracy valued most and on which its power and prestige depended: military prowess.

Games with racquets, the forerunners of modern tennis, badminton, and squash, were also historically the preserve of the wealthy and powerful. French and English monarchs played them. At the end of the sixteenth century Paris alone had an estimated 250 courts.[18]

At the oldest of all recorded individual competitions, the ancient Greek Olympic games, only men of noble background were permitted to participate.[19] Until the modern age only the wealthy had the time and the resources to organize competitions, to prepare for and to compete in them, and to set down the results for posterity. So only the individual sports they favored were part of history.

This is not to say that no trace of team sports can be found prior to the modern period. To the contrary, they too have roots that reach back well before the modern era. Traces of what seem to have been balls have been found among the artifacts of ancient Egypt and China. In Europe, team sports began as spontaneous, unorganized forms of play that sometimes became folk customs observed on feast days in which people without status or wealth could take part.

Football descends from a European custom, dating back to the Middle Ages, of dividing people into two groups, each of which tries to advance an inflated animal bladder to a designated spot by kicking, throwing, and carrying it. These events were less the organized games of the twentieth century than they were melees, celebrations, and occasions for frolicking and drinking—and sometimes for violence. The distant ancestor of cricket, the English bat-and-ball game to which baseball is related, seems to have been the rural habit of swinging tree branches at pitched balls while standing in front of tree stumps or fences built to contain sheep.

With the advent of the social leveling of the nineteenth century, the games in which people who were not part of the nobility participated came to enjoy the same status—recognized, organized, recorded—that individual sports had long had. Team games, like the people who played them, experienced a kind of upward social mobility.

The second way in which team sports express the social egalitarianism of the modern period is one to which anthropologists are particularly attuned: what baseball, football, and basketball players wear. In almost all societies clothing has denoted rank. Native American tribal chiefs wrapped themselves in animal skins that lesser members of the tribe were forbidden to wear. Officials serving the Chinese emperor had symbols embroidered on their robes indicating their particular place in the imperial hierarchy.[20] The costumes worn by the participants in American team sports reflect the social egalitarianism of the modern United States in a straightforward way: They are all fundamentally the same.

The generic name for such costumes makes the point. They are uniforms: They have a single design.[21] Like the citizens of Western countries in the modern era, the wearers of such uniforms are, in an important way, equal. None has a special advantage within the game by virtue of who he or she is outside it.[22]

At the end of the twentieth century the sameness of team uniforms produced discontent, which reflected a current of restlessness in the wider society. It seemed a way of enforcing a dull conformity and suppressing individuality. In the 1970s, in reaction, baseball players in large numbers began sporting sideburns, mustaches, and beards for the first time since the early years of the twentieth century. In the 1990s basketball and football players adopted a practice once largely confined to sailors and prisoners by having themselves tattooed. They began to wear jewelry as well, prompting one college football player to compliment his coach on the grounds that "He treats us like men. He lets us wear earrings."

When uniforms first became a standard part of team sports at the end of the nineteenth century, however, they expressed a feature of American, and Western, society—equality—that was still new and, in its way, radical.

While uniforms increase the visible sameness of team members, individual achievement in games allows some players to stand out. Similarly, in the modern world people tend to be rewarded according to what they do rather than by who they are. With conspicuous exceptions, hard work and skill count for more than the accident of birth.[23] Baseball, football, and basketball belong emphatically to the realm of achievement. Every game begins with the teams equal on the dimension that matters most: The score is always zero to zero. The outcome of each game depends entirely on what the players do during the contest. The winners earn their victory by their deeds. Team sports therefore express the principle of merit.

The preference for achieved rather than ascribed status, for making merit the basis of allocating the bulk of society's benefits, received a mighty boost from the French Revolution, which sought to disestablish the aristocracy. One of that revolution's slogans proclaimed the goal of applying the principle of merit to the world of work: "a career open to talents." While the French Revolution left a deep mark on modern society, an even deeper imprint came from the dramatic changes in the economic life of the planet set in motion by the industrial revolution, and team sports reflect these changes as well.

For almost all of the last ten thousand years, almost all human beings lived in rural settings and engaged in agriculture. The industrial revolution created a new form of work and a new setting for it: Men and women toiled in factories—and ultimately in offices—and lived in cities far more densely populated than the urban spaces the world had previously known.

Farmers had worked alone or with their families and followed more or less the same routine: planting, growing and harvesting crops, and tending domesticated animals. Industrial activity was and is organized along different lines. It brought to the world the principle of the division of labor. Industrial workers perform differing tasks, with the final product of the industrial enterprise being the sum of the many different tasks that they do. A single person can grow crops, but many people (or many robots) are required to manufacture an automobile. Modern industrial and bureaucratic enterprises can involve hundreds of thousands of workers. Such enterprises became part of American life at the same time that team sports were becoming established.

The principle of the division of labor has two parts, specialization and interdependence. Team sports reflect both, as individual sports do not. Baseball, football, and basketball players carry out different functions. In the language of sports, they play different positions. And unlike a boxer or a tennis player, each has to rely on others to achieve the goal of any competition: No baseball, football, or basketball player can win a game single-handedly. Team sports, like modern industrial life and unlike individual sports, require cooperation. Each team, like every factory, is a cooperative unit. But each game, and each sequence of games—each season—also embodies the opposite principle: competition. And that, too, is integral to modern life.

In the traditional world farmers grew food for themselves. In the modern world workers in factories produce automobiles for others, and the various automobile manufacturers compete to sell their products to the same people. That is how a market economy works. While local markets date back several millennia, the fully developed market system, reaching around the world, came to dominate the economic life of the planet only in the modern era, at roughly the same time that team sports were becoming prominent. Like baseball, football, and basketball players, almost everyone who works in a factory or an office is part of a team that not only practices cooperation among its members but also competes with other teams to survive and prosper in the commercial marketplace.

Another of the features that a modern market economy shares with baseball, football, and basketball is the presence, and overriding importance, of rules. The rule of law is indispensable for the operation of a modern economy, which involves transactions spread out over time and space. Buyers will not engage in such transactions without the certainty that the products for which they are paying will be delivered. Similarly, potential sellers require the assurance of payment for their products. The rule of law guarantees both, and has therefore established itself throughout the Western world, and imperfectly elsewhere, as the industrial revolution has proceeded and the global market it undergirds has expanded.

Where law, and its accessories, lawyers and judges, are concerned, an observation that de Tocqueville made in the 1830s remains accurate at the outset of the twenty-first century: In no country do they play a larger role than in the United States. Here, too, baseball, football, and basketball, extensively rule-governed as they are, reflect one of the defining features of the society to which they belong.

The rules governing American team sports, like the laws that govern modern societies, have three main properties. They are universal: In theory and usually in practice they apply equally to all players and to all citizens. They are transparent: Everybody knows what they are. And they are legitimate: All accept them as binding. As in the law, team sports designate individuals who are empowered to decide whether a rule has been violated. In baseball the equivalent of the judge is the umpire. In football and basketball it is the referee—the one to whom questions of right and wrong are referred. Like judges, officials in team sports wear special clothing that sets them apart. They wear black, the color of death and therefore finality that, because it is the sum of all colors, also symbolizes neutrality, and white, the color of purity that denotes their special, disinterested position. In football and basketball, officials signal that an infraction has been committed by blowing a whistle. In one of the many contributions team sports have made to the American language, the term "whistle-blowing" has come to mean calling attention to wrongs of all kinds.

In each sport the rules that the officials enforce are similar. Each has rules for scoring. In all three, these are straightforward: Either a runner in baseball touches home plate before being put out or he does not; either a football player in possession of the ball crosses the goal line before being knocked to the ground or he does not; either the basketball falls through the basket or it does not. The clarity and simplicity of these rules distinguish the three team sports from individual competitions such as diving and figure skating, in which scores are assigned by judges with wide discretion. Baseball, football, and basketball games are more clearly contests of merit than these individual competitions because the outcome depends less on subjective opinion and more on objective fact.

To be sure, the discretion of officials does affect team sports, in the enforcement of a second category of rules: those governing *efforts* to score. In each game the task of the offense is to score, that of the defense to prevent the opposing team from doing so. Each game has rules specifying how each side may and may not go about its task. Violators of these rules incur penalties.

In the American legal system, justice can be a protracted process. Trials can last for weeks, months, even years. Verdicts, once rendered, can be appealed. An old saying has it that "justice delayed is justice denied." By that standard, team sports are models of justice, for judgment is usually speedy and final. Each sport does have provisions for appeal—in professional football a select category of judgments is subject to review using videotaped replay of the action in question–but these are narrowly drawn and affect only a small part of each game.

Indeed, questioning and protesting an official's decision in all but the most narrowly defined circumstances is actively discouraged and is the basis for the third type of rule that governs the three sports. In each of them, if a player, or one of the battery of coaches and supervisors from either team, carries the dispute of an official judgment beyond a certain point—and it is the official himself who decides where that point is located—the official can eject that person from the game. By implication, at that point the protest is considered to have passed beyond objecting to the specific judgment under dispute and to have become an attack on the authority of the official to make it. It has escalated, that is, into an attack on the principle of the supremacy of rules, a principle on which the integrity of the entire enterprise rests. To protect that integrity the violator must suffer a severe penalty.[24]

While excessive argument about an official judgment is the most common attack on the integrity of the game, it is not the most serious one. The most dangerous such assault occurs not when an individual or a team tries too hard to win—the subject of the rules in the second and third category—but rather when a player or a group of players deliberately try *not* to win. In baseball, football, and basketball it is an accepted part of the game for each team to attempt to deceive the other about the tactics it employs to win. In football and basketball faking—pretending to give the ball to one player while actually handing it to another in football, seeming to be on the verge of shooting the ball and then holding back in basketball—are common. Deceiving both opponents and spectators about the goal that is being pursued, however, counts as the ultimate offense. When a contest is "fixed," its outcome decided in advance, it ceases to be a game.

To summarize, baseball, football, and basketball reflect the great changes that distinguish the modern from the traditional world: equality in the organization of society, cooperation and competition in the operation of the economy, and formal laws governing both. Team sports reflect these changes more vividly than do the longer-established individual sports and this, from the point of view of an interpretive anthropologist, helps to explain the emergence of team sports in the latter part of the nineteenth century. These modern patterns, as de Tocqueville noted, appeared first and developed most fully in the United States. But they ultimately appeared and developed in Europe and in the rest of the world as well. Outside North America hereditary privilege steadily lost ground and modern industrial economies were established. And as in the United States, team sports became part of national life. But they were, and remain, different sports. And the differences between baseball, football, and basketball, on the one hand, and the similar but also different games popular in Europe in turn reflect ways that the New World differs from the Old.

The Atlantic Gulf

The three most popular team sports outside North America bear distinct family resemblances to the three that are most widely watched and played in the United States. Cricket, like baseball, involves a bat and a ball, a pitcher (bowler), a catcher, and a batter, and scoring by running from one point to another. In rugby, as in North American football, one team tries to advance an oval ball over a line defended by the other by running with and passing it (in rugby passes must be backward, never forward), while the defending team tries to prevent this by tackling the possessor of the ball. Scoring also takes place by kicking the ball through the opponent's goal posts. What Americans call soccer (but the rest of the world calls football) resembles basketball—although the American game originated independently of it—in that each team tries to put a round ball, which neither is allowed to carry, into a goal.

Cricket, rugby, and soccer, along with the word "sport," all originated in England, the country from which came many of the social, political, and technical innovations that make up the modern world. From the British Isles cricket and rugby spread throughout the British Empire. Team sports seem to follow the flag.[25] This is true in the American case: Baseball came to be played where American economic, cultural, and military influence was strong, in Latin America and East Asia. Soccer, the third sport of English origin, spread all over the world.

Britain once governed what became the United States, of course, and each of the three sports it gave to the world were and are played in North America. Perhaps if the eighteenth century American rebellion against British rule had failed, those three would have become the dominant American team sports in the twentieth century. Instead, related but distinctive games evolved in the United States.

What accounts for the differences between the English sports and their American offspring? In part these are no doubt accidents of history, not attributable to larger social forces. But some of the dissimilarities between the rules of the English and the American games, and how the sports are organized on the two sides of the Atlantic, do reflect, in ways that an interpretive anthropologist would recognize, important differences between the Old World and the New.

And those differences are related to the meaning of sports for Americans, the purposes that baseball, football, and basketball serve in the twenty-first-century United States.

In both Western Europe and North America in the twenty-first century social equality is a fact of life and, with some exceptions, the principle of merit governs the allocation of wealth, power, and position. The games played in the Old World reflect these features of modern life just as those of the New World do: Each team has an equal opportunity to win in that the rules apply equally to both and each game begins with an even score. But equality of opportunity and merit came earlier to the United States than to the British Isles or to the European continent, and remain more deeply ingrained in North America. The American nation is more committed than are the countries of Europe to ensuring that the wherewithal needed to take advantage of opportunities is as equally distributed as possible.

The organization of professional sports in the United States reflects this American commitment to equalizing the capacity to take advantage of opportunities.[26] Individual games, and even more so championships that require victory in many games, are won by teams with more skillful players than their opponents have. All other things being equal, the most skillful players are likely to gravitate to the teams willing and able to pay them the most—and that is more or less how players are allocated among professional teams in the Old World. Baseball, football, and basketball, by contrast, deploy two mechanisms for equalizing the distribution of skillful players and thus equalizing the chances for each team to win a championship.

One is the amateur draft, in which teams gain the exclusive right to hire players entering the professional from the non-professional (amateur) ranks in the reverse order of their performances in the preceding season. The previous year's least successful teams pick first and can thereby gain access to the best players. In this way, the less successfully a team performs in one season, the greater are its chances to improve in the next one.

In none of the three American team sports may a team retain exclusive rights to employ a player indefinitely. At some point a player is permitted to offer his athletic services to other teams. But in professional football and basketball, although not in baseball, a second mechanism not found in European sports comes into play to equalize the talent among the various teams by restricting the role of money in distributing it. This is the salary cap, a limit on the amount of money each team can spend on salaries.

The American professional sports leagues did not adopt these two mechanisms purely in order to make the competition as equal as possible. In both instances the owners of the teams sought, by restricting the role of the free market, to avoid competitive bidding against one another and thereby to save money. Nonetheless, the result of these mechanisms was to make the teams more evenly matched on the field.

While less committed than is the United States to equality of opportunity, however, European societies are more committed to equality of *results*. Their extensive and expensive welfare states promote a greater degree of economic equality than is found in the United States. The greater European attraction to, or at least tolerance of, equal results is reflected in the rules governing how games can end in the team sports that originated in Great Britain, on the one hand, and baseball, football, and basketball on the other. In cricket and soccer the outcome in which neither team wins— a tie—is common. It is not uncommon for soccer matches to end without either team having scored at all.

This is not the case for team sports in the United States, where the rules of baseball and basketball prohibit ties. In each sport, if the score is even at the end of a regulation game, the teams continue to play until one wins.

For most of its history, football was different. If the score was even at the conclusion of sixty minutes of play, the game ended in a tie. But by the 1990s both the college and the professional versions of the game had altered their rules so that a tie triggered additional play, making such an outcome, although not impossible, far less frequent.

The difference in the status of ties reflects the unusual emphasis on competition in the United States. Contemporary Americans are perhaps the most competitive people since the ancient Greeks. Virtually any activity in the United States sooner or later becomes the subject of a competition, from animal husbandry to architecture and even including eating.*

In addition to the organization of professional sports and the rules of the games their respective team sports reflect

---

* An Ohio mother is reported to have managed to support her family by her earnings from winning word contests in newspapers and magazines and on cereal boxes. Terry Ryan, *The Prizewinner of Defiance, Ohio: How My Mother Raised 10 Kids on 25 Words or Less* (New York: Simon and Schuster, 2001). Competition is scarcely unknown in the societies of the Old World, especially Great Britain, where, in the nineteenth century, ancient Greece was taken as a cultural model. But firms selling consumer products in Britain often seek to capitalize not on the principle of merit but on the country's aristocratic heritage by boasting of the fact, when it is a fact, that they have been designated the exclusive purveyor of whatever it is they are purveying "by appointment" to one or another member of the British royal family.

important differences between the Old World and the New in a third way: by the different patterns of popular support for individual teams on the two sides of the Atlantic Ocean.

Spectators not only watch games, they also identify with the teams themselves. Indeed, they watch because they identify. Sports appeal to their audiences for esthetic reasons, like ballet, and because of the suspense inherent in each game, as with mystery novels. But the emotional commitment to particular teams, which is part of a basic human tendency, the identification with larger groups, also helps to account for the emergence of organized team sports as a commercially successful industry in the twentieth century. Millions of people follow the exploits of their favorite teams, watching their games on television, listening to them on the radio, and reading about them in newspapers and online.

Sports fans express their attachments to their teams not only through the time and money they spend following their favorites, but in other ways as well—their clothing, for example. The proceeds from the sale of shirts patterned after the uniforms of baseball, football, and basketball players, complete with name and uniform number, is substantial. By one estimate, the annual sales of merchandise of all kinds officially licensed by the three professional leagues was $6 billion.[27] At the home football games of the team representing the University of Nebraska, which 80,000 spectators invariably attend—a number greater than the population of Lincoln, Nebraska, the city where the contests are staged—the supporters of the local team all wear its hallmark color, turning the seating area surrounding the playing field into a sea of red. Similar scenes are created at football games all across the United States. Enthusiastic spectators at football and basketball games go even farther in their outward displays of devotion, painting their faces and bodies in their teams' colors.

Identification with a particular team has a polarizing effect. To support one team is to root against its opponent. Accordingly, outside the United States team sports tend to reflect, and sometimes to aggravate, social and political cleavages. Cricket and soccer especially have served as sources of conflict.

In the United States baseball, football, and basketball have sometimes had this effect also. But to a greater extent than their European counterparts, American team sports also have the opposite effect. They are sources of integration as well as division. They promote social solidarity.

Old World sports are divisive because they lend themselves to competition between and among different countries, and therefore correspond to the most potent source of division in the modern age, nationalism, the allegiance that led millions to fight and die in the twentieth century. Sometimes poisonous political relations between the countries seep into the game. India and Pakistan once played a large number of tied cricket matches because neither would risk employing the tactics that could bring victory for fear of suffering a defeat and therefore political humiliation. Political issues other than nationalism have also intruded on sports of English origin. In 1970, threatened protests against South Africa's system of apartheid caused the cancellation of cricket matches scheduled to be played in England against a touring South African team.

American team sports are not the subject of important international competitions. While the World Cup of soccer involves a majority of the world's nearly 200 countries, the World Series of baseball matches teams representing two

American (or, occasionally, Canadian) cities. Football's championship also pits two American teams against each other: The game is barely played outside North America. And while basketball is played at the Olympic games and in world championship tournaments in the years between Olympics, these international competitions do not have the importance of the international competitions in cricket and rugby, let alone soccer.

Even within the same country, sports rivalries in Europe often express deep-seated social conflicts. In the Scottish city of Glasgow one of the two leading soccer teams, Rangers, is identified with Protestants and the other, Celtic, with Catholics, mirroring one of the oldest and most divisive antagonisms in the British Isles. At matches between them the supporters of the two sides are separated from each other by chain-link fences topped by barbed wire, with police warily on guard. Nonetheless, violence is common.[28] Similarly, the heated rivalry between soccer clubs based in Spain's two largest cities, Real (Royal) Madrid and F. C. (Football Club) Barcelona, "accurately mirrors the very essence of twentieth-century Spanish history,"[29] one of the hallmarks of which was the estrangement of Catalonia, the region of which Barcelona is the capital, from the rest of the county. Madrid and Barcelona were on opposite sides of the Spanish Civil War of the 1930s.[30]

In England, but also to some extent in other European countries, pitched battles between supporters of rival teams, and between supporters and the police, are all too common. Indeed, in the peaceful, prosperous, demilitarized, war-averse Europe of the twenty-first century, soccer seemed to be almost the only thing over which people were actually willing to fight.

Fierce hostility surrounding team competition is not unknown in the United States, where violence or the threat of violence has caused the removal of contests to neutral sites, the barring of supporters of one or both sides from attending them, and even the cancellation of entire games. Almost without exception, however, violence among spectators has occurred in connection with games between teams representing high schools, often located in the same city.[31] Games and rivalries involving players with higher levels of skill and larger audiences, especially professional baseball, football, and basketball, have had the opposite effect, pacifying and uniting rather than inflaming and dividing Americans.[32]

In the way that their professional competitions are organized, these team sports reflect the great social and political project around which much of American history, from the eighteenth century to the twenty-first, has revolved, a project that Europe has begun to attempt only recently and in a very limited way: the creation of a single society and political unit out of many different peoples on a vast continent. Team sports reflect the goal designated on the great seal of the United States and on the country's currency: *e pluribus unum.* Specifically, they express the ongoing national effort to overcome two of the country's main sources of division, geography and ethnic differences.

The greatest national trial of the United States, the Civil War, divided it along geographic lines, pitting one section of the country against the other. Regional differences have been moderated since then by, among other things, a feature of American life lacking in Europe, with its many different countries: the geographic mobility of American citizens, which has increased in scale and tempo in the century and a half since the Civil War and serves to make the different sections of the country more similar to one another than in the past.

It is common for Americans to move several times in their lives and to live in different parts of the county, which helps to prevent regions from becoming self-contained and distinctive cultural zones. One of the many reasons that F. Scott Fitzgerald's *The Great Gatsby* has a claim to being the great American novel is that it expresses this theme: the eponymous hero moves from Minnesota to New York, changes his name from Jimmy Gatz to Jay Gatsby, and in other ways assumes a new identity.

Geographic mobility is central to professional sports. While high school teams generally draw their players from the neighborhoods in which they are located, college and especially professional teams recruit from all over the country—in the case of baseball from throughout the western hemisphere (and beginning in the 1990s, from East Asia as well) and for basketball, increasingly, from around the world. Professional athletes are Gatsbys, shifting locations and identities—one season a New York Yankee, the next a Los Angeles Dodger. It is unusual for one to play for the team located where he grew up. A career like that of Pete Rose, who accumulated more base hits than any other player in the history of major league baseball, who was born and raised in Cincinnati and played for nineteen of his twenty-four major league seasons for the Cincinnati Reds baseball team, is the exception rather than the rule; and at the end of his career even Rose moved from Cincinnati to Philadelphia and then to Montreal.

Fans come to identify with players from different, often distant, parts of the United States, and even of the world.

Mark McGwire, from San Diego, became a hero in St. Louis
for his skill at hitting home runs for the local Cardinals baseball team. Joe Namath, from Beaver Falls in western Pennsylvania and a college player in Tuscaloosa, Alabama, led the
New York Jets football team to a championship and became
so closely identified with that city that his nickname invoked
one of its most famous thoroughfares: "Broadway Joe."
Michael Jordan of North Carolina enjoyed such success as a
basketball player in Chicago that a statue of him was erected
there. In this way American professional sports, at least,
serve as an antidote to parochialism, to the local chauvinism
sometimes on display in European team sports.*

While the geography of the United States is composed of
a number of different and sometimes far-flung regions, the
country's population, especially in the twentieth century,
came to be made up of people who arrived, or whose forbears had arrived, in North America from many different
foreign countries. Here again the New World differs from
the Old. European nations are, or think of themselves as
being, communities of fate, composed of peoples whose
ancestors have lived together, in the same region, for centuries. The American nation is a community of choice and
the familiar, quasi-culinary metaphor for the way that it has
been created is the melting pot, in which different national
ingredients combine to form a concoction different from any
single one of them.

Even in the American melting pot, residues of identification with the country of origin have remained, which came

---

* In the last decade of the twentieth century, Europe's professional soccer teams
began to follow the American pattern. They became increasingly international in
composition, with the Italian and English teams especially employing players
from all over Europe and from South America and Africa as well.

to be called ethnicity. But America's ethnic groups, if they did not shed their forbears' identities entirely, did, over time, gain acceptance as full and legitimate participants in American life. In the twentieth century American sports, especially professional baseball, reflected this process. Indeed, they became a part of it.

Professional sports constituted melting pots in miniature. Representatives of the waves of immigrants who came to the United States beginning in the nineteenth century rose to prominence in major league baseball. The two most successful managers of the early years of the century were Irishmen: John McGraw and Cornelius McGillicuddy, who shortened his name to Connie Mack. The stars who shone most brightly on the most glamorous of all teams, the New York Yankees of the 1920s, were of German heritage: George Herman (Babe) Ruth and Henry Louis (Lou) Gehrig. The accomplishments of these four earned them election to the Baseball Hall of Fame in Cooperstown, New York, as did those of the slugging Jewish outfielder of the 1930s, Hank Greenberg, and the superior Jewish left-handed pitcher of the 1960s, Sandy Koufax, as well as celebrated players of Italian background such as Tony Lazzeri and Joe DiMaggio, both New York Yankees of the 1930s and 1940s.

People of non-European descent have experienced greater difficulty in gaining full acceptance into American society than those of European background. The greatest difficulties of all confronted the descendants of slaves brought involuntarily to the New World from Africa. Thus the 1947 debut of the first African-American major league baseball player, Jack Roosevelt (Jackie) Robinson, was a milestone not only in the history of the sport but in the history of the country. In the second half of the twentieth century immigrants came to the continental United States in large numbers from the Spanish-speaking countries (and the American Commonwealth of Puerto Rico) to the south. Following the familiar pattern, baseball players from Latin America achieved success in the sport: the Cuban Orestes (Minnie) Minoso in the 1940s, the Puerto Rican Roberto Clemente in the 1950s, Juan Marichal from the Dominican Republic in the 1960s, David Concepcion from Venezuela in the 1970s, Fernando Valenzuela from Mexico in the 1980s.

The names and faces of Irish-, German-, Italian-, Jewish-, African- and Latin-American players in newspapers, on baseball trading cards, and ultimately on television signaled that, in at least one part of American life, members of each group had become full, valued, and successful participants.

As a vehicle for the great historic national task of promoting cohesion in a society composed of peoples from many different backgrounds, and as an expression of the American emphasis on equality of opportunity and competition, baseball, football, and basketball resemble each other even as they differ from cricket, rugby, and soccer. But the three American sports differ from one another as well. What significance would an interpretive anthropologist impute to these differences? Why, for that matter, are there three major team sports in the United States?

Variety in this case has roots in the calendar. Each of the three sports is played in a particular time of year, although the modern professional schedules, with their many games staged in order to maximize revenues, have extended all three beyond their original bounds and created considerable overlap. In the beginning, baseball was played in the spring and summer, football in the fall, basketball in the winter.

Still, an interpretive anthropologist studying baseball,

football, and basketball could find differences among the three that reflect different aspects of American history and American social life. One way to divide that history is according to the dominant form of economic activity and the way of life to which it gave rise. By these criteria the American republic has passed through three distinct periods. In the first, agriculture dominated national life. The second consists of the decades in which the initial stages of the industrial revolution shaped the society: More and more people worked in factories, lived in cities, and relied on machines. In the third period the forging of metal was supplanted by the processing of information as the main kind of work, offices replaced factories, and people left the cities for the suburbs.

Each of the three major team sports corresponds to—because its rules and customs reflect—one of these three periods. In the twentieth century each of the three enjoyed a period in which it surpassed the other two as the representative American sport. In each case the sport's "golden age" was a moment when a generation marked by the particular era to which the sport corresponds occupied a dominant position in American society. For baseball the golden age extended from the 1920s to the 1950s; for football it spanned the 1960s and 1970s; for basketball it was the last two decades of the twentieth century. The order in which each sport experienced its golden age in turn corresponds to the progression of economic and social eras in the United States. The last of them, basketball, is the hallmark game of the post-industrial age. The second, football, expresses the world the industrial revolution made. The first and the earliest, the team sport that initially established itself as central to the popular culture of the United States, is baseball, the agrarian, traditional game.

CHAPTER 2

Baseball: The Remembrance of Things Past

He wanted to talk about old ballplayers, stadium dimensions, about nicknames and minor league towns. That's why he was here, to surrender himself to longing, to listen to his host recite the anecdotal texts, all the passed-down stories of bonehead plays and swirling brawls, the pitching duels that carried into twilight, stories that Marvin had been collecting for half a century—the deep eros of memory that separates baseball from other sports.

DON DeLILLO, *Underworld*[1]

THE TRADITIONAL GAME

For most of recorded history, most human beings in most places passed their days in small settlements scattered around the countryside. They assured their own survival by planting, growing, harvesting and eating crops; or by tending domesticated animals; or by hunting, killing and eating wild animals; or by all three. Their routines, and their beliefs about their routines, were handed down, with little or no change, from one generation to the next. It is from this world—rural, agricultural, traditional—that baseball comes; and it is this world that the rules, the techniques, and the customs of baseball reflect.

Like life in traditional society, but unlike the other two major American team sports, baseball is not governed by the clock. A football game comprises exactly sixty minutes of play, a basketball game forty or forty-eight minutes, but baseball has no set length of time within which the game must be completed. The pace of the game is therefore leisurely and unhurried, like the world before the discipline of measured time, deadlines, schedules, and wages paid by the hour. Baseball belongs to the kind of world in which people did not say, "I haven't got all day." Baseball games *do* have all day to be played. But that does not mean that they can go on forever. Baseball, like traditional life, proceeds according to the rhythm of nature, specifically the rotation of the Earth. During its first half century, games were not played at night, which meant that baseball games, like the traditional work day, ended when the sun set.

The baseball season, too, follows a traditional pace, unfolding according to the same cycle as the active part of the agricultural year. The season begins with the coming of spring, stretches through the long hot days of summer, and culminates, like the growing season with its harvest, in the fall.

From November through March the playing fields and seats for spectators are empty, the players dispersed. In the winter months, like birds in the northern hemisphere, baseball migrates to the south: Winter baseball is played in Central and South America.

Finally, just as rural societies everywhere observed the three phases of the growing season with festivals, so does baseball: The opening day of the season marks the arrival of spring; the annual All-Star Game matching the best players from the two major leagues comes in midsummer; and the October championship competition modestly known as the "World Series" is often also called the "fall classic."

As with time, the space in which baseball is played reproduces traditional, agricultural life. With a few exceptions the game takes place outdoors, in the familiar setting of rural existence: brown dirt and green foliage. The venues for the games are called parks, a word closely related, by some etymological accounts, to the term for the ultimate rural setting, paradise,[2] or fields, the places where farmers grow crops. The oldest and most storied playing sites are Fenway Park, the home of the Boston Red Sox, and Wrigley Field, where the Chicago Cubs play. The first recorded game took place outside Hoboken, New Jersey, at a site named for the playground of the gods in ancient Greece: the Elysian Fields.

The 1960s saw the construction of a number of venues built for both baseball and football that were often given the name appropriate to football: stadium. (Two of the most famous teams in baseball, the New York Yankees and the Los Angeles Dodgers, also play in stadiums, each named for the team itself.) But the baseball-only facilities built in the 1990s[3] reverted to the original designations: Bank One Ballpark in Phoenix and Turner Field in Atlanta (nicknamed, respectively, "the Bob" and, after the Atlanta owner Ted Turner, "the Ted"), Oriole Park at Camden Yards in Baltimore, Coors Field in Denver.

Baseball's parks and fields embody another feature of the traditional world that football and basketball lack. One characteristic of the modern world, which separates it from the world of tradition that it displaced, is standardization. Each of America's three major team sports, all of them distinctly modern institutions, has a standard form, with a set of universally valid rules: They could not have become national in scope otherwise. Like the settings for football and basketball, the fields on which baseball is played are all the same size, but only up to a point.

On each baseball diamond the distance between the center of the pitcher's mound and home plate is sixty feet six inches and the distance between bases is always exactly ninety feet. But in other ways baseball fields do *not* come in a single, standard size. The differences affect the way the game is played. Teams try to stock their rosters with players who can take advantage of the peculiar features of their home parks. They also design and maintain their parks in order to maximize the strengths of the players they have.

The distance from home plate to the limits of the playing field varies considerably from one major league park to another. In Yankee Stadium, for example, the distance from home plate to the fence separating the playing area from the grandstands in right field is short—a mere 314 feet down the foul line. The Yankees have prospered when their roster has included left-handed batters with a tendency to hit pitches to right field. In Fenway Park, by contrast, the shortest distance is to left field. At the terminus of the playing area there rises a high wall known as the "Green Monster," so named for the color it is painted and the influence it exerts on the course of the game. (It plays havoc with pitchers, turning what would be harmless pop flies elsewhere into home runs, but also with batters, turning hard-hit balls that would be doubles or triples in other parks into mere singles.)

The space between the foul lines and the seats for spectators also varies from one park to another.[4] The larger the dimensions of foul territory in a park the greater is the advantage to the team in the field, since more foul flies will be caught for outs, and fewer will settle into the stands and leave the batter with the continued opportunity to bat, than in a park where there is less of it.

Even the conditions of the playing surface vary from one

park to the next. In some, the grass is allowed to grow long, making it easier for the team in the field to intercept batted balls hit on the ground before they reach the outfield and throw the batter out at first base. (Teams that cultivate long grass have pitchers with a tendency to induce batters to hit the ball on the ground). Home teams also treat the base paths to make it either more or less difficult to run from one to the next. In one celebrated case in 1962, the Los Angeles Dodgers had a player, Maury Wills, who was highly skilled at base running. He set a major league record that season with 104 stolen bases. In a crucial game at the home park of the Dodgers' principal rivals, the San Francisco Giants, the groundskeeper soaked the dirt around first base, turning it into a bog, so that, when he reached first base, Wills could not get the traction necessary to steal second base. This stratagem earned the Giants' manager, Alvin Dark, who ordered the special treatment, a nickname taken from a Revolutionary War hero, Francis Marion: "the swamp fox."

Baseball departs from the pervasive modern norm of standardization, as football and basketball do not, in other ways. It is asymmetrical as they are not. In football and basketball it makes relatively little difference to the way the game is played whether a player favors his right or his left hand. In baseball the difference is crucial. When the batter and the pitcher favor the same hand, this confers an advantage on the pitcher. When the two orientations differ, by contrast, the balance of advantage shifts toward the batter.[5] Thus much of the strategy of baseball consists of maneuvering players so as to produce favorable pitcher-batter matchups, with the team in the field seeking similarity, the team at bat trying to produce dissimilarity.[6]

Asymmetries matter in baseball, as they do not in football

and basketball, in another way. To put a batter out after he has hit the ball on the ground, the infielder catches it and throws it to first base. This is much easier if the infielder is righthanded. A lefthanded infielder must twist his body awkwardly to throw to first base (or to throw to second base, as infielders often also have to do), thereby losing precious time. A baseball team will thus invariably deploy at the three infield positions other than first base—at second and third base and at shortstop—players who throw with their right hands. If the bases were circled in a clockwise rather than the counterclockwise direction the rules decree, these players would be lefthanded.[7] Throughout history people who favor the left hand have experienced discrimination. They have sometimes even been regarded as cursed: The Latin word for the left side has entered the English language as a term for something diabolical—"sinister." But this is not the case in baseball, where lefthanders, although they are missing from the ranks of infielders, do enjoy important advantages. For one thing, while batting they stand closer to first base than do righthanders. They thus have a shorter distance to run, which means that, with the same foot speed, they can get there sooner. Moreover, because the population as a whole is overwhelmingly righthanded, so too are baseball players in general and pitchers in particular. This means that a lefthanded batter is likely to enjoy an advantage at bat more often than he will incur the handicap of facing a lefthanded pitcher.

Another non-standard feature of baseball that sets it apart from football and basketball is the role of the pitcher. He is by far the most important player in the game, dominating it as no player in football or basketball, no matter how skilled, is able to do. He sets play in motion. He alone can decide in advance what he will do—that is, where he will aim the pitch. Because he knows what he is attempting, and because hitting with a bat a baseball thrown toward the plate at ninety miles per hour is an extremely difficult feat to accomplish, the pitcher has a built-in advantage over the batter. In the duels between them the pitcher wins—the batter is retired instead of reaching base safely—the majority of the time.*

While a pitcher can dominate any given game, no individual pitcher is able to dominate an entire major league season. Because the stress on his throwing arm is so great, a major league starting pitcher, who is expected to pitch most, if not all, of an individual game—delivering one hundred pitches or more—can only pitch once every four or five games. And because each game is so heavily influenced by the pitcher and because individual pitchers pitch only infrequently, each game between the same two teams varies enormously. In football and basketball variety comes from different teams playing each other. Baseball has an additional source: the same teams opposing each other but with different starting pitchers.[8]

Its incorporation of one of the defining features of tradition—non-uniformity—accounts for part of baseball's appeal.[9] The asymmetries that run through it imbue the game with a subtlety that the other two team sports lack and that commends it to its most enthusiastic followers. For them, baseball is chess to football and basketball's checkers. It is less straightforward, more complicated, more cerebral,

---

* The celebrated poem about baseball, "Casey at the Bat," which ends with Mudville's mighty slugger striking out, is in this sense misleading. It was unrealistic for the faithful fans to expect Casey to deliver a winning hit. The odds were against him. His failure was no doubt disappointing but should not have been surprising.

and therefore more interesting to watch, to think about, and to discuss.

One thing that the modern world and the world of tradition have in common is the use of tools. In the modern world the traditional axe, plough, and spear have given way to the power saw, the tractor, the machine gun and intercontinental ballistic missile. In baseball, more than in football and basketball, players rely on tools and, true to the spirit of the sport, baseball's tools—the bats that batters use and the gloves that fielders wear to help them catch the ball—are more traditional than modern.

They are specialized rather than standardized. Each major league player uses bats specially designed and made for him, a practice that began in 1884 when the Hillerich Company made a bat to order for a Louisville player named Pete Browning, from whose nickname the most popular brand of bats took its title: the "Louisville slugger." Unlike most twentieth-century products in the United States, bats are to a considerable extent handmade, as were the tools of traditional man.

Once in possession of these tools, moreover, players modify them to suit their own particular needs. They shave and treat their bats, and they oil and reshape their gloves. The material from which a major league player's tools are fashioned, like traditional tools, is organic, wood for the bat and leather for the glove. This pattern extends to the ball with which they play, which is composed of a cork center wound with woolen yarn and covered by cowhide and held together by 108 stitches, all inserted by hand. Moreover, if the tools of baseball players resemble those that men and women in traditional society used, so, too, do the habits of mind and the skills necessary to make optimal use of them.

Hunting and fishing were central activities in traditional life. Indeed, as methods of acquiring enough food for survival they predate the cultivation of crops, which is only about ten thousand years old. Not coincidentally, many baseball players have adopted them as hobbies: Ted Williams, one of the greatest of all batters, became, after his baseball career ended, a fisherman of renown. In baseball's early days a rural childhood served as a school for acquiring the skills necessary to play the game. Cy Young, who won more major league games than any other pitcher, said that he had learned to throw a baseball with velocity and accuracy, while growing up on a farm in Ohio in the 1870s and 1880s, by hurling rocks at squirrels.[10] The qualities of mind and body that the pursuit of fish and game requires also make for a successful baseball player. One such skill is patience. Hunting and fishing require long periods of watchful attention, waiting for the prey to appear. So does baseball. A player ordinarily has only four or five widely spaced opportunities to bat during a game. A fielder must be constantly prepared to catch a ball hit in his direction but can never know in advance when this will occur, and often long stretches of the game pass without it happening.

Another skill that successful baseball players share with the hunters and fishermen of the traditional world is what might be called local knowledge. A successful hunter must be intimately familiar with the terrain in which he is hunting and the habits of the animals he is stalking. Similarly, the most successful batters and pitchers almost invariably earn reputations as "students of the game." Great baseball careers are built on the obsessive accumulation of detailed information. Long before the advent of computers, players compiled, in their own memories, detailed records of the performances of their opponents. A successful major league pitcher can often recall the pitches he threw to a particular batter in a game played years previously.* And fielders consider what they know of the predilections of the pitcher and the skills of the batter in positioning themselves in the field.

A third common ingredient of success in hunting and fishing and in baseball is superior reflexes. Hitting a baseball requires the kind of hand-eye coordination that the use of a firearm or a spear or a bow and arrow involves in hunting.[11] Not only keen eyesight but also excellent hearing contribute to success in both. Hunters sometimes detect their prey by the sounds they make. In baseball, a good outfielder can tell how hard, and therefore how far, a ball has been hit by the "crack of the bat"—the sound of the bat making contact with it—and so start moving immediately toward the precise spot at which he can catch it.[12]

The affinity of baseball for the now-vanished world of tradition goes beyond a set of common skills and habits of mind. The sport fosters—in some ways requires—a set of attitudes, indeed an outlook on life and on the world, that was common in rural, agrarian, traditional society.

Baseball, like life in the traditional world, is hard. Scarcity is its natural condition. Scoring totals are lower than in foot-

* George F. Will, *Men at Work: The Craft of Baseball* (New York: Macmillan, 1990), p. 90. According to Ted Williams, "A hitter can't go up there and swing. He's got to think. Listen, when I played I knew the parks, the mounds, the batter's boxes, the backgrounds. I studied the pitchers. I knew what was going on at that plate." Ward and Burns, op. cit., p. 345. Ty Cobb, who for many years held the major league record for most safe hits, was said to have excelled at the bat because "he outstudied the pitchers." Moe Berg, "Pitchers and Catchers," in Nicholas Dawidoff, editor, *Baseball: A Literary Anthology* (New York: The Library of America, 2002), p. 170. Pete Rose, who broke Cobb's record, was not known for reading any publication other than the *Daily Racing Form*. But he studied the pitchers he faced with the intensity of a fledgling lawyer cramming for a bar exam.

ball or basketball. Sometimes a team fails entirely to score: "shutouts" are more frequent in baseball than in football, where they are rare, and in basketball, where they are unknown. And just as premodern hunters often trudged home empty-handed after a long day in the field, so to play baseball is to experience frequent, indeed chronic, failure. The best batters fail to hit safely in 70 percent of their official times at bat.[13] A successful major league team, one that wins 100 games in a season—and most fall short of this—will lose more than 60 times.

To succeed at baseball therefore requires the emotional capacity to confront and accept failure, to persevere in the face of failure, and to proceed with confidence despite the repeated experience of failure, which were also the attitudes necessary to endure the conditions of traditional existence. The required outlook was summarized by one of the greatest of all batters, Henry Aaron. Asked whether he arrived at the ballpark every day knowing that he was going to get two hits, he replied that he did not. "What I do know," he went on, "is that if I don't get 'em today, I'm sure going to get 'em tomorrow." [14]

The inhabitants of the traditional world lived at the mercy of forces they neither understood nor controlled, principally the weather and infectious diseases. That feature of traditional life, while much reduced in the modern world, survives in baseball. Because hitting a baseball is such a refined skill, one extremely difficult to master and for which the line between proficiency and incompetence is an exceedingly thin one, batters are prone to experience prolonged and often inexplicable periods of failure during which, despite strenuous efforts and frenetic experimentation, they are unable to hit safely.

The term for such periods is the same as the one used, before the Great Depression of the 1930s, to describe downturns in economic activity: slumps. Pitchers are prone to similar experiences, periods when they cannot throw the ball in the strike zone. The term for a pitcher's chronic inaccuracy suggests a reversion to an earlier, more primitive state. Pitchers are afflicted by "wildness," just as odd behavior in the traditional world was often imputed to an invasion of the person by evil spirits.

In the face of inexplicable and persistent bouts of failure, baseball players gravitate to a practice common in traditional societies: superstitition. Superstition is the error, made known to students in elementary statistics courses on the first day of class, of mistaking correlation for causation. Simply because two things occur together this does not mean that one has caused the other: Where two events coincide, this may be mere coincidence. But in the uncertainty-riddled world of tradition, and even in the somewhat-less-mysterious world of the present day, people take comfort from the belief that such relationships do exist, that wearing a particular trinket, for example, will bring good fortune.

Similarly, the accomplished batter of the Boston Red Sox and the New York Yankees, Wade Boggs, took care, throughout his baseball career, to eat a chicken dish on the day of each game, convinced that this helped him perform well at the plate.[15] Players coming in from the field at the end of an inning on defense may be observed touching—or avoiding touching—the foul lines, in the belief that one or the other brings good luck.

All of these affinities with the world of tradition, combined with the sport's early beginnings in the middle of the eighteenth century, give baseball one of its defining features:

It is backward-looking. Of the three principal American team sports, it is the one most powerfully associated with the past.

Its leisurely pace, the result of the absence of a clock, its roots in America's nineteenth-century and even eighteenth-century history, its emphasis on skills once vital for survival but for most citizens of the twenty-first century of merely antiquarian or avocational interest, and its pastoral setting make a baseball game a preserved fragment of days gone by.[16] Baseball returns the spectator, for a few hours, to an earlier, simpler, happier time. It offers a brief sojourn in a lost paradise, a sip from the fountain of youth.

It has this effect, as well, because the game is associated with the past not only of American society but of individual Americans. Baseball evokes childhood. That is when players and spectators are first introduced to it. Childhood is also the moment of the initial encounter with football and basketball, but the connection with baseball is stronger because it is played in the summer, when the child is free of the adult-imposed disciplines of school. Baseball is a powerful vehicle for escaping from the bonds of the present to the remembered freedom—from care, responsibility, and mandatory routines—of the past.

This cultural meaning is embedded in the lyrics of "Take Me Out to the Ball Game," sung at every major league game during the seventh-inning stretch, when the spectators rise in a combination of a mild form of exercise and a civic ritual. "Buy me some peanuts and crackerjack," goes the song, "I don't care if I never get back." What it is no urgent matter to get back to is the world outside the ballpark, the workaday "real" world to which the spectator must return when the game ends.

For the baseball fan, biting into a hot dog, sold at every ballpark and, the musical tribute to peanuts and popcorn notwithstanding, the food most closely associated with the game, can have the same effect that the taste of the butter cake called a madeleine had on the narrator of Marcel Proust's *The Remembrance of Things Past*. It triggers a flood of memories of the world the person knew when he or she first tasted it. Baseball thus functions as a time machine, transporting spectators back into the past. That is at the heart of its status in American culture. It has another, related feature that also locates it in the culture and distinguishes it from football and basketball: It is the team sport of the individual.

The society built by Europeans in North America beginning in the seventeenth century, while rural and agrarian, differed from the traditional societies of Europe in one important way, a difference that finds expression in baseball. Traditional Europeans lived enmeshed in a thick web of familial, social, and political obligation. They were hedged about from all directions by custom and constraint. Each individual was part of a group, or several groups. His or her life was governed by the group's norms. In the New World things were different. Immigrants arriving from Europe found a virtually blank social slate. North America lacked Europe's great landed estates owned by noble families with a panoply of inherited duties and privileges. In the New World, land, the source of almost all wealth, was free to be claimed and cultivated. The conditions prevailing in North America gave rise to a character type found less frequently on the other side of the Atlantic, a type with which America came to be identified: the independent, self-reliant, unfettered man—the "rugged individual."

This is the trait of character associated with the American

frontier, where men staked out and defended their home-steads while fighting off assaults from indigenous inhabitants of the North American continent, whom they had often dis-possessed. It is the character of the sturdy yeoman farmer whom Thomas Jefferson believed to be the bulwark of dem-ocratic government. This is the character type portrayed in Hollywood Westerns. Not coincidentally, Gary Cooper, one of the great stars of these Westerns, emphasized these tough, humble, and stoic qualities when he portrayed the celebrated baseball player Lou Gehrig in Hollywood's version of his life, *Pride of the Yankees*. Baseball is an arena for displaying the same traits of character that the frontier encouraged. Far more than the other two principal American team sports, baseball is the individual's game.

The Individual's Game

Baseball is a linear game. It unfolds in sequential fashion: Only one thing happens at a time. Each pitch inaugurates a sequence that is whole and complete and the sequences that make up a baseball game can be charted with precision. The method of charting them was invented by one of the game's pioneers, an Englishman named Henry Chadwick who con-ceived a passion for the sport when he immigrated to the United States.[17] He developed the symbolic language in which the constituent events of a game are plotted on a scorecard. The numbers and signs with which the game is scored make up a hieroglyphics that, when deciphered, give a coherent narrative history of all that has happened.

Football, too, is composed of discrete events, each of which begins when the ball is snapped and concludes when the sound of an official's whistle signals that that segment—

that play—has ended. But baseball differs from football in a very important way: Each of the acts that a scorecard records can be attributed to a single individual. In football, every player is involved in every play and it is difficult to disentangle the contributions of the various players to its outcome. Of the three team sports, baseball is the one closest in evolutionary descent to the older individual sports. For in baseball the pitcher pitches, the batter bats, the fielders field—and each does so independently of the others. The spectator can follow each part of the sequence in the order in which it occurs.

Chadwick devised another way to summarize a baseball game, patterned after an English method of recording the details of a cricket match, which organizes the action according to the individual player responsible for each part of it. The box score is the symbolic—largely numerical—account of the game that appears in the newspaper the next day, and the running tallies of the individual achievements that the box score records are the statistics that permeate baseball.

Football and basketball also generate statistics, which also appear every day in newspapers and online during the course of their seasons, but these statistics are less purely individual than are baseball's. When a football player advances the ball by carrying it, the distance he travels before being tackled is credited to him and appears in the press as part of his personal total of yardage gained. But his progress depends to a very great extent on the simultaneous and coordinated efforts of his teammates, who have the task of clearing would-be tacklers out of his way. It is impossible to isolate and objectively assess the contribution each team member makes to the outcome of the play.[18] A batter in baseball, by contrast, receives no comparable help from his teammates, and his success or failure is more fully his own.

Similarly, the number of points per game a basketball player is able to score, which is that sport's most widely noted statistic, depends heavily on how much help he receives from his teammates in creating the circumstances in which he can put the ball in the basket. During the game every basketball player is interacting with all of his teammates all the time. In baseball, by contrast, every player is more or less on his own.*

In the series of duels between pitcher and batter that make up a baseball game, one always wins and the other loses. The batter either reaches base safely—a victory for him—or is retired and returns to the dugout—a triumph for the pitcher. The fielder either handles a ball hit in his direction cleanly, and gets credit for a putout or an assist, or fails to do so and is charged with an error.[19] Baseball is therefore a realm of complete transparency and total responsibility. A baseball player lives in a glass house, and in a stark moral universe. The sport creates, for those who play it, a world like the one that some religious traditions teach that all

---

* In baseball only a few players are involved in each play, and their distinctive contributions can be readily disaggregated, with one important exception. The pitcher must depend on his fielders to put out a batter who has hit the ball. The individual contribution of the pitcher to the outcome of the game is based on the concept of the fielding error, which occurs when, in the judgment of a sportswriter designated the official scorer, a batter reaches base after hitting a ball on which he would, had the fielder performed competently, have been put out. The pitcher is relieved of statistical responsibility for the base runner. If that runner scores, this counts as an unearned run. The most important pitching statistic is *earned* runs per nine innings, which is the pitcher's earned run average. It is a more telling indication of the pitcher's skill than his won-lost record. Every game has a winning pitcher—the one in the game when his team scores the winning run, although if he is the starting pitcher he must pitch at least five innings—and a losing pitcher—the one who gives up the winning run to the other team. But whether a pitcher wins or loses depends not only on how many runs he yields to the opposing team but also on how many runs his own team scores against the opposing pitchers, something over which he has very little control.

humans inhabit, in which, at the end of his or her time on Earth, the individual presents him- or herself for divine judgment based on a complete record of all his or her mortal deeds. Everything that every player does is accounted for[20] and everything accounted for is either good or bad, right or wrong. Toward the supreme goal of winning baseball games every act counts as either a debit or a credit. Nothing is overlooked and there is no middle ground.

As the embodiment of individualism, baseball presents what seems at first a contradiction, for it happens to be not only an American game but also the national sport of Japan, a country in which individual self-assertion is actively discouraged and so, historically, extremely rare. It was introduced there from the United States in the 1870s and the first Japanese professional leagues were formed in 1936. Historically, their culture has encouraged the Japanese people to blend in with others, to take their cues from the group. The national ethos is captured by the widely popular expression "the nail that stands up will be hammered down." How, then, can baseball have achieved the status that it enjoys there?

It has done so because, while the rules of baseball are the same in Japan as in the United States, the social context of the game is different, and distinctly Japanese.[21] In this sense baseball resembles another product common to both countries, automobiles. While the cars are more or less the same, the American and Japanese factories that make them are organized and operated in strikingly different ways. In fact, Japanese baseball teams are run along the lines of Japanese factories. (Not coincidentally, most Japanese teams are owned by major Japanese corporations.) They emphasize, as their American major league counterparts do not, the coherence of the group and loyalty to the team. Japanese players spend a great deal of time together. They train constantly and in groups. They accept without question the authority of the manager and the owner. Unlike American players, they almost never employ agents to negotiate their contracts with team management—that would show disrespect and threaten team harmony.* They never display anger on the field, as American players routinely do. What is considered normal conduct in the United States would embarrass a Japanese player and alienate his fans. What pleases the fans, by contrast, what earns a player popularity, is the same in both countries: superior performance on the field.

Because baseball is preeminently the individual's team sport, the heroes of baseball are more heroic, in the sense that they are solely responsible for their achievements, than are those of football and baseball. Because responsibility is personal, baseball can involve a sense of honor, which was on vivid display on the final day of the 1941 season. Ted Williams's batting average stood at precisely .400 (four safe hits per every ten at-bats), already a very high standard that would acquire an almost mythical aura over the next sixty years as no player succeeded in reaching it over the course of an entire season. Offered the opportunity to skip the two games scheduled for the final day to assure this achievement, Williams refused, on the grounds that this would be a dishonorable way to achieve the goal. He

* Masaru Ikei, "In Japan, Another Game," *Newsday*, August 11, 2002. It was perhaps a sign of discontent with the prevailing ethos in Japanese baseball that, beginning in the 1990s, some of the best Japanese players left to play in the American major leagues. They were also undoubtedly motivated by the challenge of competing against the best players from the rest of the world and by the higher salaries they could command in North America. Their departures hurt the Japanese leagues. The country's prime minister, Junichiro Koizumi, said in 2002, "These days watching Major League baseball [on television] is more exciting than watching games in Japan." Simon Kuper, "Ballgames that can help to bridge that gap," *Financial Times*, July 6/7, 2002, "Weekend FT," p. XXVI.

played, made six hits in eight times at bat, and ended the season with a batting average of .406.

This same feature of the game, the unfailing, unerring designation of personal responsibility for everything that happens, also creates the opposite of heroes. If success is more personal, failure is also more obvious, and the blame for it more precisely assignable, than in the other team sports—or for that matter in most arenas of modern life. As well as its honor roll of heroes, baseball has its roster of goats. Because players with minimal skills never reach the major leagues, the stigmatized players are those of real ability who nonetheless made obvious mistakes in crucial situations: Fred Merkle, who failed to touch second base after a teammate had delivered what seemed to be a game-winning hit, resulting in the loss of the game, which ultimately cost his team, the New York Giants, the National League championship in 1908; Ralph Branca, the Brooklyn Dodgers pitcher who gave up a game-winning home run to the New York Giants' Bobby Thompson—"the shot heard round the world," perhaps the most celebrated hit in baseball history—in the ninth and final inning of the playoff game to decide the National League championship in 1951; Bill Buckner, who allowed an easily catchable ground ball to pass through his legs in the sixth game of the 1986 World Series, thereby depriving his team, the Boston Red Sox, of their first world championship in seven decades.

Because personal responsibility cannot be evaded, baseball is, in psychological terms, the cruelest sport. It requires of those who play it two different types of courage. One is physical courage. Baseball can be hazardous to a player's health. A baseball thrown by a pitcher can do serious damage if it strikes the batter.[22] Over the years a number of baseball players have died after being hit in the head by a pitched ball, and many more have suffered serious injury.[23]

Baseball requires a kind of moral courage as well, the courage to perform knowing that the frequent and inevitable failures will be personal ones, responsibility for which cannot be shirked, will be universally known, and will be recorded forever. Successful baseball players possess not only keen eyesight and quick reflexes but also strong nerves and resilient egos.

Baseball's individualism has yet another effect: It gives the sport an added dimension of interest to those who follow it. Over the course of the seven-month major league season they can monitor not only the fortunes of their favorite teams but also the individual accomplishments of their favorite players.

The contest among individual players to achieve the highest batting average or hit the most home runs in a particular season are subplots to baseball's central competition among major league teams to win the overall championship. The contest for individual honors is a game within the game, like the Tour de France, in which the entrants compete to win individual segments of the race as well as the race as a whole. In any given baseball season individuals often excel even when their teams do not. It is not at all unusual for the team that has the batting or home run champion, or the winner of the Cy Young Award for the league's best pitcher, to fail to win the pennant. Occasionally a player will turn in an historically superior performance for a team that is truly wretched. In 1972, Steve Carlton of the Philadelphia Phillies tied the National League record for victories by a left-handed pitcher with twenty-seven, and recorded one of the lowest earned run averages in fifty years, while his team won only fifty-nine games and finished in last place. Carlton's exploits provided what the rest of his teammates did not: a reason to attend the team's games (at least those in which he pitched) and to follow its fortunes throughout the season.

Individual statistics form the basis for yet another source of late-twentieth-century interest in baseball all apart from the success or failure of particular teams: "Rotisserie" leagues. In 1982, at the New York City restaurant La Rotisserie, a group of baseball enthusiasts devised a way that they could simulate the ownership and management of major league teams. The participants in Rotisserie leagues compete, to quote the dictionary definition, "by running imaginary baseball teams whose results are based on the actual performance of major-league players,"[24] which they allocate among the imaginary teams before the baseball season begins.

Individual statistics form part of the texture of baseball in yet another way. Like other aspects of the game, they help to anchor it firmly in the past through the best individual achievements in the history of the game, its records.

As a team game, baseball is cyclical: each major league team plays the same game—that is, with the same rules—162 times from April through September; the championship is decided in October; then, the following April, the same cycle begins again. As a series of individual competitions, however, baseball is a linear and a cumulative exercise. As in individual contests in track and field and swimming, players compete not only against each other but against the players, often long retired or even long dead, who have achieved the greatest performances.

Baseball's most celebrated records almost all involve offensive rather than defensive accomplishments, for two reasons. First, offensive achievements are more clearly individual, since defense involves a collaboration between pitcher and fielders.[25] Second, offensive achievements are more dramatic and vivid and thus more popular. As one astute student of baseball put it, "Offense is making things happen. Defense is keeping things from happening. People would much rather watch things happen."[26] This is true beyond the realm of sports. Action movies attract larger audiences than do performances of the Samuel Beckett play *Waiting for Godot*, in which the character in the title never arrives, although the play is, as superior defensive play can be, more subtle and elegant and, to someone with the requisite sensibility, more rewarding to watch.

Baseball's most celebrated single-season record is for home runs. For batting average in a single season, in the second half of the twentieth century the supreme goal came to be not the highest average on record—.424 by Rogers Hornsby in 1924—but rather an average at or above .400, which achieved an almost magical status both because of the allure in Western culture of round numbers and because, after 1941, while it was occasionally approached it was never achieved. Perhaps the most impressive single-season batting accomplishment is Joe DiMaggio's record, in 1941, of batting safely—getting at least one safe hit—in fifty-six consecutive games. In the six decades thereafter the closest any player came to that total was forty-four games. By sophisticated statistical reckoning this is the batting record that furthest exceeds what the law of averages would predict.*

The individual contest of statistical accomplishment within the team game of baseball becomes most exciting

* "DiMaggio's streak is the most extraordinary thing that ever happened in American sports. He sits on the shoulders of two bearers—mythology and science. For Joe DiMaggio accomplished what no other ballplayer has done. He beat the hardest taskmaster of all, a woman who makes Nolan Ryan's fastball look like a cantaloupe in slow motion—Lady Luck." Stephen Jay Gould, "The Streak of Streaks," in Dawidoff, editor, op. cit., p. 591.

when a player threatens to compile a season-long batting average of .400, or to break the established record for home runs, or consecutive games with a safe hit, or one of the many other categories of offensive prowess, such as runs batted in, or stolen bases, or total number of safe hits. The pursuit of individual seasonal records, like the pursuit of individual career records, is another tie that binds baseball's present with its past. Whenever a batter flirts with a .400 average, the media coverage invokes Ted Williams's 1941 season. When a consecutive game batting streak rises above thirty, Joe DiMaggio's name, and his achievement during that same year, become a vivid presence. Indeed, the 1941 season lives in the collective memory of baseball not for the winner of the World Series, which was the New York Yankees—the determination of which is, after all, the central purpose of every season—but rather for the two heroic batting feats. Similarly, the 1998 season is destined to be remembered not for the winning team performance of the New York Yankees but rather for the record-setting home run duel between two individuals playing for mediocre teams: Mark McGwire of the St. Louis Cardinals and Sammy Sosa of the Chicago Cubs.

Individualism and a close connection to the past are baseball's defining features, the basis for its place in American popular culture. They came to full development in the years between the 1920s and the 1960s, a four-decade span that constitutes baseball's golden age.

THE GOLDEN AGE

Traditional societies understand their own pasts through myths, modern societies through history. Baseball has both.

Its founding myth was orchestrated by Albert Spalding, a nineteenth-century player who became a sporting goods manufacturer. Like all myths, this one had a social purpose. Spalding decided that baseball needed a purely American pedigree and organized a commission in the early years of the twentieth century to discover the origins of the sport. In 1908 the Spalding Commission reported, on the basis of flimsy, unreliable, and since discredited evidence, that baseball had been invented in 1839 in the village of Cooperstown, New York, by Abner Doubleday, later a Union general in the American Civil War.[27] In fact, baseball evolved from the English game of rounders, which settlers from the Old World brought to North America as early as the eighteenth century. Like the evolution of species, over the years it incorporated some new features and shed some old ones.

Before the Civil War, the game began to assume its modern shape. By 1860 the distance between bases had been set at ninety feet and nine innings had been established as the normal length of a game. The role of the umpire had been created to judge whether a pitched ball at which the batter did not swing crossed home plate at a height between the batter's chest and knees and was therefore a strike, or passed outside the strike zone and so counted as a ball, and to decide whether runners were safe or out on the bases. The Civil War helped to spread the game all over the country—it was played in military bases and prison camps in both North and South—and in the wake of the war what had been an informal game was transformed into an organized sport. Permanent teams were formed and regular competitions among them scheduled.

The last three decades of the nineteenth century saw the advent of more of the rules and practices that defined baseball during the course of the twentieth century and into the twenty-first. The distance from the pitcher's mound to home plate was fixed at sixty feet six inches and pitchers began to deliver the ball overhand rather than with an underhanded motion. Three strikes and four balls were established as the totals for putting the batter out with a strikeout or awarding him a walk to first base. A ball falling into foul territory was deemed a strike. The catcher was moved from several feet to directly behind the batter and equipped with a chest protector. He also began to wear a padded glove (early on, a piece of beefsteak supplied the padding), as did the other players in the field.

A spectator observing a baseball game in the year 1900 would not have felt disoriented seeing the game 100 years later. With the rules and procedures of the game in place, in the first two decades of the twentieth century the modern sport took shape. The American League joined the longer-established National League as baseball's two major leagues at the outset of the twentieth century and in 1903 the champions of the two played the first World Series. The sixteen franchises that comprised the two leagues were, by 1903, located in ten cities (four cities had two teams and New York had three) stretching from Boston to Washington along the East Coast and as far west as St. Louis. This distribution would remain intact for the next half century.

The teams' owners took steps to make baseball a permanent, respectable, and (for them) lucrative form of mass entertainment. They cut down on drunkenness and rowdy behavior both on and off the field. They erected new concrete and steel ball parks, which were larger and more durable (because less vulnerable to fire) than those they replaced. The new parks became noteworthy specimens of public architecture, civic landmarks like the central post office and the city hall. The owners were able to attract more spectators to the new venues built in the years before 1920, with their greater seating capacities and more reliably tranquil environments. (Of these, Fenway Park in Boston and Wrigley Field in Chicago survived into the twenty-first century.) Baseball parks became so closely identified with and important to the cities in which they stood that by the 1960s new ones were being built with public funds.

In the first decade of the twentieth century mass-circulation daily newspapers began devoting regular attention to baseball, assigning reporters to follow and write about the local team for the sports section. This heightened interest and increased attendance. The first permanent teams had been founded in the wake of the Civil War for the purpose of making money; by the outset of the twentieth century baseball had long since been a business. In the century's first two decades it became a profitable (although not wildly profitable) business.

In the twentieth century's second decade the sport encountered two major problems. One was World War I, which intruded on the world of baseball. Attendance at games decreased and a number of players joined the military. Several, including the outstanding pitchers Grover Cleveland Alexander and Christy Matthewson, were seriously wounded while serving. The war ended in 1918 but soon thereafter another major difficulty befell the sport: scandal.

In 1920 several members of the American League champions of the previous year, the Chicago White Sox, admitted that, in exchange for payments (or the promise of payments) from gamblers, they had conspired to lose the 1919 World Series.[28]

The confessions created a crisis for baseball. By calling into question the integrity of the game they threatened the core of the sport: its identity as a genuine contest and not simply a planned performance. Baseball was rescued, and propelled into its golden age, by two men. One was Kenesaw Mountain Landis, a federal judge with a reputation for the strictest probity, whom the owners hired as their commissioner and invested with broad powers over the sport. Over the next quarter century, while Landis acted often in arbitrary and sometimes in unfair ways, his reputation for honesty served to certify the integrity of the game itself. The other savior was a lefthanded pitcher turned outfielder named Babe Ruth.

George Herman Ruth was born in Baltimore in 1895. Apparently a difficult child, his parents sent him at the age of eight to live at the St. Mary's Industrial School for Boys, a combination vocational training boarding academy and reform school. There he learned to play baseball and by 1914 had become so proficient that the local club, the Baltimore Orioles of the International League, a notch below the major leagues, signed him to a contract. At the age of nineteen (misinformed about his own birth date, he thought he was actually twenty), he was the baby of the team and was given the nickname "Babe," by which the world came to know him.

He performed in stellar fashion for the Orioles and his contract was purchased by a major league team, the Boston Red Sox. This was a familiar kind of transaction in those years. It was how major league teams filled their rosters and the owners of minor league teams made money. Ruth excelled on the diamond for the Red Sox as well, initially as a pitcher. In 1916 he was the winning pitcher in twenty-three games. He appeared in the World Series in 1914, 1915, and

1918 and set a record for consecutive innings pitched without giving up a run—twenty-nine and two-thirds—that stood for more than four decades.

He also excelled as a batter. So valuable were his batting skills that in 1919 he ceased to be a pitcher, playing only once every fourth or fifth game, and shifted to the outfield so that he could play, and bat, in every one. And it was as a batter, and as a member of the New York Yankees, the team to which the cash-strapped owner of the Red Sox sold him after the 1919 season, that he became the most famous and influential player in the history of baseball.

Ruth revolutionized the game. The American philosopher Alfred North Whitehead once observed that the history of Western philosophy can be seen as a series of footnotes to Plato. Similarly, the modern history of the game of baseball consists in some ways of a series of footnotes to Babe Ruth. His great contribution to baseball was the home run—the towering fly ball or hard-hit line drive that crosses the boundary of the playing field and lands among the spectators and sometimes even beyond. He did not invent the home run but he made it popular, common, and central to the strategy of run-scoring in the game; and in so doing he tilted the balance between offense and defense, a feature of every team sport, in the direction of the offense.

In the old order that Ruth overturned, the batter ordinarily gripped the bat several inches above the knob—he "choked up"—and tried to steer the pitch between the waiting infielders in order to reach first base safely. The goal was, in the words of a skilled nineteenth century batter, to "hit 'em where they ain't." Once a runner reached first base the predominant style called for his trying to advance one base at a time through the use of the stolen base or the bunt—holding the bat over home plate and allowing the ball to strike it and roll slowly toward the infielders. (One reason the dimensions of the early ball parks varied so widely was that the distance from home plate to the outfield grandstand was considered unimportant, since a ball would almost never be hit that far.)

Babe Ruth approached batting differently. He deployed his bat less like a log than like a golf club, wielding it not to bludgeon but to whip the ball as far as possible. He gripped it at the end and swung it as hard as he could, hoping to hit the ball a long way. With far greater frequency than anyone before him, he succeeded. He was assisted by a 1920 rule that made the batter's task easier by requiring that new, fresh baseballs replace dirty, scuffed ones during the course of the game. The period of baseball history before this rule, and before the ball had been given a cork center, in 1910, came to be known as the "dead ball" era. Since 1920, umpires have been obliged regularly to check the ball to make certain it is suitable for play.

Before Ruth became an outfielder the major league record for home runs in a single season was twenty-seven. He raised the record to twenty-nine in 1919, fifty-four in 1920, and sixty in 1927, where it stood for thirty-four years. Before he retired, the highest career total of home runs was 138. Babe Ruth hit 714.

The home run is the most spectacular event in baseball and the new emphasis on it made the game more dramatic and exciting. It became, like the lion-tamer in the circus, the game's main attraction. A home run can change the tone, the direction, and the outcome of the game with a single swing of the bat, as the prevailing pre-Ruthian tactics could not. The long arc of a home run as it leaves the bat and soars over the fence and into the stands, like a firework exploding high in the sky, can be seen from every point in the ballpark, even by those spectators seated far from the infield, the place where virtually all of the action had previously taken place.

The home run not only could be readily observed, it could, unlike the tactics of the dead ball era, be readily understood, even by onlookers untutored in the subtleties of the game. The 1920 New York Yankees became the first team to draw one million spectators in a single season. The home run, in sum, introduced an outsized, heroic element into what had been a game of cramped tactics; and the man responsible for introducing this mighty feat had a personality to match it, which helped to elevate his own popularity, along with that of the game, to new heights.

Babe Ruth cut an imposing figure. He was a big, striking-looking man, with a broad face and a barrel chest to which was added, toward the end of his career, a girth like that of a prosperous banker of the time, and spindly legs. The sight of him trotting around the bases, an odd combination of the majestic and the comic, became, through newsreels, as familiar to American moviegoers of the 1920s as the gait of Charlie Chaplin's Little Tramp.

Ruth was a man of large appetites. Some of them—for food, for example—were widely known. Others—for female companionship—were kept from the public by the code of discretion that prevailed among the journalists of that period. Particularly expansive was his appetite for attention. He loved the public spotlight. In the year 1934, with his career in decline, he was nonetheless by one estimate the most photographed person in the world. Journalists reported his exploits on and (with major exceptions) off the field because stories about Babe Ruth helped to sell newspapers.

At the height of his career, newspapers all over the country carried a feature entitled "What Babe Ruth Did Today."[29] In 1929 he was hospitalized with an intestinal abcess. The press coverage was so intense that his illness was termed "the bellyache heard 'round the world."[30]

Like Chaplin and other movie stars of the period, and gangsters and plutocrats as well, Ruth was part of the first wave of twentieth-century celebrities. (The other athletes whose renown approached his in the 1920s competed in individual sports: the boxer Jack Dempsey and the racehorse Man O'War.) Like them, he incurred the cost of celebrity, the omnipresence of enthusiastic admirers. He had the celebrity's experience of sequestering himself in hotel rooms and sneaking in and out of public places by side entrances in order to avoid the crush of adoring fans.

Testimony to Ruth's enormous popularity were his paid endorsements of a vast array of consumer products, from pajamas to automobiles. His salary was, by the standards of the day, stratospheric. In 1930, when he was paid $80,000, the next highest paid baseball player, his teammate Lou Gehrig, received $30,000.[31] Asked whether it was proper for him to earn more than the president of the United States, he is supposed to have replied, "I had a better year than he did." In fact, no record of any such conversation exists. The story is a legend, as is the story that during the 1932 World Series Ruth "called his shot" by pointing to an area of the outfield bleachers while at bat and then proceeding to hit the next pitch to precisely the spot he had indicated. Babe Ruth was, even in his own lifetime, a legendary figure.

His larger-than-life personality entered the wider culture as a figure of speech. A prodigious feat became "Ruthian." Someone who towered over his colleagues in any particular field of endeavor became the "Babe Ruth" of tennis, or of chess players, or among cheesemakers. Not the least of his accomplishments was to make the New York Yankees the most famous and successful team in all of American sports, a distinction it retained long after he had retired from the game.

In the eighty-four years after Babe Ruth joined the team, the Yankees were American League or division champions forty-two times, and in twenty-seven of those years went on to win the World Series. Between 1918 and 1965, with the exception of the war years, the Yankees finished lower than third in an eight- and then a ten-team league only once.* The team became the symbol of success, and to some a symbol of the arrogance that often accompanies success. Such was the dominance it exerted that an imperial aura came to surround the team, and it was the first in sports to carry the label borrowed from the oldest empire of all. Like the reigning houses of China, the Yankees became a "dynasty." The place where they played, which opened in 1923, was no mere park or field. It was named for the structures associated with imperial Rome, and was the first to bear the name of the team itself: Yankee Stadium.

The Yankees came to be regarded with the same mixture of admiration, envy, and resentment that characterized other Americans' attitude toward New York and New Yorkers, and with which other nations regarded the richest and most powerful country in the world. When in 1954 the author Dou-

---

* Individual Yankee teams became the subjects of books, notably Richard J. Tofel, *A Legend in the Making: The New York Yankees in 1939* (Chicago: Ivan R. Dee, 2002). The most celebrated and influential book about a particular team is Roger Kahn, *The Boys of Summer* (New York: Signet Books, 1973), about the Brooklyn Dodgers of the 1950s.

glass Wallop published a modern version of the Faust legend, the prize for which the protagonist sells his soul is the victory of the lowly Washington Senators over the perennial champions. The book, called *The Year the Yankees Lost the Pennant*,[32] was turned into a Broadway musical, the title of which captured the frustration of millions of baseball fans outside New York: *Damn Yankees*. A 2003 *New Yorker* cartoon depicted a man telling his son, "Daddy doesn't hate the Yankees. Daddy has issues with the Yankees."

Adding to the luster of the team's public image were the accomplishments of individual Yankees. At one time Babe Ruth held the record for home runs for both a single season and a career. The single-season mark was surpassed in 1961—by a single home run–by another Yankee, Roger Maris, who then held it for thirty-seven years. Lou Gehrig, Ruth's teammate, established the standard for consecutive games played—2,130, almost fourteen years' worth—which stood for six decades. Joe DiMaggio's consecutive-game batting streak survived without serious challenge into the twenty-first century. Perhaps the most notable single-game pitching performance in baseball history was turned in by a Yankee. In the fifth game of the 1956 World Series against the Brooklyn Dodgers, Don Larsen, an otherwise undistinguished player, achieved one of the game's rarest feats, pitching a perfect game by retiring twenty-seven consecutive batters over nine innings without a single one reaching first base.[33]

Babe Ruth was not the only Yankee to leave a mark on the wider culture. His teammate, Lou Gehrig, became, through his consecutive game streak, a symbol of consistency and durability. He was as sturdy and reliable as a railroad train, as his nickname, the "Iron Horse," suggested. Gehrig was struck by amyotrophic lateral sclerosis, a disease of the motor neurons, from which he died in 1941 at the age of thirty-seven. The uncomplaining way that he bore his fatal affliction made him a symbol of courage in the face of tragedy and the illness that killed him became known as "Lou Gehrig's disease."

Joe DiMaggio, the greatest Yankee star of the 1940s, was noted for the effortless grace with which he excelled in every aspect of the game, at bat and in the field. If Gehrig was a powerful engine, he was a sailing ship—the "Yankee Clipper." His status as an icon of purity and integrity, in a world all too short of both, was ratified nearly two decades after he had stopped playing, when a lyric from the song "Mrs. Robinson" written by Paul Simon for the 1967 film *The Graduate* included a longing reference to him.[34] Upon retiring, DiMaggio cemented his status in the firmament of popular culture by marrying one of the few people in the United States as famous as he, the movie star Marilyn Monroe. A story told about them illustrates the celebrity status of the star player, which Babe Ruth had pioneered. The two went to Japan for their honeymoon and the bride made a side trip to Korea to entertain the American troops stationed there. She received a rapturous response. When she returned, she said to her new husband, "Joe, you never heard such cheers." "Yes I have," he replied.[35]

While Ruth was an epic figure and Gehrig and DiMaggio heroic ones, two of the most famous Yankees of the 1950s— their manager, Charles Dillon Stengel, known as "Casey" because his home town was Kansas City, Missouri, and Lawrence Peter Berra, nicknamed "Yogi" because his stocky build and large hands once reminded someone of a picture he had seen of a Hindu holy man—entered the wider culture as comic characters. Although each excelled at his job—Stengel's twelve Yankee teams won ten pennants and seven world championships between 1949 and 1960 and Berra was, in the view of at least one well-informed observer, the best catcher in the history of baseball[36]—both became known for their distinctive uses of the English language. Stengel wrapped nuggets of insight in mounds of confusing verbiage. He would regale his listeners, usually sportswriters but on one occasion a Congressional committee, with rambling disquisitions that strayed far from the designated subject only to arrive, unexpectedly, at an acute insight. He was baseball's version of a standup comedian, entertaining audiences with singular verbal routines.

Berra earned a reputation, within the world of baseball but extending far beyond it, as a kind of syntactical idiot savant, the source of observations illogical on their face yet readily intelligible and somehow all the more striking for the fractured way in which they were expressed. Of a popular restaurant he said: "Nobody goes there any more. It's too crowded." Of the problem of attracting spectators to baseball games: "If the fans don't want to come out to the ballpark, we can't stop them." Of the shadows that enveloped the left field area of Yankee Stadium midway through afternoon games in the fall: "It gets late early out there." As with Babe Ruth's deeds, some of Yogi Berra's words may be apocryphal. "I didn't say half the things I said," he once said—or is said to have said.

The most memorable Yankees of the 1970s were baseball's version of a constantly bickering couple, the owner, George Steinbrenner, who purchased the team in 1973, and the manager he hired and fired on five separate occasions, Billy Martin. Martin had the personality of a juvenile delinquent. He was cocky, smarmy, knowing, sneaky, angry, and with a powerful self-destructive streak that ultimately killed him—he died in an auto accident while driving drunk. Steinbrenner was every employee's nightmare of a boss: harsh, arbitrary, capricious, and not entirely above board. Including Martin's multiple tenures Steinbrenner hired and fired eighteen different managers in the first seventeen years that he owned the team. His feuds and reconciliations with Martin gave baseball its own ongoing soap opera, and the same newspapers that had recorded Babe Ruth's daily activities chronicled its almost-daily episodes in their pages. (In the 1990s a somewhat calmer Steinbrenner saw his Yankees establish yet another period of domination, this one uncharacteristically free of memorable characters, with six American League championships and four World Series victories between 1996 and 2003.)

Ruth, Gehrig, DiMaggio, Stengel, Berra, Martin, and Steinbrenner's team cast so large a shadow over all the rest of baseball that two of the other most celebrated and popular clubs became noted in no small part for their futility in comparison with the Yankees. The Boston Red Sox and Chicago Cubs were known for their old and agreeably intimate home ballparks, which were set in urban neighborhoods and retained their antique aura. But the two also shared the dubious distinction of having gone for the longest periods of time without winning a World Series. By the beginning of the 2004 season the Cubs' non-winning streak stood at ninety-four years, that of the Red Sox at eighty-four. Among the more successful teams before 1920—the Boston team won the world championship six times, the Cubs twice—from the moment Babe Ruth joined the Yankees neither won the championship again.[37]

Because they competed directly with the Yankees in the American League, the failures of the Red Sox were the direct result of the Yankees' success. Indeed, the connection was even closer. It was, after all, the Boston team that had sold Babe Ruth, its star player, to New York.* For the long-suffering Red Sox fans, this was a sin that cast a pall over the subsequent fortunes of the team. The term Bostonians coined for the stigma the Red Sox bore used one of Ruth's nicknames, the Italian word for *baby*: "the curse of the Bambino."

Ruth and the Yankees were crucial to the rising status of baseball beginning in the third decade of the twentieth century. It became the most popular of the team sports and a leading form of summer entertainment. Its status gave substance to the description of baseball, which first appeared in the nineteenth century, as America's national game.

It was national in the sense that its appeal crossed the boundaries of race, class, geography, ethnicity, age, and religion. In its golden age, as the novelist and baseball fan Philip Roth put it, "Baseball was a kind of secular church that reached into every class and region and bound us together in common concerns, loyalties, rituals, enthusiasms, and antagonisms. Baseball made me understand what patriotism was about, at its best."[38]

It was national as well in that it deliberately identified itself with patriotic themes. During World War I the custom of playing "The Star-Spangled Banner" before each game

---

* The offending Red Sox owner was Harry Frazee, a theatrical impresario who found himself short of cash at the end of the 1919 season. He later launched the Broadway hit *No, No, Nanette*, and legend has it that he used the payment for Ruth's contract to put up the money for that particular show. In fact, the play opened five years later. It proved a financial success, raising the possibility that if it had been running in 1919 Frazee would not have felt the need to sell his star player and the history of baseball would have taken a different course.

began (it was not until 1931 that the song became the official national anthem) as did the practice of decorating with red, white, and blue bunting the ballparks where the World Series was played. The game asserted its special national standing as well by its identification with the president of the United States. In 1886 Grover Cleveland became the first president to welcome a championship team—the Chicago White Sox—to the White House. And in 1910 William Howard Taft, once a catcher on an amateur team in his home town of Cincinnati, inaugurated what became an annual rite of spring by throwing out a symbolic first pitch at the opening game of the baseball season.

Perhaps the high point of baseball's tenure as America's national game came in January 1942, a mere five weeks after Pearl Harbor. In response to an inquiry from Commissioner Landis, President Franklin Roosevelt sent what became known as the "green light" letter, expressing his view that major league baseball should continue during World War II—as it did, although without many of its best players, who joined the military. "I honestly feel that it would be best for the country to keep baseball going," the president wrote. "Everybody will work longer hours and harder than ever before. And that means that they ought to have a chance for recreation and for taking their minds off their work even more than before."[39]

During its golden age baseball came to be known not only as the national game but also as the national *pastime*.[40] The dictionary definition of pastime is "something that serves to make time pass agreeably, a pleasant means of amusement, recreation, or sport,"[41] but the term also underscores the game's connection to the past. So, too, did the fact that, in important ways, the game and the sport remained unchanged for what counts, in contemporary American life, as a long time.*

Some developments did take place, but two of the most significant served to reinforce the sense of baseball's timelessness based on its ties to its own, and the nation's, past. In 1939 the National Baseball Museum, known as the Hall of Fame, opened in Cooperstown, New York. The site, chosen because of its supposed connection to the game's beginnings, evoked the nation's rural past: a small village located among mountains at the tip of a lake. The main business of the Hall of Fame turned out to be the annual election to membership of retired players whose achievements had, in the opinion of a panel of designated sportswriters, earned them a place there. Without any fixed standards for membership, the process of choosing new members, and the discussion and debate that surrounded the process each year, inevitably involved comparing the accomplishments of candidates for admission with those of players already enshrined, an exercise that seemed entirely plausible precisely because the game had changed so little. In yet another way, therefore, baseball's past was injected into its present.

Similarly, the broadcasting of baseball games over the radio, which began in 1921, although the product of twentieth-century technological innovation, harked back to the world before printing, even before written manuscripts, when all information was transmitted orally. The broadcasters were

---

* The same sixteen teams remained in the same ten cities for half a century, from 1903 to 1953; and for the three decades after 1923 major league games were played in the same parks. The rules of the game and the schedule of the season—opening day, the pennant races stretching over 154 games, the World Series—all remained the same. The dominance of the Yankees was a recurrent theme. Judge Landis presided over the major leagues as commissioner for almost a quarter century, from 1921 to 1944. Even the uniforms the players wore remained largely unchanged from year to year.

akin to the poets and troubadours who preserved and handed down the great tales of their cultures by committing them to memory and reciting them publicly.*

The dominant style of baseball broadcasting, moreover, turned out to be folksy, with the liberal use of the language of rural and small-town America. The signature phrase of the Brooklyn Dodgers' Mississippi-born broadcaster Walter "Red" Barber, for example, which he used to refer to a favorable situation for one team or the other, was "the catbird seat." Catbirds were rare in Brooklyn.†

The generation that dominated American life during baseball's golden age, if it did not emerge directly from rural, traditional America, did have memories of the older way of life. It was born toward the end of the nineteenth century, when that way of life was disappearing.[42] The 1920 census showed that the United States was, for the first time, a predominantly urban rather than a rural country. But this generation was raised by one that had had the opportunity to experience the frontier at first hand. And the many Americans of this age group who immigrated to North America came originally from sections of Europe that remained rural and traditional. The traditional, rural past was near enough in time for baseball to evoke nostalgia for it.

---

* Occasionally the radio broadcaster was not even present at the game. He sat in a studio, received a bare-bones account of the events of a distant game by telegraph, and supplemented the basic facts with his imagination to paint a vivid picture for his listeners. Ronald Reagan narrated Chicago Cubs games over station WHO in Des Moines, Iowa, in this way. Such games were not, officially, broadcast: They were "re-created."

† The humorist James Thurber used the phrase as the title of a short story. Thurber also wrote a short story about baseball. "You Could Look It Up" concerns a fictional team that sends a midget to bat in order to draw a walk. A decade later, life imitated art. As a way of gaining publicity for a bad team, the St. Louis Browns signed a midget and sent him to bat in a major league game. He walked.

A measure of baseball's standing at the heart of American life is its transcendence of the boundary between popular and high culture. More than either of the other two major team sports, baseball has had "crossover appeal"—attracting interest from groups with little else in common. It is, of course, first and foremost a form of popular entertainment. But it has also been the subject of serious literary treatment and rigorous quantitative analysis. In the national life of the United States, baseball has made a place for itself in both the arts and the sciences.

ARTISTS AND SCIENTISTS

Were there a Hall of Fame for American novelists, Mark Twain, F. Scott Fitzgerald, and Ernest Hemingway would be charter members. And in the work of each can be found a reference to baseball. In Twain's *A Connecticut Yankee at King Arthur's Court* the American who is transported to medieval England introduces the game to the Knights of the Round Table. Meyer Wolfsheim, one of the characters in Fitzgerald's masterpiece *The Great Gatsby*, is based on Arnold Rothstein, the gambler alleged to have been the ringleader in the fixing of the 1919 World Series.* And Hemingway's *The Old Man and the Sea* refers to "the great DiMaggio."

Baseball, along with writers from Herman Melville to

---

* Rothstein turns up in another classic work of popular American storytelling, this one on the screen rather than in print. In Francis Ford Coppola's *The Godfather*, the criminal impresario Hyman Roth, played by Lee Strasberg (and modeled after the real-life gangster Meyer Lansky), tells Al Pacino's Michael Corleone, as they watch a game on television in a scene set in the late 1950s, "Baseball's been my favorite sport ever since a friend of mine, Arnold Rothstein, fixed the 1919 World Series." His life is described in David Pietrusza, *Rothstein: The Life, Times and Murder of the Criminal Genius Who Fixed the 1919 World Series* (New York: Carroll and Graf, 2003).

James Baldwin and subjects such as the debates about the American constitution and reporting on World War II, but unlike football and basketball, has its own volume in *The Library of America* series. By 1889, when *A Connecticut Yankee* was published, not to mention in 1925 and 1952, the publication dates of *The Great Gatsby* and *The Old Man and the Sea*, baseball was lodged firmly enough in the general American cultural consciousness that a writer could feel confident that allusions to it would be widely understood.

Further evidence of baseball's place at the center of the national life comes from popular figures of speech that originated in the language of the sport. To "strike out" connotes failure of almost any kind. To defer acceptance of an invitation is to "take a rain check."[43] Something unexpected arrives "out of left field."

So familiar was baseball to the American reading public by the second half of the twentieth century that novelists not only referred to it in telling their stories, they also used it as the setting for some of these stories. The sport had an appeal to writers of fiction beyond its cultural familiarity, an appeal stemming from the nature of the game itself.

The novel, as distinct from other narrative forms, emphasizes the development of individual character rather than the presentation of an archetype. It portrays people who are different from all others. They are original, "novel." Character is revealed over time in a setting rich enough to display its various features. The novel blends psychology and sociology. Baseball supplies both elements. It is a narrative of individual success and failure, which lends itself to the exploration of character; and it is an activity, indeed a world, as familiar to readers of American novels in the twentieth century as the customs and beliefs of the rural gentry in early-nineteenth-century England would have been to Jane Austen's contemporary readers.[44]

Coincidentally, the first serious work of baseball fiction took the same unusual form as the book often considered the first modern novel. Ring Lardner's *You Know Me, Al*, like Samuel Richardson's 1741 novel *Pamela*, is an epistolary novel, consisting of a series of letters from Jack Keefe to his friend Al that portray life as a member of the Chicago White Sox. Jack is an earnest *naif*, a "hayseed" to use the term of the time, in the tradition of Voltaire's Candide.[45]

In 1952 Bernard Malamud published *The Natural*, which sets the English legend of King Arthur in twentieth-century America, with baseball as the context. The hero who appears from nowhere to conquer the metropolis is Roy Hobbs, a ballplayer. The equivalent of Excalibur, the magic sword Arthur pulls from the stone to prove his legitimacy, is Roy's bat, named "Wonderboy."

In 1953 Mark Harris published *The Southpaw*, the first of what would be four novels that explore the world of baseball. In 1968 there appeared Robert Coover's *The Universal Baseball Association Inc., J. Henry Waugh, Prop.*, which uses a fan's involvement with an imaginary baseball league of his own creation in the same way that other authors have used other obsessions to explore the line between passion and madness.

The opening scene of Don DeLillo's *Underworld* is the epochal playoff game between the New York Giants and the Brooklyn Dodgers on October 3, 1951, that the Giants won on Bobby Thompson's ninth-inning home run. In his description of that game the themes that the author develops in the course of the book, which are major themes in the life of the nation in the second half of the twentieth century, come together. Baseball symbolizes the sunny uplands of

American life, the open, pastoral reverie, which contrasts with the dark, secret, subterranean current embodied by the atomic bomb, the first full-fledged Soviet version of which was tested on the same day as the game.

While baseball became a subject for writers of serious literature, writing about baseball also took on a literary character. This was particularly evident in the articles by Roger Angell that appeared *The New Yorker*. Like a novelist, Angell depicted the game as an arena for the revelation of character. He portrayed, for example, the post-baseball life of Bob Gibson, one of the best pitchers in the history of the game and the possessor of a "proud, obdurate personality"[46] that was the key both to his success in the game and his difficulties after he left it. He portrayed as well the baffled, helpless Steve Blass, also a pitcher of significant albeit lesser distinction, whose ability to throw the ball in the strike zone, the necessary basis for success in pitching, vanished—suddenly, without warning, and without explanation. Like the work of novelists, Angell's writing makes liberal use of metaphor. The batting stance of Hall of Fame outfielder Frank Robinson, for example, "was that of an impatient subway traveler leaning over the edge of the platform and peering down the tracks for the D train."[47] Angell came by his affinity for literary techniques naturally: His full-time job was as fiction editor of *The New Yorker*.

In his own principal job George Will has been a professional analyst of and commentator on public life. He has undertaken, twice a week, to explain to his readers why public officials were doing what they did, and what they should be doing. He, too, brought the techniques of his full-time occupation to the exploration of the summer game.

Like electoral politics and international relations, baseball is a competitive activity that requires of its participants strategies that lend themselves to explanation and criticism. In his principal book about baseball, *Men at Work: The Craft of Baseball*, like his newspaper columns an exercise in both reporting and analysis, Will explored the foundations of baseball strategy. He followed, and interviewed, four accomplished figures of the 1980s to discover how they approached the game and why they excelled in one particular aspect of it: the batter Tony Gwynn, the pitcher Orel Hersheiser, the infielder Cal Ripken, and the manager Tony LaRussa.

Baseball lends itself to an even more rigorous form of analysis, the kind practiced in science. Scientific investigation of the natural world relies heavily on controlled experiments. In the study of the social world, where such experiments are rarely possible, the scientific equivalent of experiments is the analysis of statistics. And statistics are, of course, things that baseball generates in abundance.

The publication of Macmillan's *Baseball Encyclopedia* in 1969 marked an important moment in the history of baseball statistics. It contained the most complete compilation of baseball records that had ever been assembled and so made widely available a treasure trove of information about the game.[48] In the 1970s a small number of devoted baseball fans began to use the now-available statistics to analyze the game. They gave their field of statistical inquiry the title "sabermetrics," after the acronym of the Society for American Baseball Research to which they belonged, which had been founded in Cooperstown in 1971.[49]

The sabermetricians approached the game of baseball the way the modern economist approaches the understanding of economic life. As in the work of economists in the second half of the twentieth century, where the predominant way of understanding their subject had been descriptive, they made it analytical. They did so by posing questions—why do the records of some teams improve dramatically from one year to the next?, for example, or how large a contribution do stolen bases make to winning games?—and then conducting statistical tests based on the abundant data available to determine the answers. Many of the tests depended on the use of computers and had been impractical to conduct before their advent.

Some of their findings proved difficult to accept. One of the questions posed was whether some batters hit particularly well in "clutch" situations, when the stakes are unusually high because a hit can win the game. A series of studies failed to uncover any evidence that particular players were prone to rise to such occasions, leading to the following exchange between a reader and a sports columnist of *The Wall Street Journal*: "Q: You've often said you don't believe in clutch performance, yet you talk about it frequently. Do you believe in it or not? A: I agree with the Irish woman who was asked if she believed in leprechauns. 'I do not,' she replied, 'but they're there.'"[50]

The term "sabermetrics" was coined by the most prominent of its practitioners, Bill James, who turned his childhood fascination with baseball into an influential adult career. After college and military service he took a job as a boiler room attendant in a meat-packing plant in his home state of Kansas, an undemanding position that gave him considerable time to scrutinize and analyze baseball statistics.[51] He began to publish his findings in 1977, first privately for friends and then, beginning in 1982 and for most of the rest of that decade, through a commercial press as the annual *Bill James Baseball Abstract*. The publication, which last appeared in 1988, proved popular both for the pithy, witty way in which it was written and, more importantly, because it presented what were, for virtually all of its readers, new insights into a game they thought they knew well.

Sabermetrics, combined with the use of the computer, had the same effect as the invention of the microscope. It permitted people to see the inner structure and the fundamental dynamics of something that had seemed familiar. In so doing, sabermetrics clarified features of baseball that had been obscure and corrected widely held beliefs about the game that, when held up to the light of scientific scrutiny, turned out to have been mistaken.[52] One of the most comprehensive accounts of the findings of sabermetrics was entitled *The Hidden Game of Baseball*.[53]

In the spirit of Benjamin Disraeli's assertion that "there are three kinds of lies: lies, damned lies, and statistics," the sabermetricians discovered that the most familiar offensive statistics, the ones printed in newspapers every day and by which the offensive prowess of individual players is widely judged, are misleading because they do not fully measure how much players actually contribute to the goal of the offense in baseball, and the key to winning games, namely scoring runs. The three most familiar individual statistical achievements were, and continue to be, home runs, runs batted in, and batting average. A player who leads his league in all three categories—a rare feat and one never accomplished by Babe Ruth or by anyone at all in the last three decades of the twentieth century—is said to have won the "Triple Crown."

While home runs measure individual achievement, runs batted in do not. A player's total depends on the ability of his teammates to reach base. A good player with a poor team is likely to drive in fewer runs than a lesser player whose team-mates are better able to put themselves in position to be "driven in."

Batting average is the oldest and most prestigious category (the statistic was first computed in the 1870s and as early as 1910 the batting champion, as he was called, earned a new car)[54] and the one listed first in the newspapers; and it is, if anything, an even more misleading measure of offensive ability than runs batted in. Sabermetricians discovered, through statistical research, that the two most important contributions to the overriding goal of scoring runs are getting on base and advancing runners already on base. Batting average provides a very partial, and therefore imperfect, measure of both. It is an imperfect measure of the ability to reach base because it excludes one important method of doing so, the walk. A player who walks frequently is more valuable, all other things being equal, than one with a slightly higher batting average who, because he is impatient, or a poor judge of the strike zone, walks far less often.

The measure of a player's capacity to reach base is his "on-base average," which includes walks (and the times a batter is safe because of an error and is hit by a pitch) as well as safe hits. But that statistic has far less currency, despite the proselytizing of the sabermetricians, than the batting average.

Similarly, the batting average offers an imperfect gauge of the ability to advance runners because, in compiling it, every safe hit, be it a single, double, triple, or home run, counts equally: the average is reckoned by dividing safe hits of all kinds by official times at bat. For the purpose of advancing runners, however, hits are decidedly not of equal value. For this important purpose a double is at least twice as valuable as a single, a home run worth four times as much. A player with a relatively low batting average but a propensity for extra-base (non-single) hits may therefore contribute more to his team than someone with a higher batting average that is based almost exclusively on singles.

The statistic that measures the ability to advance runners and thereby to contribute to the scoring of runs is slugging percentage: total bases achieved divided by times at bat. In 1920 Babe Ruth set a record that stood for eight decades by compiling a slugging percentage of .847. But while his total of sixty home runs seven years later became the most famous individual achievement in all of baseball, perhaps in all of sports, the earlier mark—as a contribution to the basic purpose of baseball, the winning of games, a greater achievement—was known to perhaps one in a thousand baseball fans.

The sabermetricians proposed new statistics, usually combining on-base and slugging percentage, as truer measures of offensive ability. None caught the baseball public's imagination. The triple crown statistics continued to occupy pride of place in the daily newspapers. But attentive baseball fans absorbed the sabermetricians' basic point, and these fans' perspective on the game, and on individual batting activity, changed accordingly.

The sabermetricians' findings had implications for how baseball ought to be played, but for the first quarter century after the movement began the people responsible for selecting and managing teams ignored them. In the 1990s this began to change. One executive, Billy Beane, the general manager of the Oakland Athletics, having read what Bill James and other sabermetricians were writing, built successful teams by emphasizing the qualities that the sabermetricians had discovered were most important, above all the ability to get on base and to hit for power.[55] His team's success—it reached the playoffs for four consecutive years between 2000 and 2003 and in 2002 won the Western division of the American League with 102 victories, which equaled the total of the mighty Yankees—was all the more noteworthy because Beane had far less money to spend on building his team than did his wealthier rivals. The sabermetricians' findings helped to offset the advantages that the gusher of revenue from local television fees conferred on teams operating in the largest cities. And in 2002 the long-suffering Boston Red Sox hired Bill James himself as a consultant.[56]

Sabermetricians discovered that the most frequently compiled offensive statistics mislead in yet another way. A player's achievements are assessed in comparison with those of other players. Seasonal achievements—winning the championships in batting, runs batted in, or home runs—involve exceeding the totals in these categories that all other players compile. The pursuit of records—for a season or a career—pits the pursuer against the record-holder of the past. But these comparative assessments omit a crucial dimension. Individual numbers are meaningful only in the context in which they are achieved, and the context for baseball achievements, as the sabermetricians' research demonstrated, varies substantially across both space and time.

Every player plays half of all his games in his home park, and major league ballparks are not uniform. Besides the distance from home plate to the fences that delimit the playing field and the amount of foul territory, the predominant wind patterns, the backgrounds against which the batters see the pitch coming toward home plate, and other conditions differ from one field to another. Some parks are therefore friendlier to the batter, and thus to the scoring of runs, than are others. The average number of runs scored per game displays surprising variation across the American and National Leagues.

Players whose teams inhabit batter-friendly home parks will tend to compile more impressive statistics than will those of equal or even superior ability who play half their games in parks that favor the pitcher. Because the New York Mets play in pitcher-friendly Shea Stadium, for example, the team's pitchers have often led the National League in strikeouts and earned run average but no Mets player has ever won the batting championship. When the Houston Astros played their home games in the Astrodome, a park notoriously unfriendly to batters, players who moved from the Astros to another major league team often raised their seasonal batting averages by thirty or forty points in their new surroundings.

This means, of course, that where a player plays exerts a major influence on his career totals as well as his seasonal achievements. It was decidedly advantageous to Babe Ruth to play in Yankee Stadium, where the short distance to the right field boundary favored lefthanded home run hitters. The same conditions disfavored righthanded batters, such as Joe DiMaggio, who, had he played for a team with a more accommodating home field, would have hit more home runs during his career.

Moreover, some periods in baseball's history, like some ballparks, were far friendlier to batters (and thus more unfriendly to pitchers) than others. The shift in the balance of advantage in the game in favor of the offense, which began with Babe Ruth and the "lively ball" of the 1920s, was reversed in the 1960s. A series of subtle changes, which were not formally legislated by the sport's ruling authorities, strengthened major league pitchers and weakened batters. Two in particular were important: the umpires expanded the strike zone, and the pitcher's mounds were raised slightly so that the angle at which the ball approached the batter was greater, making pitches move faster.

The average number of runs scored per game decreased throughout major league baseball. So did batting averages and home run totals. In 1968, the zenith of the period of the supremacy of the pitcher, Carl Yaztrzemski of the Boston Red Sox captured the American League batting championship with the lowest winning number in the history of major league baseball: .301. In that same season, the St. Louis Cardinals' pitcher Bob Gibson recorded the lowest earned run average—1.12—in sixty-two years, since the pre-Ruthian dead-ball era, and Denny McLain of the Detroit Tigers became the first pitcher in thirty-four years to win at least thirty games (he won thirty-one). In the subsequent thirty-five years no pitcher achieved that total. In the 1970s the balance began to shift back, gradually but steadily, toward the batter. In the 1990s the movement in this direction accelerated, leading to an explosion of home runs in which the single-season record was broken twice in four years, by Mark McGwire with seventy in 1998 and by Barry Bonds with seventy-three in 2001.

The proper comparison of batting and pitching performance across time, the sabermetricians concluded, required statistical adjustments to allow for differences in the overall balance between offense and defense in the periods being compared, just as economists must make statistical adjustments to account for inflation or deflation in comparing prices across time. And the balance between offense and defense was not the only aspect of baseball that changed over the course of the twentieth century.

THE SILVER AGE

For all its continuities, and for all of its appeal as a preserved fragment of the past, baseball did not remain frozen throughout the twentieth century. It did change, and with increasing rapidity beginning in the middle of the century. Two of those changes count as important events not only in the history of the sport but also in the history of the United States, for they were milestones in trends that transformed American society. These milestones were the racial integration of the sport in 1947 and the transfer of two major league franchises from New York to California in 1958.

The architect of the end of segregation in baseball was Branch Rickey, at the time the general manager and part owner of the Brooklyn Dodgers. Before coming to Brooklyn he had earned a reputation as an executive of uncommon shrewdness with the St. Louis Cardinals, where he had invented the system of developing players on minor league teams that the major league team owned. Between 1919 and 1942 the Cardinals won six National League pennants and four world championships, a record of success second only to that of the Yankees.

In 1946 he signed Jackie Robinson, then under contract to the Kansas City Monarchs, a team in the Negro Baseball League, to play for the Dodgers' minor league affiliate in Canada, the Montreal Royals. The next season Rickey brought Robinson to the Dodgers and on April 15, 1947, he became the first known American of African descent to play in a major league game in the twentieth century.[57]

Robinson's debut began the process of integrating the sport, which reached its zenith in 1974, when 26 percent of all major league players were African-Americans.[58] The integration of baseball followed a well-established pattern. The sport had served, since the nineteenth century, as a vehicle for including, in a visible arena of national life, representatives of ethnic groups subject to disdain and discrimination in the society at large. As was the case for Jackie Robinson, some of the ethnic pioneers initially encountered considerable hostility. A contemporary player said of Hank Greenberg, the Jewish slugger for the Detroit Tigers in the 1930s and 1940s, "There was nobody in the history of the game who took more abuse than Hank Greenberg, unless it was Jackie Robinson."[59]

Moreover, Jackie Robinson's significance for baseball lies in the fact that he opened the way not only for African-Americans but also for players, many of them also of African ancestry, from the Spanish-speaking parts of the western hemisphere, to which the game had spread from North America in the nineteenth century. This prefigured the most important demographic trend in the United States in the last third of the twentieth century, the growing proportion of Hispanics in the population. Following in Robinson's footsteps came a trickle, which turned into a torrent, of skilled players from Cuba, Puerto Rico, Venezuela, Mexico, Panama, Nicaragua, and other places in Latin America.

By the year 2003 almost 24 percent of all major league players were Latins, the largest number of whom came from the Dominican Republic, a small country situated on the eastern half of the island of Hispaniola in the Caribbean Sea.[60] Baseball there was more than a pastime: It was a passion that consumed virtually the entire male population, a pathway out of poverty in a predominantly poor society, and a source of individual and national identity, its status matched only by that of soccer in Brazil and perhaps cricket in India. Dominican players were notable for their impatience at bat. They brought to the game a propensity to swing even at pitches out of the strike zone, a logical habit considering that thousands of them competed as youngsters to attract the attention of scouts for major league teams in order to earn contracts to play in the United States. The way to stand out from the crowd in those circumstances was not to wait for four pitches out of the strike zone and then move to first base, but rather to hit the ball hard, often, and far. The unofficial motto of aspiring young Dominican baseball players accordingly was, "You can't walk off the island."

Of the Dominican players in the major leagues, a formidable number hailed from just one city, the port of San Pedro de Marcoris, population 100,000, which produced major league shortstops with odds-defying frequency.

Yet the surpassing significance of Jackie Robinson's entry into major league baseball had to do with the experience of African-Americans in the United States. For all the similarities of that experience to those of Irish, German, Italian, Jewish, and Hispanic immigrants, black Americans have never been simply one ethnic group among many. No other group was brought to North America involuntarily, forced into slavery upon arrival, and then subjected, after slavery had formally ended, to a century of forced separation from all other groups in all the major spheres of American life, including baseball.

Jackie Robinson is an important figure in American history because of the particular, and particularly oppressed, status of African-Americans in the life of the nation and because baseball was the first visible institution in American civilian life in which they were able to participate on equal terms with whites. Before the Supreme Court decision outlawing segregated schools, *Brown v. Board of Education*, in 1954, before the civil rights movement and the civil rights legislation of the 1960s, came the Brooklyn Dodgers versus the Boston Braves on April 15, 1947. Jackie Robinson's career in baseball helped to end the enforced separation of African-Americans throughout American life because, from the moment it began, it gave the lie to the beliefs on which segregation in baseball—and, in modified form, segregation in American society as a whole—had rested. One of those beliefs was that white players would not accept black teammates or opponents. Although subjected to racially motivated abuse, Robinson was accepted by the Dodgers. A few major league players threatened to boycott games in which he took part, but none carried out the threat.

A second belief that Jackie Robinson's performance undercut was that African-American players could not compete in the field with their white counterparts. Robinson, and the black and Latin players who followed him, more than held their own. Robinson was voted the Rookie of the Year in the National League for 1947 and the league's Most Valuable Player in 1949. He retired from the game following the 1956 season and five years later was elected to the Hall of Fame. The Dodgers won the National League championship six times during his ten years with the club.

A third prediction that evaporated during Robinson's first year with the Dodgers was that fans would shun games played by integrated teams. To the contrary, in 1947 the Dodgers had the highest attendance in their history, drawing over one million spectators for the first time, and the total attendance in the National League surpassed its previous all-time high.[61] Branch Rickey was, by all accounts, a man committed to racial justice[62] and that commitment no doubt underlay his decision to break baseball's color line. But Rickey was also an intense competitor and a shrewd businessman, devoted to the pursuit of victories and profit. Jackie Robinson brought both, and the Dodgers' successes on the field and at the box office, regardless of whether Rickey fully anticipated them, were scarcely unwelcome to him. More importantly, that success impressed the owners of other teams, who proceeded, albeit at differing speeds (the Boston Red Sox did not field their first black player until 1958), to follow his example.

When Jackie Robinson stepped on to a major league diamond for the first time he put the Brooklyn Dodgers, for a moment, at the center not only of the baseball world but of American life. So, too, did another decision a decade later by the Dodgers' ownership, which by this time did not include Branch Rickey: the decision to move the team to Los Angeles.

For fifty years major league baseball was played in the same cities. Then, in 1953, its geographic scope began to change. In that year and the next, three teams in cities with two major league franchises relocated to cities with none: the Boston Braves moved to Milwaukee, leaving the Red Sox as the only team in town; the same year the St. Louis Browns decamped to Baltimore and became the Orioles, with the Cardinals remaining in the Midwest; and after the 1954 season the Athletics ceded Philadelphia to the Phillies and transferred to what became the westernmost outpost of major league baseball, Kansas City. In each case, the new city lay close enough to the sites of existing franchises that teams could continue to travel by rail.

A more radical break with the past came in the 1958 season: The Dodgers moved to Los Angeles and, simultaneously, their National League rivals, the New York Giants, abandoned their park in upper Manhattan, the Polo Grounds, for San Francisco. Three years later four teams were added to the major leagues, two in each league, and by 2003, a half century after the changes began, major league baseball consisted of thirty teams located in twenty-eight cities all over North America: in the Pacific Northwest (Seattle), the Rocky Mountains (Denver), the deep South (Atlanta, Miami, and Tampa), Texas, and even in Canada (Montreal and Toronto) as well as the Northeast and Midwest. Only New York and Chicago retained two teams.

Baseball changed because the country changed. The American population moved, in ways that compelled baseball to follow. The people who made up baseball's paying audience moved from the inner cities to the suburbs. Baseball had difficulty persuading them to return to attend games both because these neighborhoods became increasingly unappealing places to spend leisure time and because of the lack of space to park the cars they needed to drive there.

At the same time, the population in the regions beyond the original scope of major league baseball grew more rapidly than the Northeast and Midwest, where the original teams were located. On the eve of World War II, Los Angeles, with no major league team, had a population bigger than all major league cities except New York and Chicago. It had 700,000 more people than did St. Louis, where two teams played.[63]

The significance of the two New York teams' move to the West Coast, like that of Jackie Robinson's debut, transcended baseball. It symbolized a new stage in the geographic integration of the United States, one in which regular commercial air service by jet aircraft, which carried National League teams to and from San Francisco and Los Angeles, made transcontinental travel unprecedentedly swift, accessible, and easy—and therefore routine. It symbolized as well the emergence of California as an economic, political, and cultural center to rival New York.

The removal of the Dodgers also symbolized, and hastened, the decline of Brooklyn, from the middle of the nineteenth century to the middle of the twentieth a community with a flourishing commercial and civic life and, even as a borough of the larger New York City, with its own distinctive identity. In the 1950s, when the *Brooklyn Eagle*, the borough's last daily publication, shut down, a sportswriter wrote, "Brooklyn is the only American city of two million people without a newspaper, a mayor, or a leftfielder."[64] After 1957 it had no fielder of any kind and less of the vitality that had made it, among other things, a natural home for a major league team.[65]

The implicit covenant between baseball and its followers promised loyalty in exchange for changelessness; but the two mid-century changes, far from ruining the sport, gave it a shot in the arm. Baseball could hardly have sustained its claim to being the national pastime as a game reserved for white North American players and played at the highest level of skill only in the Northeast and Midwest of the United States. The period that followed integration and the move to California, if not the golden age that the sport enjoyed in the decades after Babe Ruth transformed it, qualifies as baseball's silver age.

Racial integration brought to the major leagues some of baseball's greatest players. Two of them came from the

Negro League in the early 1950s. Willie Mays was signed by the New York Giants from the Birmingham Black Barons. In his twenty-three-year career in the major leagues he established himself as the Picasso of the game, excelling at every aspect of the craft and performing each with the flair of a gifted, flamboyant artist. On defense he was perhaps the best centerfielder ever to play the game. On the base paths he led the league in stolen bases four times. At bat he ended his career with 660 home runs and would surely have hit more had he played in a ballpark friendlier to hitters than San Francisco's Candlestick Park.

Henry Aaron came to the Milwaukee Braves from the Indianapolis Clowns. Like Mays, he was a rarity in baseball, a "five-tool" player, with exceptional abilities at hitting for average, hitting for power, running, fielding, and throwing. He played for twenty-three years and his consistently strong offensive performances left him, when he retired, the major league career leader in home runs, his total of 755 surpassing Babe Ruth's 714. In the 1956 All-Star game, Mays and Aaron comprised the starting outfield for the National League along with Frank Robinson, another stellar African-American player: He was the only man to win the Most Valuable Player award in both major leagues and when he retired he was the fourth leading home runner hitter in baseball history. Of the 1956 game baseball fans could have said, paraphrasing President Kennedy's observation that a White House gathering he hosted for American Nobel laureates represented the greatest collection of talent in one room since Thomas Jefferson had dined alone, that it was the occasion for the greatest collection of baseball skill ever assembled in a single outfield—including those moments when Babe Ruth stood by himself in rightfield.

In this period teams other than the Yankees rose to the pinnacle of success in baseball. The Dodgers dominated the National League during their final decade in Brooklyn and in Los Angeles their two Hall of Fame pitchers, the peerless lefthander Sandy Koufax and the righthander Don Drysdale, led them to four pennants and three world championships between 1959 and 1966, when Koufax, his arm battered by a decade's worth of pitching mastery, retired at the early age of thirty.

In the 1970s the Athletics, by now having moved a second time, from Kansas City to Oakland, across the San Francisco Bay from the city of San Francisco, became the only team other than the Yankees to win three consecutive world championships. The team's leading personality was its owner, Charles O. Finley, who had made a modest fortune selling insurance. He believed that baseball had become too stodgy. To enliven it, he paid his players bonuses to grow mustaches and assigned them colorful nicknames, such as Jim "Catfish" Hunter and John "Blue Moon" Odom.[66] He proposed a number of innovations, some of which, such as night World Series games and brightly colored uniforms to replace what he called the "eggshell white" and "prison grey" of the standard home and road baseball wear, were widely adopted. Others, the idea of coloring baseballs orange for better visibility, for example, were not. Finley was what sportswriters have traditionally called colorful, but, like the other highly visible owner of the period, the Yankees' George Steinbrenner, he was not lovable. When he decided to take his team out of Kansas City, one of the senators representing the state of Missouri, Stuart Symington, called Oakland, to which Finley intended to move, "the luckiest city since Hiroshima."[67] His championship teams, which included a heterogeneous assortment of highly skilled players, had little in common with one another save a strong resentment of Finley's stinginess when it came to salaries. The players left for other, better-paying teams as soon as they could and the Athletics' reign came to an end in the mid-seventies.

Another dominant team of the 1970s was the Cincinnati Reds, which won five division championships, four pennants, and two World Series titles between 1970 and 1976. Although thin in pitching, the "Big Red Machine," as the team came to be called, fielded an array of batters comparable to the New York Yankees of the 1920s: Pete Rose, the career leader in base hits who was later banned from baseball for gambling on games while managing a team; the inappropriately named Johnny Bench (a star player who was almost never found on the bench), who was, on the basis of his combined offensive and defensive skills, one of the two or three best catchers ever to play the game; and Joe Morgan, on the same basis arguably the best second baseman in baseball history.

In the decade of the 1980s the competitive balance among major league teams was more even than ever before. For the first time since the second decade of the twentieth century, the Yankees failed to win a single world championship.

Baseball's silver age also witnessed the breaking of records. The most celebrated of them, Babe Ruth's total of sixty home runs in 1927, had stood until Roger Maris hit 61 in 1961. Thirty-seven years later, in 1998, Mark McGwire of the St. Louis Cardinals raised the record to what seemed at the time an unbeatable (and pleasingly round) number: seventy. But only three years after his feat Barry Bonds of the San Francisco Giants, the game's best all-around player of the 1990s but one whose highest previous single-season home run total had been forty-six, hit seventy-three. In that same year Bonds broke the longest-standing and, from the sabermetricians' point of view the most impressive of all seasonal batting records: His .863 slugging percentage exceeded Babe Ruth's 1920 mark of .847.

Most of the other single-season offensive records, all of them set before World War II, remained intact into the twenty-first century: Joe DiMaggio's fifty-six-game hitting streak; Rogers Hornsby's .424 batting average (1924)—not to mention Ted Williams's more recent .406 mark; the record for runs batted in—190—set by Robert "Hack" Wilson in 1930; the highest total of safe hits, 257 by George Sisler in 1920; and Babe Ruth's total of 177 runs scored in 1921.[68]

On the other hand, a number of career records were broken in the silver age, including the two most celebrated of them: Henry Aaron surpassed Babe Ruth in home runs (and established career records for runs batted in—2,297—and total bases—6,865) and Pete Rose reached 4,256 career hits, exceeding the previous high of 4,190 set by Ty Cobb, a Detroit Tigers outfielder in the early years of the twentieth century and charter member of the Hall of Fame. Rose also became baseball's Methuselah by setting career records for games played, 3,562, and times at bat, 14,053.

In 1995 the Baltimore Orioles shortstop Cal Ripken broke yet another familiar record when he exceeded Lou Gehrig's total of 2,130 consecutive games played. Ripken's streak ultimately reached 2,632 games over sixteen years. Rickey Henderson, who played with nine teams (with one of them, the Oakland Athletics, on four separate occasions) over twenty-five seasons between 1979 and 2003 recorded the most runs scored, walks, and stolen bases in the history of major league baseball. And a number of players achieved totals that, although not records, had come to be regarded as the measures of distinction: 300 career victories for pitchers and 3,000 career base hits for batters.

So many of baseball's single-season records proved invulnerable during its silver age, even as so many career standards were being exceeded, because of two powerful trends in the game, trends related to developments in American society as a whole in the second half of the twentieth century. The first was the improvement in the quality of play and the skills of the players. As in other areas of American life, the techniques of baseball and the ways of teaching them were steadily refined, and the population pool from which baseball could draw for its players widened with the growth of the country, the opportunity available to African-Americans, and the increasing recruitment from Latin America. Baseball became a better-played game for the same reasons that the American economy grew: a broad advance in knowledge and training, which formed the basis of what economists call "productivity," combined with an increase in the number of workers available.

One effect of this general improvement was for the players to bunch together in ability over time, an example of a more general trend in the natural and social words by which, according to the distinguished scientist and baseball fan, the late Stephen Jay Gould, "systems tend to equilibrate as they improve."[69] The distribution of talent becomes more compressed. It thus became more difficult for an individual player to stand out in any statistical category in a single season. The best batters were not as much better than the average ones (and not as successful against the average pitcher), for example, as Babe Ruth had been. In 1920, when Ruth set the major league record for home runs with fifty-four, the next highest total was nineteen.[70] When Mark

McGwire hit seventy, the next highest total, Sammy Sosa's, was sixty-six.[71]

The second trend, which contributed to the breaking of career records and also mirrored a broader American development, was the rise in players' salaries. This gave them greater incentives to continue playing, and their careers grew correspondingly longer. Just as important, improvements in diet and conditioning—again the result of advances in knowledge and its application—made it possible for players to sustain a high level of performance deep into their careers. (The two are related: With their high salaries players ceased to have to take full-time off-season jobs as their predecessors had done and could devote themselves to conditioning.) Babe Ruth spent his time off the field eating and drinking in ways now recognized as unhealthy. (He died of cancer at the age of fifty-three.) Barry Bonds spent his time following a strict diet and an assiduous program of weight training and managed the unusual, if not unprecedented, feat of recording his best offensive statistics at what in sports is considered an advanced age—his late thirties.[72]

Whereas seasonal records depend on the gap between outstanding and ordinary players, which narrowed in the second half of the twentieth century, career records depend on the length of time a player can play at a high level, which expanded.

Racial integration and the geographic movement of franchises changed where major league baseball was played, and by whom. How the game was played, and how the championship was decided, also changed, and the pace of these changes accelerated in the last three decades of the twentieth century.

The most dramatic change was the reversal, beginning in

the 1970s, of the trends favoring the pitcher. For the next thirty years the balance between offense and defense tilted progressively in favor of the batter. Scoring underwent inflation. This trend had a number of causes: major league batters used systematic weight training (and, it was alleged, steroids and other chemicals) to make themselves stronger. Bats were refined to make them more suitable for hitting for greater distances. The strike zone as the umpires defined it narrowed. The pitcher's mounds in major league parks were lowered.[73] The most dramatic result was the cascade of home runs of the late 1990s and the early years of the new century, an iceberg of offense of which the record-setting efforts of Mark McGwire and Barry Bonds were the tip.

At the same time, baseball became more specialized. Managers used more pitchers in each game. In 1985 Steve Bedrosian of the Pittsburgh Pirates reached a milestone by becoming the first starting pitcher to pitch 200 innings without completing a single game. In the next decade and a half a pitcher finishing a game that he started became a rarity and the use of several pitchers in each game became the norm. From 1992 until 2003 no pitcher finished a World Series game that he started. The frequent substitutions of one pitcher for another, with the consequent intermissions as one left and the other entered the game, extended the time it took to play an average major league game.[74]

From 1903 through 1996 National and American League teams never played each other except in the World Series. In 1997 baseball inaugurated interleague play during the regular season. In the golden age each team played every other team the same number of times, with an equal number of games in each home park. As the number of teams expanded, this symmetry disappeared, in favor of an "unbalanced" schedule in which teams played some of their rivals more often than others. And as the number of teams expanded, the format in which the champions of the two leagues played each other in the World Series in the first week of October, immediately following the end of the regular season, gave way to a format in which each league was divided into two, and then three, separate divisions. Ultimately four teams from each league (the three division champions plus the non-winner with the best overall record, the "wild card" team) qualified for postseason play, which consisted of three stages of playoffs rather than one. All this resulted in the World Series being played at the end rather than at the beginning of October.

These changes made for a contradiction at the heart of baseball. On the one hand, the changes were reasonable, even necessary, contributions to the economic health, and therefore to the survival, of the major leagues. Offensive prowess, high scoring, and especially home runs were popular with the game's ultimate constituency, its fans, and helped attract them to games. Attendance flagged in the 1950s and 1960s.[75] It increased in the century's last three decades. Expansion made major league games accessible to far more people who wanted to attend them. Night World Series games could be watched by millions of fans who, because they had to work during the day, would otherwise have missed them.

On the other hand, these changes—defensible, popular, even necessary though they might have been—contradicted the spirit of the sport. They violated baseball's promise of changelessness. They made the game different from what it had been when fans first encountered it; and because in so many ways, and especially in comparison with football and basketball, baseball did remain the same, the changes were all the more glaring. They made baseball less a preserved fragment of the past and more like everything else in the fluid, hectic national life of the United States.

The changes from mid-century onward are one reason that the second half of the twentieth century, for all the improvements that took place in the game, does not qualify as baseball's golden age. For a social institution so deeply linked to traditional life and so strongly identified with a static, timeless image, the golden age is the unchanging past, not the dynamic, ever-evolving present.

Even playing games at night and broadcasting them on the radio—two innovations in the first half of the century that powerfully strengthened baseball by expanding its audience—occasioned sharp criticism when they were first introduced, on the grounds that the wholesome American sport was meant to be played only in natural daylight and not in the sinister atmosphere of the artificiality illuminated nighttime, and that once a running account of games became available in every home via radio no one would pay to watch them in person at the ballpark.[76]

As with night games and radio broadcasts, the other changes in the game, especially those affecting how it was played on the field, evoked ambivalence. Three in particular provoked resistance.

One such innovation was artificial turf. In 1965 the Houston Astrodome, the first domed, enclosed stadium in the United States, became the home field of the local National League team, which changed its name from the Colt .45s to the Astros. A problem arose almost immediately: Grass would not grow under the dome. In its stead was installed a plastic carpet called AstroTurf. At one time or another ten teams played on turf fields. Turf was adopted because it was easier to maintain than grass. This made the fields easier to prepare for football as well as baseball games, and a number of parks built in the 1960s were used for both sports.

The new surface affected the strategy of the teams that played on it. They tended to place more emphasis on the foot speed of their players and less on the ability to hit home runs than had been the norm since Babe Ruth's day. Because batted balls skipped and rolled much faster on turf than on grass, speedy players could reach second or third base on balls they had hit on the ground to the outfield, while swift outfielders could intercept such balls before the batter could advance that far.

Artificial turf never earned full acceptance in baseball. A stigma attached to it from the beginning because it was at odds with the rural, traditional, natural essence of the game and thus violated the heart of baseball's appeal. A comment by Dick Allen of the Philadelphia Phillies expressed the feelings of much of the baseball world about artificial turf: "If the horses won't eat it, I won't play on it."[77]

The new ballparks built in the 1990s all featured grass and were designed to resemble the parks built before 1920, not the dual-purpose (for baseball and football) stadiums of the 1960s. None played host to football games. Several had retractable roofs to provide the weatherproof advantages of indoor baseball without the necessity of artificial turf. Two of the permanently domed facilities where baseball (as well as football) had been played, the Kingdome in Seattle and the Astrodome itself, were abandoned by their baseball teams.

The second controversial innovation of baseball's silver age was the designated hitter rule. Beginning in 1973, each American League team could designate one member of its roster per game to bat in place of one of the players in the field—invariably the pitcher—while not himself playing in the field. The rationale for the rule was the widespread incompetence of pitchers as batters. While no other position was regularly filled by someone with feeble batting skills, the singular role of the pitcher in a baseball game meant that someone with a strong, accurate arm could pitch regularly in the major leagues even if he had no aptitude at all as a batter. Giving pitchers a regular turn at bat, as the rules of the game required until 1973, exerted a drag on the game since, in George Will's words, it meant that "every ninth at-bat is unserious."[78]

The designated hitter rule was intended to make the game more interesting for the spectators; and with its introduction, scoring in American League games increased, as did attendance. But like artificial turf, the designated hitter rule was never fully accepted. While baseball teams and leagues, amateur and professional (including the Japanese leagues), did adopt it, the National League steadfastly refused to do so.[79] The opponents of the rule argued that it reduced the degree of strategic calculation in the management of the game by eliminating one decision that, under the old rule, it fell to the manager to make. With the pitcher as part of the team's batting order, when the team trails in a game the manager must decide whether to send another, better batter—a pinch hitter—up to bat in place of the pitcher. This increases the chances that the team will score enough to catch up in the game but runs the risk that, since under the rules the pitcher for whom he has batted must leave the game, the new pitcher will be less effective at stifling the opposing batters. The designated hitter rule allows the manager to have both a better hitter and the continued services of the pitcher, and so deprives the game of some of the risk that it is the responsibility of the manager to weigh.

The designated hitter rule was also criticized for introducing an unwarranted, un-baseball-like degree of specialization into the game. Baseball is preeminently the game of individual responsibility because every player must take part in every aspect of the game. Each player has, or rather before the designated hitter rule had, to play both offense and defense. The rule creates two exceptions—the pitcher does not bat and the designated hitter does not play in the field. After 1973 it was perfectly possible for a pitcher to have a long and successful American League career without a single time at bat; and a number of designated hitters compiled impressive batting statistics while almost never appearing in the field.

A third, related objection to the designated hitter rule involves what might be called the moral consequences of this particular form of specialization. Pitchers often seek to gain an advantage over batters by means of intimidation. They aim an occasional pitch close to the batter to create discomfort and anxiety. Sometimes they aim directly at the batter. Under the rules prevailing until 1973, a pitcher who "brushed back" or actually struck a batter of the opposing team would have to take a turn at bat himself, at which point the opposing pitcher had the opportunity to aim a pitch directly at him.

Practicing the technique of intimidation required the courage to face retaliation—until the introduction of the designated hitter rule, as a result of which, to use a familiar phrase, pitchers could dish it out but did not have to take it.[80] Among the most successful, and intimidating, pitchers of the 1960s were Bob Gibson and Don Drysdale, both of whom frequently aimed pitches near or at batters, but both of whom regularly subjected themselves to the possibility of retaliation. (Both were, for pitchers, unusually good hitters, as was the most successful of all lefthanders, Warren Spahn, who won 363 games in his career.) In the era of the designated hitter, Roger Clemens, another hard-throwing righthanded pitcher, was often compared to Gibson and Drysdale. He, too, made a habit of "pitching inside," inducing caution in opposing batters that reduced their effectiveness at bat. Unlike them, however, he did not have to run the same risk he posed to the batters he faced.[81] This exemption made him, despite a glittering won-lost record and six Cy Young awards, a lesser figure in the history of baseball. And in general the designated hitter rule, precisely because of this exemption, wrenched the moral universe of the sport out of alignment.

The third late-twentieth-century innovation in baseball that encountered serious resistance was a new kind of bat, made of aluminum rather than wood, which first appeared in 1970.[82] The aluminum bat offered the same advantage as artificial turf: It lowered the cost of staging baseball games. Wooden bats tend to have short careers of useful service. When a pitched ball strikes them at a weak point they crack or even break apart entirely. Aluminum bats do not break—a single bat can last for many seasons. Baseball leagues with limited budgets, a category including virtually all of amateur baseball from youth leagues to college teams, therefore adopted bats of this kind.

But professional baseball resisted, for many of the same reasons that artificial turf had provoked dismay and opposition. For one thing, aluminum bats changed the game, tilting the balance between offense and defense even more sharply in favor of the batter than did the series of small adjustments in the way the major league game was played from the 1970s onward. To hit a baseball hard with a wooden bat requires making contact on a limited part of it, the center of which is called the sweet spot. Making contact near the bat's handle usually results in a weak ground ball or a pop fly to the infield. With an aluminum bat, by contrast, contact virtually anywhere will send the ball flying, and solid contact will propel it so swiftly that it can endanger the pitcher, who has less time to react than in the case of a wooden bat. Aluminum bats used by amateur baseball players caused more injuries to pitchers than wooden ones in the hands of professionals.[83]

Moreover, as a synthetic rather than a natural product, aluminum, like AstroTurf, violates the spirit of the game. Baseball belongs to the world of wood and grass. Removing it from that world eliminates an important satisfaction of playing and watching it. Baseball played on turf using aluminum bats is like Shakespeare's plays staged on television: recognizable, to be sure, but somehow different, diminished, inauthentic.

While artificial turf, the designated hitter rule, and aluminum bats had not, by the outset of the twenty-first century, gained full acceptance, they did bring benefits as well as disadvantages. They had their supporters and had established themselves in part, if not all, of the world of baseball. One change in the sport in the last quarter of the twentieth century, by contrast, had an unmitigatedly malign effect: the poisonous turn taken by relations between major league players and their teams' owners.

Those relations resembled the battles between miners and mine owners and auto workers and auto companies in the early part of the twentieth century for acrimony and mistrust, although not, fortunately, for violence. The bitterness had its roots in the sport's pattern of labor relations in the years before the 1970s, when all of the power resided with the owners. Every player's contract included a "reserve clause," which first appeared in 1876 and gave the team the exclusive right to the players' services for as long as it liked. (Teams could "reserve" those services indefinitely beyond the life of the contract.) A team could trade or release a player but he could not of his own accord become a free agent. He therefore lacked the source of leverage in negotiating his salary on which workers in virtually every other industry and profession could draw: the availability of other opportunities. Team owners, by contrast, had considerable power over the income they received. They could charge whatever they liked for tickets to the game. They could bargain with media outlets for the right to broadcast their home games. They could, and did, threaten to move their franchises if the host city did not confer favors on them, such as the construction of a new ballpark. And players could not alter their status as employees through legal recourse because of a 1922 Supreme Court ruling that baseball did not qualify as an example of interstate commerce and so the federal statutes prohibiting the kind of power the owners possessed did not apply to it.[84]

In these circumstances the baseball owners developed an attitude toward the players that had something in common with that of feudal European landholders toward the serfs who worked their land. The owners saw the players as children: talented, often lovable, and certainly valuable, but also irresponsible and both incapable and undeserving of controlling their own professional destinies. Then, beginning in the 1960s, the player-owner relationship changed dramatically.

In 1965 the players' association, previously a tame and not very active group, hired as its executive director a shrewd and determined employee of the steelworkers' union, Marvin Miller, who set out to challenge the power of the owners. The crucial change in baseball's labor relations came in 1976. A number of court rulings had expressed reservations about, without explicitly overturning, the special status conferred on the sport by the 1922 Supreme Court decision. In this climate of skepticism an arbitrator effectively ruled the reserve clause in the standard player's contract illegal, and the decision was upheld in court.[85]

Instead of accommodating themselves to the new circumstances and trying to forge a mutually beneficial relationship with the players, the owners resisted the shift in the balance of power and the struggle turned bitter. In the last three decades of the twentieth century, baseball experienced nine of what were euphemistically termed "work stoppages"—strikes initiated by the players and lockouts by the owners. As a result of the 1994 players' strike, no World Series was played for the first time in ninety years.

Although creating ill will on both sides and disenchantment among the sport's fans, baseball's rocky post-1976 labor relations did not stop one trend that the 1976 ruling set in motion: a sharp rise in players' salaries. In 1976 the average major league salary was $45,000. In 2002 it was $2,380,000.[86] In 2000 the All-Star shortstop Alex Rodriguez signed a contract to play for the Texas Rangers for ten years at a total salary of $252 million dollars, a sum larger than the total cost of building his home field, the Ballpark in Arlington, which opened in 1994.[87]

One justification for the reserve clause had been the fear that, without it, the inevitable increase in salaries caused by rival teams bidding for players' services would lead to a competitive imbalance in the major leagues, with the wealthiest team corralling the best players and monopolizing the championships. In fact, the early years of free agency had the opposite effect. The American and National Leagues became more evenly balanced than ever before. In the decade after 1976 all twelve National League teams and eleven of the fourteen American League clubs won division championships and reached postseason play. But in the 1990s the more affluent teams dominated. One of them, the Atlanta Braves, captured twelve consecutive division championships between 1991 and 2003. (The 1994 season was ended prematurely by the strike.) The wealthiest team of all, the Yankees, won three consecutive world championships and four in five years. Dividing the teams into quartiles according to their total payrolls, in the five seasons after 1994 no team in the bottom two quartiles won any of the 158 playoff games; every winner of the World Series came from the top quartile; and no team below the first quartile won a single World Series game.[88] Of the forty-eight playoff spots from 1995 through 2000, only three went to teams in the lower two quartiles, and they won only three out of 189 postseason games.[89]

The dominance of the wealthy was hardly unknown in baseball, as the history of the Yankees after the arrival of Babe Ruth testifies. Nor was the competitive imbalance as lopsided in the 1990s as it had been in the 1950s, near the end of baseball's golden age, when the three teams from New York won fifteen of the twenty pennant races over ten years and eight of the ten World Series. But by the second half of the 1990s the disparities had again become extreme, and this was clearly because the disparities in team payrolls had become extreme. In 1991, thirteen of the other twenty-five teams had payrolls at least 75 percent as large as that of the Yankees. By 2002 this was true of only four of the other teams. In 2002 the Yankees paid their players $97 million more—$135 million to $38 million—than did their division rivals, the Tampa Devil Rays[90] But coming in the wake of a period in which many more teams had enjoyed success, and in an era in which even the weaker, poorer teams were paying salaries in the millions of dollars—something unimaginable for most of the sport's history—the inequality seemed less tolerable than it had been during baseball's golden age.

It seemed less tolerable, as well, because remedies were available. One was sharing equally among all major league teams the proceeds from the sale of rights to televise games, which had become, by the final decade of the twentieth century, the largest source of baseball revenues. Under the prevailing system each team kept all the income from the rights to its own home games, which channeled the most money to the teams playing in the biggest cities, above all New York. Another remedy was to impose a common limit on the total amount of money each team could pay its players—a salary cap.

Baseball did not, as the new millennium began, have either a well-developed system of revenue sharing or a salary cap. (The labor agreement negotiated in 2002 did include a "luxury tax" on payrolls exceeding a certain amount, an indirect and modest type of salary cap.) But the professional league of another major American team sport had both, and indeed had been the pioneer in adopting them. Football had a large, if seldom explicitly acknowledged, influence on baseball during its silver age.

Some of the changes in baseball imitated features of football: the increases in scoring; the multiplication of postseason games so that more teams than the mere two that had traditionally played the World Series could participate; the appearance, in major league ballparks, of what George Will called "planned distractions"[91] having little or nothing to do with the game itself, especially the playing of loud music over the public address system and the encouraging of spectators to chant in unison.

Football exercised this influence because, beginning in the 1960s, it experienced a surge in its own popularity, which baseball naturally sought to match. Among the things that made baseball's golden age golden was its unchallenged standing as the national game. But in the second half of the twentieth century football contested that status, and by some measures displaced baseball as the nation's favorite game.[92] It was like a younger sibling who, as he or she grows, vies with increasing success with his or her elder for parental attention and approval.

In 1942 Franklin Roosevelt had expressed the view that the absence of major league baseball during wartime would be bad for the nation's morale. A half century later, during the 1994 strike, the country coped with the absence of the game without apparent difficulty. Of course the world and the United States were vastly different places in 1994 than they had been in 1942, but one reason that baseball was missed less than it would have been earlier in its history was that, when the games stopped in August, American sports fans could look forward to the imminent beginning of the football season, which, at the outset of the new century, was in full swing by the time the World Series was played. In the last third of the twentieth century football's popularity had put it in the place that baseball had once monopolized: at the center of American popular culture.

CHAPTER 3

Football: The Spectacle of Violence

[In football] you can fight without being arrested. We're paid
for violence. You've got to love that.

DERRICK DEESE, *professional football player*[1]

THE INDUSTRIAL GAME

The industrial revolution, which began in England in the latter half of the eighteenth century and spread throughout the
planet thereafter, changed the world in three ways. It led to
the widespread use of machines. It made possible steady economic growth, whereby more and more people gained access
to more and more possessions. And it caused human societies
to be organized differently: People came to live in cities that
were larger, denser versions of the villages and towns that
had existed since antiquity. Workplaces in these cities
brought together substantial numbers of people in one place,
in factories or office buildings.

It is from the industrial world of the nineteenth and
twentieth centuries that football emerged. And it is the distinguishing features of this world that football reflects.

A cardinal feature of industrial society, largely absent in the traditional, agrarian world, is the importance of measured time. Industrial life is lived by the clock and football, unlike baseball, is played by the clock. Measured time is indispensable for the coordination among the different members of the team on the field that football requires. Football players must do things together. They must perform their assigned tasks at precisely coordinated moments. Synchronization is as important in football as it is in the choreography of the dance numbers in Broadway musicals.

Football is the sport of the machine age because football teams are like machines, with specialized moving parts that must function simultaneously. Players are like workers in a factory. They must perform their tasks in a precise sequence, and the failure to do so leads to the kind of disaster depicted in the film *Modern Times* in which Charlie Chaplin, working on an assembly line, gets tangled up in the machinery.

Measured time governs football in another way. The game, like much of industrial life, proceeds under externally imposed deadlines. Each game consists of a series of individual plays and the team in possession of the ball has only a limited period of time—thirty seconds—after the conclusion of one play to initiate the next. A team that exceeds this limit suffers a penalty for delay of the game. Each football game, moreover, unlike a baseball game, must be played within sixty minutes of elapsed time. (Explicit rules govern what counts against the designated hour—when the clock is running—and what does not—when it is stopped.)* Thus in

---

* This means that a period of game time can last far longer in real time if the clock is constantly stopped. Sympathetic timekeepers have occasionally helped the home team stretch the time on the game clock in order to be able score a winning touchdown. After one such episode the coach of the losing team began

football, as in the industrial world but unlike baseball and the rural, agrarian way of life that baseball reflects, time has considerable value. It is a precious resource, to be expended scrupulously and never wasted.

In fact, in a football game the clock is a participant. The team in the lead will attempt to use as much time as possible, hoping to run out the clock and win the game. It will employ the technique, in a phrase that combines the agrarian with the industrial, of milking the clock. As the end of the game approaches, the team that is trailing finds itself battling against two adversaries: the opposing team, which is trying to prevent it from scoring, and the clock, which is winding down to the point at which the game, and so the team's efforts to win, must end. The final minute of a close game resembles in this sense the climactic scene in James Bond films, in which the hero must fight his way past the villain (or the villain's powerful and dangerous henchmen) to reach and disable the bomb that is set to explode at a designated moment. Bond invariably succeeds in disarming the doomsday machine in the nick of time. In football games, by contrast, one of the teams runs out of time before it can prevent defeat.

The role that time plays in football means that the pace of a game can be frantic in a way that industrial life often is but that baseball games and agrarian life are not. Unlike baseball, football does not offer to twenty-first-century spectators a respite from the rhythm of daily life.

As in the industrial world, football involves the precise

continued

to race across the field shouting, "I want to find the timekeeper." An assistant tried to restrain him, warning, "If you do anything to harm the timekeeper you'll be kicked out of football." "You don't understand," the coach replied, "I don't want to hurt him. I want him to time the rest of my life."

calibration of space as well as of time. To keep possession of the ball a team must gain ten yards in four attempts. A length of chain of exactly that distance is periodically brought on to the field (unlike in baseball, in football all fields have the same dimensions) to check on whether the ball has been advanced the required distance.

The space that is football's natural habitat differs from baseball's. Baseball is a rural game, played on grass and dirt. Football is played on grass (or artificial turf, but not, except when unavoidable, dirt) but the sport's setting is urban. Its distant ancestor is the combination game and ritual involving kicking an inflated animal skin that dates back to medieval Europe. To play a football game, or even to acquire the skills necessary to play one, requires a concentration of people. The ball game that became baseball has its origins in farms and villages. Football originated in schools located in cities in the Northeast, then the most densely populated and urbanized part of the United States.

Moreover, baseball, like life in rural, traditional society, accommodates nature. It defers to the weather. A rainstorm of even modest severity stops the game. Football, by contrast, defies the elements, in the spirit of the industrial age, the aim of which has been to master the natural world. Football games are played nonstop in rain, sleet, hail, and even snow.[2]

The world of the industrial revolution is one of specialization, another feature that football incorporates in a way that baseball does not. Football, since the advent of unlimited substitution, the rule that was introduced in the 1940s and became permanent in the 1960s that permits every player to enter or leave the game at any time, has been a two-platoon game: Some players specialize in offense, some in defense, and none plays on both offense and defense as do baseball and basketball players. In fact, since yet a third group of players takes the field when the ball is being kicked, it is actually a *three*-platoon game.

Football's specialization extends farther. On offense and defense players play different positions. This is true of baseball players in the field as well, but players at every position in baseball can and do catch and throw the ball. In football the division of labor is stricter. Some players throw the ball, some catch it, some run with it, and some do none of these things—indeed are forbidden by a rule of the game from doing them. The differentiation of function in football is reflected in the uniforms the players wear. Unlike in baseball, football players playing specific positions must wear certain numbers. Those playing on offense with numbers in the fifties, sixties, and seventies, for example, play positions that are barred from handling the ball.

With the division of labor in the industrial world came interdependence. Workers came to specialize in one small part of a large task. Many different specialists working together are required to complete that task—to assemble an automobile, for example, or build a bridge, or operate an insurance company. Baseball and football, as team sports, both embody the principle of interdependence: No individual player can win a game by himself. Each player depends on his teammates. But the two sports exhibit different kinds of interdependence.

Baseball consists of a sequence of individual acts. One player pitches the ball, a second bats it, a third fields and throws it, a fourth catches it and tags a base to put the batter or another baserunner out. Football consists of a sequence of *collective* acts, in each step of which every player participates.

In the common baseball sequence just described, only four of the eighteen people involved in the game have active roles. The rest are, in effect, bystanders.

In each play in football, by contrast, every one of the twenty-two players on the field has a specific assignment and the failure to carry it out can prove costly to his team. While baseball players act as individuals within the context of a team game, therefore, football players always play as part of a group.

The more collective character of football, and the division of the team not into individual players but, as with industrial enterprises, into sub-groups, is reflected in a custom common to all sports: the assignment of nicknames. A nickname is a sign of familiarity and so reduces social distance. It is also often a metaphor, highlighting a particular characteristic of the person who bears it. Baseball nicknames apply to individuals: Babe Ruth was the "Sultan of Swat." Ted Williams, tall and thin as a young man, became the "Splendid Splinter." Football more often bestows collective nicknames, with groups within the team rather than individuals having distinctive identities. Thus the Minnesota Vikings' defensive behemoths of the 1960s were the "Purple People Eaters,"[3] the even more formidable defensive players of the Pittsburgh Steelers of the 1970s became the "Steel Curtain," and beefy blockers of the offensive line of the Washington Redskins teams of the 1980s became the "Hogs."[4]

Football differs from baseball in yet another way that reflects a fundamental difference between the traditional and the industrial worlds. Change in the game of football is normal, natural, deliberate, and constant. While a spectator transported from a baseball game at the outset of the twentieth century to one being played at the beginning of the twenty-first would be witnessing essentially the same sport, a football fan similarly transported would not.

In the course of the twentieth century almost every feature of football changed markedly. When the game began, the players wore no special uniforms. By the twenty-first century they were swaddled in high-tech protective gear. The rules of the sport changed, including the rules governing scoring. The goal posts were moved back and forth several times between the goal line and the back of the end zone.

The techniques of the game changed as well. To take one example among many, once the principal method of scoring by kicking was the dropkick. The player held the ball, dropped it, and just as it touched the ground kicked it toward the goal, seeking to send it between the goal posts. But the dropkick gave way to the placekick, in which one player places the ball upright on the ground and, while he holds it, another kicks it toward the goal. The technique of placekicking also changed. Once the holder placed the ball on a small plastic tee, making it easier to propel the ball accurately. Then the tee was banned and the holder was required to put the ball on the ground. Until the 1960s the placekicker approached the ball head on and struck it with the front of his foot. (The most famous place kicker of the 1950s was Lou "The Toe" Groza.) Then soccer-style placekicking came into vogue, with the kicker approaching the ball from the side and propelling it with the side of his foot.

For football, as in the industrial world and unlike in baseball, change has a positive connotation. It is deemed progress. The game of baseball also changed, but slowly, gradually, through small adjustments usually made anonymously and often to a dismayed reception. Domed stadiums and artificial turf found readier acceptance in football than in baseball. Technological innovation infiltrated the rules of the game: Teams may challenge officials' decisions and when they do, video replays are consulted to assess these challenges. No such procedures are available in baseball.[5]

One man, Walter Camp, contributed so much to the shape of the game in its formative years, the last quarter of the nineteenth century, that he became known as the "father of American football."[6] He is credited, among other things, with stipulating eleven as the number of players permitted on the field for each team at any one time, with developing verbal signals to coordinate offensive play, and with creating the basis for the game's scoring system.[7] Camp's full-time job was symbolically faithful to one of the defining features of the game over which he exercised sweeping influence: He was president of the New Haven Clock Company.*

Because the history of football is one of pronounced, fre-

---

* After Camp's era the predominant method for deploying offensive players, and especially those handling the ball, changed several times, and each of the changes can be traced to a single individual who was searching for, and found, a more effective way to advance the ball toward the opposing team's goal. In 1906 Glenn "Pop" Warner, one of the most successful of all coaches, invented the single-wing formation, in which play begins with the ball being passed several yards backward from the center to the tailback. Richard Wittingham, *Rites of Autumn: The Story of College Football* (New York: The Free Press, 2001), p. 37. The T formation, which dominated football in the second half of the twentieth century, in which play begins with the center handing the ball through his legs to the quarterback stationed immediately behind him, was devised by Clark Shaughnessy in the early 1940s. In the T formation the ball carriers ("backs") stationed behind the quarterback were aligned in various ways. In 1949 Tom Nugent, a college coach, introduced the I formation, in which the backs were placed in a straight line behind the quarterback. Ibid., p. 44. Darrell Royal, a successful coach at the University of Texas, developed the wishbone, so named because the three backs were arrayed behind the quarterback in a V-shape that resembled the breastbone of a chicken. In 1961 Howard "Red" Hickey of the professional San Francisco 49ers brought back a version of the single wing, which he called the "shotgun" formation. Beginning in 1975, one of the greatest of professional coaches, Tom Landry of the Dallas Cowboys, used the shotgun so successfully for the purpose of passing that it became common throughout the game.

quent, and rapid change, and because the achievements on the field are collective rather than individual, its statistics have less significance and command less attention than those of baseball.[8] The batting exploits of Babe Ruth and Barry Bonds may be meaningfully compared because they played, five decades apart, essentially the same game. The statistical achievements of Sid Luckman, the leading passer of the 1940s, and Dan Marino, the most prolific passer of the 1980s and 1990s, by contrast, are not readily comparable. This is so not only because of changes in the rules and prevailing strategies of the game (which made advancing the ball by passing easier and therefore more popular, and relieved offensive players of the burden of having to play defense as well) but also because the football season grew longer over the course of the twentieth century, making the comparison of single-season accomplishments, the staple of baseball records, virtually meaningless for football. In the 1950s, professional teams played twelve games each season, and then two of them competed for the championship. By the end of the 1990s the teams played sixteen games, and the playoffs to determine the championship had four stages, so that a player's season could be half again as long as it had been four decades earlier.

So while baseball's past is an important part of the game's present, in football the sport's history is, on the whole, gone, discarded, forgotten.[9] Still, football does have a connection with the past. It embodies the spirit, the goals, and many of the tasks of one of the most widespread and most influential of all human practices. Of the three major American team sports, the game of football is the one that bears the closest resemblance to the age-old human practice of armed conflict.[10] If a football team is like an industrial enterprise, a football game is like a war.

THE WAR GAME

War involves the organized, deliberate use of force to attain a goal, often the control of territory. So does football.* At the heart of every football game are violent physical encounters between and among players on the opposing teams. The offensive team blocks the defensive side, trying to clear the way for the teammate carrying the ball or to allow time for their quarterback to throw a forward pass. The goal of the defense is to knock to the ground the offensive player in possession of the ball.[11]

Like opposing armies, football teams seek to conquer and defend territory. Each half of the field is said to be the "property" of the team defending the goal at its end. If a team is in possession of the ball five yards from its own goal, it is said to be on its own five-yard line. If it is twenty yards from the opposing goal it is on the opponent's twenty-yard line. Since a touchdown is the method of scoring with the highest value, it is the ultimate aim of all teams and thus roughly corresponds to the capture of an important city in war.

Just as a war is composed of a series of battles, so a football game consists of a series of individual plays, which are small-scale, non-lethal versions of battles. Like most battles, football plays have a beginning and an end, after which the outcome can be assessed: The offensive team has either retained or surrendered possession of the ball, and, if it has retained the ball, has either gained or lost yardage toward the

---

* In the 1960s a Brazilian television company purchased films of American football to show locally and confronted the problem of what to call the North American game, since "football" in Brazil—and almost everywhere else on the planet—means the game that Americans call soccer. The name finally chosen was "military football." Faced with the same problem several decades later the British called the game "gridiron."

opponent's goal line, or ended the play in exactly the same place where it began.

Seen from a distance, a football play looks like a premodern Western battle. Two groups of uniformed, padded men swarm against each other. Each play, like each battle, is a melee of tangled bodies, pushing, pounding, and grabbing one another.[12] And like the battles of an earlier era, football plays consist of a series of individual but interrelated skirmishes. The confrontations between and among the biggest players are reminiscent of Japanese sumo wrestling—large men pushing and pawing each other, trying to throw the opponent off balance.*

The ways that football teams customarily seek to advance the ball correspond to the familiar battlefield tactics of armies throughout history. Offensive teams often attempt to concentrate their personnel at a certain point to clear the way for the ball carrier to break through the defenses of the opponent, just as armies have sought to do since the days of Alexander the Great. Alternatively, the offense will try to turn the opponent's flank, making it possible for the man carrying the ball to run around the end of the defense and advance down the field. For both breakthroughs and flanking maneuvers, speed of movement in getting personnel to the designated point of attack is the key to success.

In addition, teams on offense, like armies, regularly practice deception. They try to fool the defenders into believing

---

* The Oakland Raiders' owner Al Davis investigated the possibility of using sumo wrestlers on his team but found "two things wrong with the idea . . . One, you couldn't pay them enough. They make big money there and don't get the hell beat out of them. No. 2, no stamina. Their bouts last a few seconds. Make 'em go much longer than that and they'd give out." Paul Zimmerman,   "Chief concerns," ESPN.com, June 13, 2003.

that the play is proceeding in a direction other than the one it is in fact taking, or that someone other than the actual ball carrier is in possession of the ball. A quarterback will fake a handoff to one player and instead give the ball to another, or gaze at one receiver as if intending to throw the ball to him and then pass it to another. Occasionally teams will deploy in a formation ordinarily used to kick the ball but instead pass or run with it. Most plays include some version of the elaborate ruse by which the Allied armies gave the defending Germans a mistaken idea of the site of the invasion of France before D-Day in World War II.

As with the offense in football and the attacking side in warfare, the task of the defense is the same in both endeavors: to disrupt and foil the opponent's advance, and above all to avoid yielding ground.

If football games are like wars and the plays that comprise them less lethal versions of battles, the structure of the offensive platoon of a football team resembles the organization of an army. A military observer from a previous era would recognize in a team the standard, tripartite division of an armed force.

The line—the large, powerful men who squat along the line of scrimmage and, when the play begins, launch themselves at the equally large men crouched opposite them, trying to knock them aside—are the equivalent of the infantry. Like the ground troops of armies, they are both the hammer and the anvil of the football team. They inflict and absorb punishment and do so anonymously, as part of an undifferentiated group.

The running backs function as the cavalry of the team— highly mobile agents of swift advance. Like the horsemen of the premodern era, they are marked out as special, privileged, of a higher status than the infantry. The cavalry was recruited from the ranks of the nobility, who were wealthy enough to maintain horses. Running backs, unlike linemen, are permitted to handle the ball.

A football team has the equivalent of the third arm of the military as well. The artillery attacks the foe through the air, hurling deadly objects over the adversary's first line of defense. Similarly, football teams attempt to advance the ball toward the opponent's goal by having the quarterback throw it downfield, over the heads of the defensive linemen, to a waiting receiver.

The preparations for a war and a football game follow parallel paths. Responsibility for these preparations rests, in both, with a staff, which functions as the brain of the organization. The coaching staff of a football team corresponds to the general staff of an army, a Prussian innovation that formally separated those in the military who think and plan from those who actually do the fighting. The general staff became a standard feature of modern armed forces. Like its football counterpart, it carries out three tasks.

A general staff determines its forces' overall approach to warfare, its strategy. The football team's general approach, over which the coaching staff presides, consists of its offensive and defensive systems, or schemes. The general staff draws up war plans that determine how the army will fight in specific circumstances, just as the coaching staff prepares game plans for each contest. In doing so, both draw on the close study of as much information as possible about the opponent. The football term for the person who observes the opposing team and gathers this information is the same

as the name for those who, before the age of aerial recon-
naissance, performed this service for armies: the scout.*

Besides choosing strategies and devising tactics, general
staffs and coaching staffs must make their troops and players
ready to fight and play properly. In both cases this involves
inculcating the appropriate techniques through regular training: Both armies and football teams spend far more time
preparing for the activity they exist to carry out than actually
engaging in it.

The techniques are taught and mastered in both cases by
breaking them down into their component parts and repeat-
ing them constantly, until they can be performed instinc-
tively and proficiently even under the severe pressures that
combat and game conditions impose. And to introduce
recruits to the routines of their jobs, both armed forces and
football teams take them to isolated places and subject them
to a particularly intense period of training. Boot camp for
soldiers and training camp for football players are always
psychologically taxing and physically exhausting experiences,
often unpleasant and occasionally unbearable.[13] Some
recruits and some players drop out. In 1956 Paul Bryant,
then the coach at Texas A&M University, took 111 players
for a week to an isolated, drought-stricken town in central
Texas called Junction. At the end of the week only thirty-five
remained with the team. All the rest had left the camp and
the team.[14]

---

* Like armies, football teams occasionally engage in the clandestine gathering of
information—that is, espionage. When it became standard practice for coaches
on the sideline to relay the plays they wanted to be run to the team on the field
via a telephone connection to the quarterback, some teams hired lip readers to try
to decipher the messages being sent. Mike Freeman, "Some Coaches Reading
Lips to Steal Plays," *The New York Times*, October 28, 2001, p. S11.

Warfare is among the oldest of human institutions. Football, by comparison, is recent. But their histories exhibit similar features. One similarity is the trend, which pervades the modern world, toward increasing specialization. The armies of ancient Greece consisted of several thousand men armed with swords, shields, and spears who presented themselves for battle when necessary. Their twenty-first-century counterparts include millions of people performing hundreds of different, specialized tasks. In football, where once every player played on both offense and defense, now each concentrates on one or the other. And while in the early days of the game a star player could pose a "triple threat" to the opposition through his ability to kick, pass, and carry the ball, now no player is regularly called upon to do more than one of these tasks.

The expansion, over the centuries, of the destructive power at the disposal of armed forces also has a parallel in football. Over the decades football players have become stronger, faster, and, most conspicuously, through diet, weight training, and sometimes chemical stimulants to growth, bigger. Players weighing three hundred pounds or more, once rare, had, by the end of the twentieth century, become common.[15]

As with the history of warfare, the history of football is marked by an ongoing contest between the techniques of the offense and the methods of defending against them, with innovation in one calling forth countervailing adjustments in the other. In war, it has usually been technological change that has upset the existing equilibrium between offense and defense, giving one or the other at least a temporary advantage. In football, changes in the rules have prompted changes in the prevailing methods by which teams have sought to score and to prevent scoring. In 1978, for example, rule changes made it easier to protect passers against onrushing defensive linemen and more difficult to defend against pass receivers down the field. The effect of this shift in the balance between offense and defense in favor of the offense was to increase the average number of passes attempted and points scored per game.

In the modern era, armed forces have competed not only on the field of battle but also in making preparations to fight, especially in the development and accumulation of ever more powerful weaponry. Similarly, in the second half of the twentieth century, football became a full-time, year-round undertaking, with its own version of arms races. During the months of the year when games are not played—the off-season—players continue to train[16] and coaches continue to study their own teams and their prospective opponents and to plan for the contests ahead.

The many affinities football has with war find expression in terminology the game has borrowed from armed conflict. A pass far downfield is a "long bomb." The offensive and defensive lines, like the infantry on the western front in World War I, operate "in the trenches." The quarterback, whose signals initiate the play and who regularly handles and distributes the ball, is the "field general."[17] An all-out assault on a quarterback attempting to pass the ball, a "blitz," takes its name from the comparable German offensive tactic in World War II—the *blitzkrieg*, or lightning war.

Football and war have yet another common feature: Both are dangerous. Because football involves frequent violent collisions, injuries to players are normal byproducts of the game. The protective equipment that football players wear attests to the hazards that come with playing the game.

Deaths in football are rare, although not unknown. In the early years of the sport they came from brain injuries, more frequent then because it was only after the turn of the twentieth century that the first primitive helmets—known as "head harnesses"—were worn.[18] Recently, the major cause of football fatalities has been heatstroke or cardiac malfunction, with the exertion of the game sometimes aggravating an existing condition.

In addition to fatalities, football is plagued with major injuries, serious enough to cause the player to miss several games or even require surgery that keeps him out of action for the entire season: Broken arms, legs, wrists, and ankles, and especially tears to knee ligaments are common.[19]

Those who play football over a long period of time—in high school, college, and the professional ranks—very often pay for their careers with chronic conditions of one kind or another, which frequently manifest themselves after the player has left the game. The human body is not built to resist years of the regular pounding that football players absorb.[20] The joints, especially, suffer. Chronic arthritis is an occupational hazard of playing the game. But it is not only the bones and joints that are vulnerable. The violent collisions on the field can cause concussions, which, if repeated, can permanently damage the brain.[21] Pithy testimony to the toll the game takes on those who play it was once provided by O. J. Simpson, a superior football player before going on to even greater celebrity in the annals of American crime and justice. Asked whether a gifted athlete who had the ability to play professionally in both sports should choose baseball or football, Simpson replied, "Baseball. He'll play longer, make more money, and he won't walk funny when he retires."

Because each is dangerous, fighting a war and playing in a

football game both require doing what comes unnaturally. Commanders and coaches must find ways to overcome the natural inhibitions to taking part in both.[22] Here again, the array of techniques they use, and the incentives they offer, exhibit marked similarities.

In both, symbolic rewards are provided. Armed forces award medals for valor. Football teams offer comparable forms of recognition. High school and college players earn "letters"—usually the first initial of the name of the school—that signify a substantial contribution to the team and that they can display on a sweater or jacket. On some teams, a valuable exploit—a touchdown scored or a pass intercepted—earns the player a token that is pasted on his helmet: for the Florida State team this is a decal of a tomahawk; for Ohio State, a replica of the school's symbol, a buckeye, the brown nut of a tree native to the state. For outstanding play in a particular game a player may receive a game ball—one actually (or purportedly) used in the game itself.

Both armies and football teams exalt, by keeping alive through retelling their stories, those who have vividly displayed the qualities related to success. The equivalent for football of Sergeant Alvin York, the battlefield hero of World War I whose feats formed the basis for a Hollywood movie, are the men who insisted on playing despite serious injuries—broken arms or legs.

Victory on the battlefield and on the football field require physical courage—the willingness to behave in ways that bring with them vulnerability to physical harm. But in both enterprises courage by itself does not suffice. Another essential ingredient of success in both cases is discipline. History is filled with examples of men who conducted themselves with great courage in battle but whose cause was lost because they did not carry out their military operations in a coherent, disciplined fashion. Western armies consistently defeated courageous and more numerous non-Western forces because the Western soldiers held their positions, discharged their responsibilities, and carried out the orders they received from their commanders while their opponents, although willing to expose themselves to the risk of death, did not.[23]

Football players, too, must carry out their assigned roles on each play in order for their teams to win. And, like soldiers, they must persist in doing so even when they are tired or injured or both. Persistence, along with courage and discipline, are the martial virtues that loom large, as well, on the football field. "Fatigue makes cowards of us all" is a maxim illustrating the point that is popular in the world of football, as is the approbation routinely bestowed on those who, although injured, "play with pain" or "play hurt."[24]

If performing acts that court serious injury runs counter to normal human impulses, doing so persistently, and while already injured, is even more unusual. Beyond symbolic (and, because the players are paid, material) rewards for such behavior, the impulses for overcoming the inhibitions to what soldiers and football players must do have two additional sources. One is the drill in which both continually engage. Constant repetition makes the conduct that is desirable in battle and in a game reflexive and almost automatic.[25] The other is the social solidarity that develops among soldiers, football players, or indeed any group that spends extended time together apart from the rest of the world, has its own rules and customs, cooperates closely, and undergoes common and stressful experiences.[26] Aristotle thought that courage on the part of the Greek soldiers of his day stemmed, in the words of one military historian, from "their fear of cowardice before their commonwealth and fellow citizens" as well as "their desire for recognition of virtue that such public bodies offer to selfless men."[27] Soldiers, studies show, are generally motivated to fight not for their country, its principles, or even their families, but out of loyalty to their comrades.[28] The worst offense a nineteenth-century European officer could commit was to act in a way that sullied the honor of the regiment, the military unit to which he owed his first allegiance. Similarly, football players endure the discomfort and danger they regularly encounter out of, among other reasons, a disinclination to "let down" their teammates.[29]

Courage, discipline, and perseverance have their roots in human psychology. That is why Napoleon said that, in determining the outcome of a war, moral factors are three times as important as material ones.[30] There is no doubt that on both the battlefield and the football field morale counts for a great deal, especially when the opposing sides are evenly matched in other ways. And here, again, there are parallels between the two. Three common methods for elevating the morale of a football team correspond to familiar practices in the history of warfare: one comes from primitive, or, as it has come to be called, preliterate or "archaic" warfare, the second from the way war was waged in Europe in premodern times, and the third is a familiar feature of warfare in the modern age.

Primitive warriors often identified with animals. They carved or painted likenesses of lions, tigers, bears, and wolves on the clubs and shields they carried into battle. They even wore the skins of the animals they took as their totems so that they could absorb and make use of the power and ferocity of these creatures.

Contemporary football players presumably do not believe that they can capture for their own purposes the spirits of animals, but football teams do adopt mascots, which serve as their totems, that are noted for the qualities on which success on the football field depends.* Some of these totems have their origins in actual wars. From the Civil War came the names borne by the football teams (and therefore teams in other sports) of the University of Tennessee—the Volunteers—and the University of Mississippi—the Rebels.

Large, predatory felines—wildcats and tigers, especially—are favored as the mascots of college teams. The Universities of Kentucky and Arizona adopted the wildcat as their mascot, Princeton and Louisiana State Universities the tiger. Professional football teams include the Detroit Lions, the Cincinnati Bengals, the Jacksonville Jaguars, and the Carolina Panthers. Not all the animals with which football teams are associated are large, powerful mammals, but even the totemic birds tend to be predatory: the Philadelphia Eagles, the Atlanta Falcons, and the Seattle Seahawks. The winged creatures adopted by baseball teams, by contrast, are generally smaller and pose little threat to creatures larger than a worm: the Baltimore Orioles, the Toronto Blue Jays, and the St. Louis Cardinals.[31]

In premodern times armies marched into battle to the sound of music. Drums, bagpipes, and even entire bands accompanied them, beating out martial rhythms or blaring martial melodies to inspire them. The custom has persisted

---

* The state of Oregon stands as the exception to this pattern. The teams representing its two major state universities are the Oregon Ducks and the Oregon State Beavers, both worthy animals but neither noted for its ferocity—except, in the case of beavers, against trees. Perhaps the least bellicose mascot was the one adopted by Scottsdale Community College, the (presumably oxymoronic) "Fighting Artichokes."

over the decades, despite sweeping changes in warfare. Even the American armed forces of the twenty-first century, which rely more on technical wizardry than in previous eras, retain military bands in all four armed services.

The sound of music rings throughout football stadiums as well. Bands play stirring marches known, as if to emphasize the connection with war, as fight songs. Their purpose, as with military music, is to raise the morale and increase the fervor of the men in uniform in the struggle on the field.

In the modern era, a country's entire population became increasingly involved in the wars that it fought. Especially in the two world wars of the twentieth century, almost all able-bodied men up to a certain age were taken into the ranks of combatants; and those who did not wear a uniform—men and women alike—worked to produce the materiel with which the war was fought. Thus in the modern era the entire country came to identify with the army, which was certainly not the case before the nineteenth century, and wars were waged not by small bands of mercenaries but by the entire "nation in arms."

Similarly, football teams draw on the enthusiasm of those who do not play but who identify, sometimes passionately, with them. At universities, students stage pep rallies on the eve of games in order to demonstrate their support for their team. During the games themselves students and others in attendance, often clad in the team's colors, chant rote phrases loudly and in unison. These cheers, as they are known, are intended, once again, to fire the spirits and thus improve the performance of the team with which the cheerers identify.

In football, as in baseball, a team gains an advantage from playing in its home arena. In both sports, the home team wins more than half the time. Whereas the advantage in baseball stems largely from the fact that teams assemble players whose skills are suited to the particular features of their home parks, in football, in which all the fields are the same size, the benefit comes from the powerful emotions, which can on occasion spill over into violence, that the spectators express on behalf of the home team.[32] A noisy, enthusiastic audience is believed to provide the kind of advantage that an extra player on the field would, and so to function as the home team's "twelfth man."

The numerous affinities between football and war suggest the possibility that they have a common source. And the practice of war is sufficiently widespread in human history to raise the question of whether it arises from human nature itself: whether, that is, organized human conflict (and thus, perhaps, football as well) has a basis in the genetic makeup of the species. The traits of all living creatures and the genes that underlie them persist over time in the relevant populations when they are helpful to the process of reproduction. It is surely possible that some of the features that football has in common with war—group solidarity, controlled aggression, and a proprietary attitude toward territory—favor the reproductive success of those who possess them and have thus been "selected" over the many generations of the human presence on the planet.

No consensus exists on the extent to which human conduct in general, let alone warlike behavior, has a genetic basis: This is in fact one of the most contentious issues in all of science. But whether war and football have a common origin in the building blocks of human nature, they have been closely associated, one with the other, over the course of American history.

During the first and especially during the second world

wars of the twentieth century, so many young men entered the armed forces that the peacetime football teams had difficulty in filling their rosters. But the military itself considered football a valuable enough activity, for the entertainment it provided and for the example of the martial virtues that it set, to field its own teams, which recruited some of the most talented players in the country. At the beginning of 1919 the Rose Bowl game, the climax of the college season, pitted a team from the Great Lakes Naval Training Center, outside Chicago, against one from the Mare Island Marine Base, located near San Francisco.

The nation's colleges did continue to play football during World War II and the outstanding team in the war years was the one representing the United States Military Academy at West Point, whose players ran no risk of being drafted into the armed forces because, as West Point cadets, they were already in the army. When the team won its final game of 1944 against its arch-rival from the Naval Academy in Annapolis to complete a season without a defeat, the Army coach received a telegram from General Douglas MacArthur, the commander of allied forces in the southwestern Pacific. MacArthur had faithfully followed the fortunes of Army football since his own days as a cadet, when he had served as the team's student manager. His telegram read: "The greatest of all Army teams. We have stopped the war to celebrate your magnificent success."[33]

War and football were linked even before the twentieth century, in 1898, when the United States fought Spain and emerged from that conflict in possession of the nearby Caribbean island of Cuba and a distant Pacific archipelago, the Philippines. One of the heroes of that war was Theodore Roosevelt, the assistant secretary of the Navy, who resigned his government post, raised a battalion, took it to Cuba, and led a successful attack on a fortified Spanish position at the top of a hill. The publicity he received propelled him into elective office, first as governor of New York and then as vice president of the United States, from which position he ascended to the presidency upon the assassination of William McKinley in 1901.

Roosevelt was an enthusiastic supporter of the game of football.[34] He and other champions of war and empire in 1898 considered football valuable because it fostered precisely the qualities of character necessary for success on the battlefield, which he, like many others of his era, regarded as the supreme and necessary test of men and nations.[35] In assembling his band of "Rough Riders" to fight in Cuba he was particularly interested in finding men with experience in playing football.[36] And he was able to find them, because by that time the game had been played, mainly but not exclusively in the northeastern part of the United States, for almost three decades.

THE COLLEGE GAME

The contest that has come to be regarded as the first game of American football took place on November 6, 1869. It matched players from two New Jersey universities: Princeton and Rutgers. (Rutgers won.) The game they played that day resembled soccer. Five years later, in 1874, a group of students from McGill University in Montreal traveled south for two contests with players from Harvard. The two sides played the first game according to the rules that Rutgers and Princeton had followed. The second, however, at the suggestion of the McGill players, was governed by the rules of the other of the two branches of football into which the game had divided in England: rugby.[37] The Harvard students decided that they preferred the second game to the first and because they, and students from Yale and other, similar institutions in the Northeast adopted this second set of rules, so, too, ultimately did the rest of the country.

Over the next quarter century the rules of football were modified, with Walter Camp taking a leading role. Two changes in particular shaped the way the game came to be played and set it apart from its English forbear. The first change provided for play to stop when the knee of the man carrying the ball touches the ground,[38] after which the two teams regroup and begin play again. The second crucial rule change of the early years concerned possession of the ball. Play stops as well in rugby, although less frequently than in football, but when it does it is resumed in such a way that each team has a more or less equal opportunity to gain possession of it. But by the second rule change, the team in possession of the ball can retain it by advancing it a certain distance in a set number of attempts, or downs. At first the requirement was five yards in three tries; ultimately it became ten yards in four downs.*

In combination these two changes made American football a more organized and planned exercise, because each team has the opportunity to regroup and plan its strategy anew after each play, and a less fluid and spontaneous one than rugby.

---

* In the Canadian version of football the team has only three downs to gain ten yards. For this reason risky, spectacular plays are more frequent there than in the game south of the border, making it perhaps the one area of Canadian life that is more flamboyant than its American counterpart.

In football's early years the favored approach to advancing the ball was to bunch as many bodies as possible as tightly together as possible and hurl them forward as the advance guard of the ball carrier against the massed ranks of the opposing team. Each play was like an infantry charge against a formation of opposing soldiers, a collision of two human walls—one moving, one stationery—producing a tangle of bodies with the ball carrier pushed and pulled by his own team and pummeled by the opposing side. Weight, momentum, and brute force usually carried the day. Speed, agility, and elusiveness counted for far less. Deliberate assaults on star players to force them to leave the game were common.

Unlike in rugby, moreover, in football it became legal to tackle the ball carrier below the waist. Together with the other rule changes this made American football not only a less fluid game than rugby but also a more violent one. Its violence led to the demands for reform that Theodore Roosevelt was attempting to accommodate while preserving the basic features of the game when he convened his White House meeting on football in 1905. Reform did come to football, in the form of further rule changes that, by the eve of World War I, had given the game the shape it would retain into the twenty-first century.

The reforms made football less violent. The game recaptured some of the freewheeling openness of rugby while retaining the controlled rhythm that Camp's possession rules had imposed on it. One new rule made it more difficult to concentrate players by stipulating that a certain number had to be stationed side by side, strung out along the line of scrimmage, when each play began. A second lessened the shock of the human collisions that occurred on each play by prohibiting more than one player from being in motion before the play started.

A third rule barred the offensive team from pushing or pulling forward their teammate who was carrying the ball and a fourth designated a neutral zone along the line of scrimmage separating the two teams before the beginning of the action, making it easier for officials to enforce a fifth set of rules, against fighting and other forms of rough play.

A final change made in response to the outcry against violence in football further distinguished the American game from its English ancestor and had, over the long term, a monumental effect on it. In rugby the ball may be passed backward or sideways from one player to another but not forward. At the end of the nineteenth century and the beginning of the twentieth, gradually, in several stages, the forward pass, launched behind the line of scrimmage, became legal in American football.

The forward pass came to play the same role in football that the home run did in baseball, and rule changes pertaining to the ball itself encouraged both: In the early part of the century the shape of the football was streamlined to make it easier to throw, just as discoloring the baseball was outlawed in order to make it easier to hit. A long pass is the visual equivalent of a home run, and has the same emotional effect. The ball sails high and far, describing an arc, and as it moves through its trajectory suspense mounts among the spectators about its ultimate fate: in baseball, whether it will be caught for an out by a fielder or clear the boundary to record one or more runs for the team at bat; in football, whether the offensive player at whom it is aimed will succeed in catching it before it hits the ground, a task complicated by the efforts of the defensive team to prevent this from happening, efforts that cannot, however, involve bumping, pushing, or otherwise impeding him.

The event that revealed the potential of the forward pass, the equivalent of the impact of Babe Ruth's 1920 season on how the home run was perceived in baseball, was the November 1, 1913, football game between West Point and the University of Notre Dame. The Army team was heavily favored but Notre Dame made adroit use of the forward pass to score an upset victory, 35–13.[39]

For most of the next seven decades most football teams attempted to advance the ball by having a player carry it as far as he could before being tackled. Rushing, as this was called, was generally far more popular than passing. But toward the end of the twentieth century the priority for many teams reversed, and they came to rely ever more heavily on the forward pass. For most football teams most of the time over the seven decades following the seminal game between Army and Notre Dame it was unusual to attempt more than twenty passes in a game. But in the 1980s and 1990s, in no small part because of rules enacted at the end of the 1970s making it easier to complete passes, the average number of passes per game soared: forty per game became common. In a college game in 1998, one team went so far as to attempt eighty-three passes.

Because this represented a tilt in the balance between offense and defense toward the offense, the average number of points scored per game also increased. While in football individual statistics have less significance than in baseball, team statistics do correlate with success on the field and the team statistic most accurately predicting a team's success in a game and over the course of a season came to be the average yardage gained per pass attempted.[40]

Just as baseball's most storied events are dramatic home
runs that decide close and important contests at the very end
of the game, so the most celebrated individual plays in football history are long, last-minute passes that turn a looming
defeat into victory. For the college game the most famous
play is probably the fifty-two-yard pass for a touchdown,
with six seconds left to play, by Boston College's star quarterback Doug Flutie to defeat the University of Miami (Florida)
on Thanksgiving weekend of 1984. The comparable play in
professional football is the pass by the Pittsburgh Steelers,
again at the last moment of their 1972 playoff game against
the Oakland Raiders that bounced off one player and into
the arms of Pittsburgh's Franco Harris, who snatched it and
ran with it for the game-winning touchdown.

Because success was so improbable in both cases—in the
first, three defenders collided with one another, in the second, the ball ricocheted wildly—requiring the kind of
remarkable good fortune that, when it occurs, raises suspicions that divine intervention is involved, each play had a
religious image attached to it: the first became known as the
"Hail Mary" play, the second as the "Immaculate Reception."

The way football evolved in its early years provoked a
second kind of criticism, which focused not on the way the
game was played but on how the sport was organized. The
game began in universities because these institutions provided the required concentrations of able-bodied young men
and because, in the latter part of the nineteenth century, they
were home to the belief, which first appeared in the British
private schools, that competition in games helps instill desirable traits of character and thus qualifies as a legitimate educational activity.

But as the game actually developed it seemed to many observers to have little or nothing in common with the norms and the mission of higher education, and indeed appeared flagrantly to violate some of them. In 1932 the Marx Brothers made a film about college football called *Horse Feathers*. The plot revolved around an effort by the president of Darwin College, played by Groucho, to improve the institution's football team by hiring skilled players, who were available to the highest bidder and who spent their time not in classrooms or libraries but in local speakeasies. Embedded in the plot are the two principal vices, as the critics saw them, of college football: that the players were not regular students, for whom football was simply an extracurricular activity, and that they were in violation of the amateur spirit appropriate to college sports because they were paid to play.

By the time *Horse Feathers* appeared, these criticisms were at least four decades old. The first recorded "slush fund" to pay football players was made available at Columbia University in 1879.[41] Ten years later Andrew White, the president of Cornell University, vetoed a trip by the football team, saying, "I will not permit thirty men to travel four hundred miles merely to agitate a bag of wind."[42] But over the next century and beyond, many more than thirty students traveled much greater distances than four hundred miles for precisely that purpose, and the same criticisms were frequently repeated.

In 1910 the rules committee of college football became the National Collegiate Athletic Association (NCAA) and the organization ultimately assumed responsibility for policing college sports. In this capacity, over the years it imposed penalties on colleges and universities that violated its rules. [43] Almost every major institution incurred such penalties at one time or another.[44]

The recurrence of such penalties might at first seem to show that, where these issues were concerned, in college football's first century and a quarter nothing changed. But such a conclusion would be incorrect. In fact, two important changes occurred. First, while some institutions of higher learning competed in football at the highest level of skill, others—the majority—chose not to do so. The distinction was made formal in 1973 by the division of NCAA member institutions into several different categories, only the first of which—Division I, including such schools as Notre Dame, the University of Alabama, and Texas A&M—which numbered 126 out of the total 667 schools, devoted substantial resources to the pursuit of success on the football field.

NCAA-mandated rules governed the operation of the football programs at Division I schools but—and this was the second major change—in the second half of the twentieth century those rules were amended to *permit* precisely the practices that had been the subject of criticism since the last decade of the nineteenth. What critics had decried as incompatible with the ethos of academic life the NCAA's rules established as permissible.

Players were required to be full-time students, but they could be treated differently in a variety of ways from students who were not members of the football team. They could live and eat separately from the rest of the student body and miss classes for the sake of their football duties. Most importantly, by NCAA rules they could legally be paid, through the provision of athletic scholarships. These scholarships pay for the recipient's tuition and give him (or, in some sports, her) money for room, board, and other expenses. Universities also routinely furnish their athletes with summer employment, which is seldom difficult and often lucrative.

True, universities with major football programs frequently violated the NCAA rules, in an effort to attract skilled players for whose services rival schools were also competing. But these violations did not involve paying the players, which was now permissible. The schools were penalized, rather, for *over*paying them. NCAA rules tacitly conceded that football players differ from other students, that the principal purpose of their presence in the institution is not educational, that college football is, for its players, a vocation not a hobby, and that the phrase that the NCAA uses to refer to them—"student-athletes"—is an oxymoron.

From its earliest days, the principal purpose of college football where it has received the most attention and has been played with the greatest skill has not been to contribute to the education of the players but to provide a diversion for the far larger number of spectators—fellow students, alumni, and the general public—that the games attract. The football program has constituted an almost completely independent department devoted to mass entertainment, lodged anomalously in an institution concerned with very different things. Football is to the university what the appendix is to the human body: unrelated to its functioning but also generally harmless.* Universities did from time to time suffer the equivalent, for football, of acute appendicitis, usually when the expense of sustaining a major football program became prohibitive.

* Football and other comparably organized sports are not regarded as harmless to universities by all observers. The contemporary indictment of major college sports has three principal points. The first is that they injure the institution of which they are a part because they conflict with their educational norms, a point made as early as 1929 in a report sponsored by the Carnegie Corporation of New York. Watterson, op. cit., pp. 164–176. The second is that the time they require deprives participants of the opportunity for a genuine education. And the third is that sports act as a kind of narcotic for students who do not play on the teams, diverting them from the tasks for which they have enrolled in the institution. The

When this happened, the institution in question would undergo a version of an appendectomy, either abolishing or severely downgrading—"deemphasizing"—the sport.[45]

The rules governing football on the field and the way the sport was organized on college campuses throughout the twentieth century and into the twenty-first were in place by the time World War I began. But it was not until the 1920s that the game became a prominent part of the popular culture of the entire nation, helping to satisfy a growing demand for entertainment. Having begun in the private universities of the Northeast, by the 1920s football had spread to the rest of the country, gaining particular popularity in the Midwest and the South. Universities in these regions constructed large stadiums—the one in Ann Arbor, Michigan, dedicated in 1927, has the capacity to hold more than 100,000 people—in which football games could be played.

The universities' teams commanded the enthusiastic support of their students, who helped to fill the stadiums on Saturday afternoons. There they were joined by alumni, many of whom became, if anything, more avid supporters of the team than the students[46] and some of whom contributed sub-

continued

critic who has given most prominent voice to these charges is Murray Sperber, a faculty member at the University of Indiana, in a series of books that include *College Sports, Inc.: The Athletic Department vs. The University* (New York: Henry Holt, 1990) and *Beer and Circus: How Big-time College Sports Is Corrupting Undergraduate Education* (New York: Henry Holt, 2000).

Even the nation's most selective institutions of higher education, most of which do not compete at the highest levels in football and basketball, have come in for criticism on the grounds that they nonetheless give preference for admission to some students on the basis of their athletic skills and these students perform worse academically than the rest of the student body. William G. Bowen and Sarah A. Levin, *Reclaiming the Game: College Sports and Educational Values*, (Princeton, New Jersey: Princeton University Press, 2003).

stantial sums of money to support the football program. In recognition of the continuing interest in the team even after graduation, (and in the hope of encouraging donations to the school), universities took to designating one football game each year as the occasion for "homecoming." Alumni were invited to return to campus, attend the game, and participate in other festivities.

By coming to be seen as representing the entire state, the teams of the large state universities even earned the loyalty of people who had never attended the institution. Pride in the teams reached particular heights in the South, which had no major league baseball teams with which to identify until the 1960s. There success in football became a form of symbolic self-assertion in a part of the country that, in the early decades of the twentieth century, was poor and still bore the psychological scars of defeat in the Civil War.[47] As a Catholic university in an era—the years following World War I— scarcely free of anti-Catholic sentiment, Notre Dame attracted a special following. Its teams' successes on the football field earned the institution a place in the affections of Catholics all over the country, most of whom had never been within a hundred miles of its campus. Because many were urban workers, they became known as Notre Dame's "subway alumni."

In the 1920s news of college football, as of baseball, was featured prominently on the sports pages of the large-circulation daily newspapers that had blossomed at the end of the previous century. It was also disseminated over the airwaves and on screens in movie theaters through two new inventions, the radio and the newsreel.

As with baseball, star players became national celebrities. The first football player to achieve something like the status of Babe Ruth was the University of Illinois player Harold "Red" Grange, whose elusiveness while carrying the ball earned him the nickname of the "Galloping Ghost." On October 18, 1924, in the inaugural game of the University of Illinois' football stadium against arch-rival Michigan, until then the dominant team in the Midwest, Grange captured the nation's attention with a remarkable performance. He scored four touchdowns in the first twelve minutes of play and five overall, while passing for another and gaining 402 yards in the twenty-one times he carried the ball—an astonishing total in any era. He led his team to a 39 to 14 victory. That game, and Grange's performance, had an effect on football's national popularity comparable to the impact of the 1913 Notre Dame-Army contest on the game's offensive strategy. Grange became known throughout the country. He was able to leave college in 1925, join the new and struggling professional football league, and command a salary and endorsements that earned him $250,000,[48] putting him on a par with, perhaps even ahead of, Ruth himself.

By the 1920s major league baseball had become national in scope in the sense that, although the teams were located only in the Northeast and Midwest, within both of the two leagues each team played all the others and in the World Series an overall champion was chosen. By contrast, major college football, although played in every part of the United States, was organized on a regional basis. The Ivy League was not formally established until 1955, but in 1895 what would become the Big Ten conference, encompassing the large state universities of the Midwest, came into being and there followed the creation of the Southeastern Conference, which included much of the Old Confederacy, the Southwest Conference centered on Texas, the Big Eight in the Great

Plains, and the Pacific Coast Conference. Each team played mainly other teams in its own conference or situated nearby.

Of particular importance to players and supporters were the annual games against traditional rivals, often the final game of the season. These games matched teams representing schools that were similar, located close to each other, and that had played annually over a long period of time. The potent emotions they often aroused exemplify, perhaps, what Sigmund Freud termed "the narcissism of small differences."[49] These contests are ordinarily the best-attended games of the football season, and even a team with a dismal record can fill its stadium for this contest. For many spectators, attending this particular game becomes an annual social ritual.

Like individual statistics in baseball, "rivalry games" offer a focus of attention for fans and players other than a team's overall record. Victory in this game, like an heroic statistical achievement by an individual player on an otherwise unsuccessful baseball team, can compensate for the disappointment of a losing season.

The oldest of all traditional rivalries is the one between Yale and Harvard, which was first played in 1875. Walter Camp, then a New Haven high school student, witnessed that game. When the Ivy League schools de-emphasized football in the 1950s, the game became more a social occasion for the spectators than a major event on the nation's football calendar, but in the first half century of the sport's history the stakes were high when the two teams met. In the 1920s the Yale coach T. A. D. Jones told his team, "Gentlemen, you are about to play football for Yale against Harvard. Never in your lives will you do anything so important."[50]

In the year-end game between the military academies at West Point and Annapolis the teams came to represent not only the institutions that their players were attending or even the officer corps of which their alumni were members, but the entire armed service: The contest came to be known as the Army-Navy game. The rivalry was heated from the start. It began in 1890 and soon thereafter, in 1893, an argument over a detail of the game between an Army brigadier general and a Navy rear admiral became so intense that each challenged the other to a duel. President Grover Cleveland thereupon banned the game, which was not resumed until 1899.[51]

An even longer hiatus marked one of the fiercest of the intra-state rivalries, between Auburn University and the University of Alabama. The series began in 1895 and games were played between 1900 and 1907 but then were discontinued, not to be reinstated until 1948, when it was agreed that they would be played at neither team's home stadium but rather at a neutral site in Birmingham.

In the Midwest the most consequential year-end game, the one that, after World War II, often decided the championship of the Big Ten conference, matched Michigan and Ohio State, a rivalry that began in 1897. So intense was the dislike of Woody Hayes, Ohio State's coach from 1951 to 1978, of his school's chief rival that on those occasions when he found himself forced to drive through the state of Michigan he refused to purchase gasoline there.

In the Southwest, Texas and Oklahoma began an annual contest in 1900. They play the game in the first half of the football season, not at the end, and in Dallas rather than at the home stadium of either of the two teams. Until the mid-1990s, moreover, the two schools belonged to different conferences and so the game did not affect either's efforts to win a championship. Because the two states involved are neighbors, however, and because both number among their alumni people who have earned fortunes in the oil business, some of whom fly into Dallas on private jets to attend the game, it achieved the intensity of a traditional rivalry.

The oldest football rivalry on the West Coast is the one between the two major institutions in the San Francisco Bay area, the University of California at Berkeley and Stanford University in Palo Alto. The first game took place in 1892. The student manager of the Stanford team was Herbert Hoover, later the thirty-first president of the United States. As part of the rivalry, students from each school have often played pranks on the other, such as stealing the trophy awarded to the winner each year, an axe enclosed in a glass case.

The 1982 "Big Game," as it is called in northern California, was the occasion for perhaps the most bizarre single play in the entire history of college football. On the last play of the game, Stanford kicked off to the Berkeley team, which needed to score a touchdown or lose. As they carried the ball toward the Stanford goal, the California players spontaneously revived one of the staples of rugby, the backward or lateral pass thrown beyond the line of scrimmage, which, although permitted, is rarely employed in American football. As the player with the ball was about to be tackled, ending the game, he lateraled to another. This occurred no fewer than five times, and the last recipient found himself approaching the Stanford goal line with no opposing players in front of him. He did, however, encounter the Stanford band, which had rushed from the stands on to the field in anticipation of a victory celebration. He knocked over a trombone player and crossed the goal line to score, giving California a wholly unexpected victory on what entered the lore of West Coast football as "the Play."

One reason that college football came to be organized on a regional basis had to do with logistics. In the days before regular air service it was costly and time-consuming for teams to travel long distances.[52]

Another reason was the practice of racial segregation in the South. In the first part of the twentieth century college football teams outside the South did not have many black players, but they did have a few. Among the notable players of African descent were Paul Robeson, a star at Rutgers in 1917 and 1918 who later gained fame as a singer, actor, and sympathizer with Communist causes, and Jackie Robinson himself, who played football at the University of California at Los Angeles before breaking the color barrier in professional baseball. Teams from the segregated South refused to play opponents that fielded African-American players, which meant that Northern teams either left such players off their squads in games with Southern schools or, more commonly, did not schedule games with such schools at all.

The closest equivalent for football of Jackie Robinson's debut for the Brooklyn Dodgers in 1947 took place a decade later, in a game in New Orleans, when a black player named Bobby Grier played for the University of Pittsburgh against a team representing Georgia Tech. Not until the 1970s did teams located in the states of the Confederacy include black players in any appreciable numbers on their own rosters.

Although not the norm, games between teams from different parts of the country—"intersectional" contests—did take place before the age of air travel. Beginning in 1926, for example, the University of Southern California, located in Los Angeles, and Notre Dame played annually, with each making the 2,000-mile train trip to the other's stadium in alternate years. And teams did travel long distances to play in games staged after their season schedules were completed, in what came to be called bowl games.

The earliest, the "granddaddy of them all," was the Rose Bowl. In 1890 the city of Pasadena, just east of Los Angeles, staged a New Year's Day festival called the "Tournament of Roses," to display the city's flowers and publicize its balmy winter climate to would-be vacationers in colder parts of the United States. In 1902 the sponsors decided to capitalize on football's growing popularity by adding a game to the festivities, and invited the University of Michigan, the leading team in the Midwest, to play Stanford. (Michigan won, 49–0.) Thereafter the Rose Bowl pitted the Pacific Coast champion against a team chosen from among the best in the rest of the country. After World War II the regular participants were the Pacific Coast Conference and the Big Ten champions. By that time, however, the Rose Bowl was not the only opportunity for postseason play available to successful teams.

Pasadena's model was replicated in 1935 by New Orleans, which established the Sugar Bowl, and Miami, which established the Orange Bowl. In 1937, Dallas launched the Cotton Bowl. Over the years, bowl games proliferated. In 2002–2003 a total of twenty-eight were staged, including the Continental Tire Bowl in Charlotte, North Carolina, the Alamo Bowl in San Antonio, Texas, and the Humanitarian Bowl, played on a field of blue artificial turf in Boise, Idaho.

Although college football dominated most of the sport's first century, football teams that were not based in colleges, with explicitly paid players, appeared as early as the 1890s. In the first two decades of the twentieth century most were based in the Midwest, many in the state of Ohio. On August

20, 1920, what became the major association of professional football teams, the National Football League (NFL), was formed in Ralph Hay's Hupmobile (an automobile of the era) dealership on the ground floor of the Odd Fellows building in Canton, Ohio.[53]

The fledgling league became more widely known five years later when Red Grange agreed to play for one of its teams and a new team was simultaneously established in New York. It was called, like the city's National League baseball team, the Giants.

Franchises came and went during the league's first decade, but by the 1930s it had achieved a measure of stability. Almost every team was located in a city with a major league baseball team, which meant that it could rent for its own games the stadium in which the baseball team played. The NFL teams were split into two divisions, all played the same number of games, and a playoff determined the champion each year.

The years following World War II were for professional football what the era after World War I had been for baseball: a time of rapid growth. So financially promising did professional football appear that, in 1946, a new league was organized, the All-American Football Conference. In 1950 it merged into the NFL, adding several teams to the older league. By that year two of the league's twelve teams were located on the West Coast, in San Francisco and Los Angeles. The Los Angeles team, called the Rams, attracted enormous crowds to its home stadium, the Los Angeles Coliseum, a building modeled after the original coliseum in Rome and constructed for the 1932 Olympic Games.[54]

College teams could attract spectators, especially to

games against traditional rivals, by appealing to institutional and regional loyalty. But they also offered another kind of attraction, which was even more important for the professional teams: star players. And the brightest stars on the field, the ones whom people would pay to see, were deployed in two particular positions. When the rule changes of the late nineteenth and early twentieth centuries transformed football from a sequence of collisions of massed bodies to a more open and fluid, albeit controlled, exercise, the two positions most responsible for advancing the ball and scoring, the positions whose players handled the ball most often and on whose activities the spectators concentrated their attention most avidly and that therefore came to be surrounded by an aura of glamour, were the quarterback and the running back—the first responsible for passing the ball downfield, the second for carrying it forward.

The players at these two positions received more attention than all the others combined. A popular song of the 1920s was titled "You've Got to Be a Football Hero to Get Along with a Beautiful Girl." The heroes were quarterbacks and running backs. In 1898, the custom of choosing "All-American" teams designating the country's best college players at each position began. (Walter Camp inspired it and for many years offered his own selections.) But not all All-Americans were equally celebrated. In the second half of the twentieth century these selections came to be overshadowed by an award given to the outstanding individual player in the United States. It was named for John Heisman, a successful coach for many years who was, at the time of his death in 1936, the athletic director of the Downtown Athletic Club of New York.[55] The club polled sportswriters across the country and awarded the Heisman Trophy to the player with the highest vote total.* The winner of the Heisman Trophy was almost always either a quarterback or a running back.

While they shared public visibility, the two positions required different skills. For a running back, foot speed, durability, and the ability to dodge around or bulldoze through would-be tacklers are the keys to success. For much of the twentieth century the last two qualities customarily belonged to different players, who filled different positions in the backfield. The tank was the fullback. (Indeed, one of the best fullbacks of the 1950s, the Los Angeles professional player Paul Younger, was nicknamed "Tank.") The artful dodger was the halfback. But increasingly in the last three decades of the century there appeared ball carriers—O. J. Simpson was one—who combined the two abilities.

While the admiring adjective often applied to a running back is "explosive," the desirable qualities in a quarterback are cerebral as well as physical. He must be able to scan the field in front of him, with players running in all directions, pick out a likely receiver for his pass, and throw it to the designated (and moving) target accurately, all the while contending with large, menacing players from the defense struggling to push past his protective screen of blockers and knock him to the ground. The successful quarterback is said to be cool under the pressure he regularly encounters. The two professional quarterbacks generally regarded as the best of all,

---

* As a coach Heisman presided over the most lopsided game in college football history. His 1916 Georgia Tech team defeated Cumberland College, 220–0. The Cumberland team had been organized only the week before and suited up just nineteen players. At halftime, with Georgia Tech leading 126–0, Heisman told his players, "Men, don't let up. You never know what those Cumberland players have up their sleeves." Wittingham, op. cit., p. 238.

Johnny Unitas, who spent most of his career with the Baltimore Colts,[56] and Joe Montana, who won four championships with the San Francisco 49ers, both fit this description.[57] Each had an understated personality, seldom displaying emotion, and each seemed to perform best under pressure. They embodied the virtues singled out in the Rudyard Kipling poem "If," which begins, "If you can keep your head/While all about you are losing theirs and blaming it on you."

While running backs and quarterbacks are invariably the most visible and celebrated players on a football team, they are almost never the individual most responsible for that team's success or failure. That distinction belongs to someone who doesn't actually play at all: the coach. For football, more than either of the other two major American team sports, is the coach's game.

THE COACH'S GAME

The history of baseball is the history of successful teams and outstanding players. The history of football is the history of successful teams and outstanding coaches. Books about baseball concern teams and players. Books about football take as their subjects teams and coaches. Babe Ruth, Joe DiMaggio, and Mickey Mantle symbolize the great New York Yankee teams of their era. The symbols of the great college and professional football teams are their coaches. In baseball, the person to whom responsibility for victories and defeats is assigned is the pitcher. In football it is not a player but rather the head coach whose career wins and losses are tallied and regularly published.

During games the head coach is a conspicuous presence on the sidelines, often dressed distinctively to set him apart from others there, pacing back and forth, barking orders. The stadiums in which the football teams of the Universities of Tennessee, Auburn, and Alabama play are all named for men who coached at these schools. Coaches can accumulate considerable power, able to hire and fire anyone in their organization. These are prerogatives that managers of major league baseball teams do not have. Coaches can also accumulate significant wealth. By the beginning of the twenty-first century professional coaches routinely received multimillion-dollar annual salaries.[58] The incomes of college football coaches tend to be modest by the standards of their professional counterparts, but not in comparison to what others working in their institutions are paid. The coaches at several large state universities have received the highest salary of any of their hundreds of thousands of fellow state employees, including the governor.[59]

The coach towers over the players in importance—and sometimes literally towers over them by observing practice sessions from an elevated platform—because he is both the playwright and the director while they are mere actors. He writes the script and supervises the way they enact it. To use another metaphor, the industrial revolution ushered in the age of the machine and so gave rise to the man who designs and maintains it—the engineer. The coach is the engineer of the football team. This is so because football is the most hierarchical of the three major American team sports, and the coach stands at the top of the hierarchy.

Because it unfolds in defined, discrete sequences, and because for each sequence both the offense and the defense must coordinate the action of all eleven players, which cannot occur spontaneously but must be arranged in advance, football both requires and permits coordination from a single, central source, in a way that baseball and basketball do not.

Before the games are played, each play (and professional teams have hundreds) must be designed and rehearsed, with each player being taught his particular role. Both are the coach's responsibility. Throughout the games each team, on both offense and defense, must decide which play to select. For most of the twentieth century the quarterback decided on the offensive play, based on the choices designed by the coaches and rehearsed frequently in practice sessions, and communicated it to his teammates in the group meeting held before each play known as the huddle. By the century's last three decades, however, the coach increasingly appropriated the task of play-calling, determining the play on the sidelines and communicating his choice to the quarterback on the field electronically, or by hand signals, or by sending a player to join the huddle with his message. By the twenty-first century a quarterback who called his own plays had become a rarity.

Before the season and between games, finally, players must be instructed on the basic techniques needed to carry out their responsibilities on each play. It is the coach—or rather the head coach and his assistants—who provide the instruction and organize the setting in which it takes place.

All this responsibility, which stems from the structure of the game, invests coaches with enormous authority. In this sense the job is comparable to two others: the chief executive officer (CEO) of a commercial firm and, not surprisingly, given the commonalities between football and war, the general. All three make decisions that others carry out. Unlike political leaders or leaders of educational or religious institutions, however, coaches, CEOs, and generals preside over organizations that are in direct competition with others and the performance of which is subject to an objective assessment of success and failure. For all three there is, to borrow an expression from accounting, a bottom line, which makes it relatively easy to hold all three responsible for the performance of the organization: losing football games, battles, and money is ordinarily cause for dismissal.

Because so much depends on the organization's performance, each of the three jobs tends to reward people who work long hours and attend scrupulously to the details of their work. But neither a coach, a CEO, nor a general can supervise his organization single-handedly. Each must delegate authority to subordinates, the selection of whom is one of the most important tasks for each.

Each of the three bears special responsibility for the morale of the organization, which in turn affects its performance. A large body of literature is devoted to how management techniques can foster conditions in which the employees of a business can work most efficiently. For military commanders and football coaches the motivation of soldiers and players is an essential part of the job, and not an easy one, given that what they are urging their charges to do with enthusiasm and persistence is dangerous. Their words just before the battle or the game begins, sometimes delivered in dramatic fashion,[60] are designed to lift the spirits of those to whom they are addressed. These words are especially important because, although a coach's and a general's demeanor does influence those he leads, neither can lead by example. Both are far removed from the action—unlike premodern war, when the commander led his troops on the battlefield, and the early days of football, when the team captain assumed the duties of the coach.

The coach's pregame pep talk, in which he exhorts the players to exert themselves, echoes a custom that dates back to the beginning of recorded history: the commander's eve-of-battle oration, the best-known literary rendition of which is King Henry's speech before the battle of Agincourt in Shakespeare's *Henry V.* Coaches invoke team solidarity, as did the king: "We few, we happy few, we band of brothers." And they hold out to the players the glory to be won in the contest about to be played, in the spirit of Henry's declaration to his troops that

> *Gentlemen in England now abed*
> *Shall think themselves accurs'd they were not here*
> *And hold their manhood cheap while any speaks*
> *That fought with us upon Saint Crispin's Day.*[61]

Coaches, CEOs, and generals have recognized the similarities in what they do and each has paid the others the compliment of close study. Football coaches are frequently aficionados of military history.[62] So devoted was Woody Hayes of Ohio State to pondering the great battles of the past that in his memory his former players endowed a professorship in strategic studies in his name at Ohio State.[63] Generals have reciprocated coaches' interest, on the grounds that the qualities that underlie success on the football field are equally useful on the battlefield. The earliest and best-known statement of this proposition is the assertion credited to the Duke of Wellington, the conqueror of Napoleon, that the battle of Waterloo was won on the playing fields of Eton. When he served as superintendent of West Point, Douglas MacArthur echoed that sentiment in causing to be inscribed on the wall of the gymnasium these words: "Upon the fields of friendly strife/Are sown seeds that/Upon other fields, on other days/Will bear the fruits of victory."[64] Similarly, the lessons of football have been deemed applicable to the world of business. Successful coaches have been invited to share, often for substantial fees, their approaches to the management of their teams with business executives.[65]

Because the basic unit of football is the group rather than the individual, the game lacks the appeal to writers of fiction that baseball has had. But because the exercise of hierarchical authority looms so large in football, as it does not in baseball, the fictional treatments that football has received have been a series of variations on the theme of authority: deflations of its pretensions, as in the novels *Semi-Tough* by Dan Jenkins and *North Dallas Forty* by Pete Gent, and attacks on its misuse, as in Oliver Stone and Eric Hamburg's film *Any Given Sunday*. Perhaps the most notable football player in American fiction is Gary Harkness, the central figure in Don DeLillo's novel *End Zone*, whose own free and sometimes rebellious spirit stands in contrast to the discipline that the game requires and that the coach of the Logos College football team imposes.[66]

In the annals of coaching, the pioneer, the first paid, fulltime director of a major football team, was Amos Alonzo Stagg.[67] A disciple of Walter Camp who played at Yale from 1888 to 1894[68] and was a member of Camp's first All-American team,[69] Stagg was hired in 1892 by William Rainey Harper, the president of the newly founded University of Chicago, to establish a football program there. Harper, like later college presidents, saw football as a way of garnering attention for his school in the wider community and generating loyalty among its students and alumni.

As it happened, the University of Chicago set the precedent not only for establishing a major football program where none had existed but also for terminating one. In 1939 a different president of the university, Robert Maynard Hutchins, decided that Chicago would no longer have a football team. This was the first, but by no means the last, instance of "deemphasis." By then Stagg had left Chicago. But he had stayed for forty-one years, and from Chicago went to the College of the Pacific, in Stockton, California, where he coached for another sixteen, ending his career with 314 victories.[70]

If one of the hallmarks of Stagg's career was its longevity—born during the presidency of Abraham Lincoln he was still active in college football (although not as a coach) when Dwight D. Eisenhower was president—another was the rectitude he brought to the game. A devout Christian who regarded football as a vehicle for moral instruction, he permitted none of his players to curse, and the strongest expression of disapproval he himself would utter was "jackass."[71]

If Stagg was the first full-time football coach, the prototype of the coach as charismatic leader and national celebrity was Knute Rockne of Notre Dame. As a player there he made a major contribution to the 1913 victory over Army, catching a number of the passes that helped to win the game. As the head coach from 1918 to 1930 he won 105 games, lost twelve and tied five, a winning percentage of .891 that remains the highest of any coach at a comparable institution. Although Rockne made some innovations in the way the game was played, his trail-blazing accomplishments came in two other areas.

He was a renowned pregame orator and motivator. In 1930 his team was traveling to Los Angeles for its annual match against the University of Southern California (it would turn out to be Rockne's last game as coach) and stopped in Tucson, Arizona, to practice. Rockne was so unhappy with his players' effort that he announced that he was resigning as coach on the spot. The shocked players begged him to stay. He agreed to do so, and, thereby presumably inspired, they trounced their opponent 27–0.[72]

Rockne also excelled at the art of gaining publicity. He drew attention to himself, becoming one of the sports celebrities of the 1920s. Like Babe Ruth and Red Grange, he was paid to endorse a range of consumer products from sporting equipment to Studebaker automobiles.[73] His teams also attracted attention. Members of one of them earned the most famous nickname in the history of college football. In his account of Notre Dame's victory over Army in 1924, the most widely read sportswriter of his day, Grantland Rice, used a Biblical image to describe the exploits of the team's principal ball carriers: "Outlined against a blue-gray October sky, the Four Horsemen rode again. In dramatic lore they are known as Famine, Pestilence, Destruction and Death. These are only aliases. Their real names are Stuhldreher, Miller, Crowley and Layden...."[74] A photograph of the four of them in warmup coats mounted on horseback was distributed to newspapers throughout the country the following week and their place in the annals of football—and of publicity—was assured.

Rockne also did a great deal to promote the sport itself. According to one contemporary, he "sold football to the men on the trolley, the elevated, the subway, to the baker, the butcher, the pipe fitter who never went to college. He made it an American mania."[75]

The episode for which he is best known combined his two great talents—giving pep talks and generating publicity. In 1920 one of his star players, George Gipp, died of pneumonia. Eight years later, addressing the Notre Dame team at halftime of its game against Army, Rockne recalled Gipp's dying words: "Rock, I know I'm going … but I'd like one last request … some day, Rock … some time—when the going isn't so easy, when the odds are against us, ask a Notre Dame team to win one for me, for the Gipper. I don't know where I'll be then, Rock, but I'll know about it and I'll be happy."[76] Suitably inspired, Notre Dame won the game 12 to 6. It is doubtful that the deathbed scene actually occurred as Rockne later recounted it. He had never mentioned it before this particular game and, indeed, had not been present when Gipp died. Nor was Gipp, who was described by a sportswriter who had known him as "a womanizer, a pool shark, a gambler and a drunk,"[77] the kind of person ordinarily given to expressing such sentiments. Whether or not true, however, it made for a good story and earned a place not only in the lore of football but also in the history of American popular culture when, after the coach's death in a plane crash in 1930,[78] Hollywood made a film about his life entitled *Knute Rockne, All-American*, with the veteran actor Pat O'Brien in the title role. Ronald Reagan, then a newcomer to the movies, played the part of George Gipp, and in his subsequent political career he and his supporters often invoked the player's supposed dying request to "win one for the Gipper."

The man who did the most to define the duties of the modern football coach was Paul Brown. A graduate of Miami University of Ohio, a school that produced so many successful coaches that it became known as "the cradle of coaches,"[79] he compiled winning records at every level of football competition: Massillon High School in Ohio, Ohio State University, the Great Lakes Naval Training Center during World War II, and the professional Cleveland

Browns[80] and Cincinnati Bengals. His greatest success came with the Cleveland team. From 1946 to 1949 it won four consecutive championships in the All-American Football Conference. Then it joined the NFL and played in six consecutive championship games, winning three.[81] Brown established what came to be the dominant trend in the game by calling all his team's plays, which he relayed to his quarterback via substitute players who regularly shuttled back and forth between the sideline and the field.

His greatest influence came in establishing what a coach must do before the games to prepare his team.[82] He compiled playbooks for his players, taught their contents in classroom settings, and regularly tested them on what they were supposed to have learned. He maintained up-to-date statistical analyses of his team's performance in all relevant categories as well as of the performances of its opponents. He obtained film of his opponents' previous games, which he studied in preparing to play them. In the professional ranks he organized a system for observing and evaluating college players who would subsequently become eligible to join his team. With all these additions to it, he made coaching a year-round job.

The most celebrated of all the thousands of men who followed in the footsteps of Amos Alonzo Stagg as football coaches, however, the one whose name was still widely recognized three decades after his death, who commanded such respect during his lifetime that he was discussed as a vice presidential candidate by both major political parties in 1968,[83] the person for whom the trophy given annually to professional football's championship team is named, and the nose on whose bust at the professional football Hall of Fame in Canton, Ohio, is shiny from having been rubbed by countless visitors seeking a symbolic and posthumous connection with him,[84] is Vincent T. "Vince" Lombardi.

Lombardi played college football at Fordham University in New York City, graduating in 1936. There he was a member of a unit with a nickname second in celebrity only to Notre Dame's Four Horsemen. He and his fellow blockers and tacklers on the team's line became known, thanks to their own proficiency and an enterprising publicist, as the "Seven Blocks of Granite."[85] He coached in high school and then in college, first at his alma mater and then on the West Point staff of Earl Blaik, the impresario of the powerful Army teams of World War II and the decade thereafter.

Lombardi crossed over into professional football as an assistant coach with the New York Giants and then, in 1959, became the head coach of the Green Bay Packers, an old but languishing franchise in the National Football League, where his achievements elevated him to football's pantheon. In nine years there his teams won 89 games, lost 24, and tied 4, captured their conference title six times, and on the last five of these occasions went on to defeat the winner of the other conference for the league championship. Lombardi's Packers won the first two Super Bowls.

His specialty was offensive football. He emphasized a rushing attack based on a few plays honed to precision through constant repetition, which instilled confidence in the players that the plays would work under actual game conditions. He wielded absolute and unquestioned authority over all aspects of the team. The strict discipline he imposed on the players had an intimidating effect but also produced maximal effort. They drove themselves to carry out his instructions out of both the desire to please him by succeeding and the fear of his wrath if they failed. He had a volcanic personality, but it was a volcano that could be turned on and off for optimal effect.

Lombardi became the most famous of all football coaches

not only because of his personality and his on-field successes but also because his team achieved dominance at an important moment in the history of the game, the moment when football surpassed baseball as America's favorite sport and the professional version overtook college football in the nation's affections. He was the most famous figure in football at the advent of its golden age.

In the rise of professional football three games stand out as landmarks, and Vince Lombardi was involved in all three. The first was the December 28, 1958, championship game in which the Baltimore Colts defeated the New York Giants, with Lombardi on the Giants' coaching staff. Staged in Yankee Stadium in the nation's media capital, it was a close, thrilling contest in which the Colts scored a last-minute field goal to tie the game. So, for the first time in the history of football, extra time was added to decide the championship. Baltimore scored a touchdown to win, 23–17. The excitement of the game captured the attention of the country. When it ended, Bert Bell, the commissioner of the NFL, said, "This is the greatest day in the history of pro football."[86] At the time *Sports Illustrated* proclaimed it the best football game ever played.[87]

Eight years later, in January 1967, Lombardi's Packers took part in the first of the games that came to be known as the Super Bowl. That game, and the tradition of holding it, originated in the creation, in 1960, of a rival to the NFL, the American Football League (AFL). After a costly competition for players the two leagues merged in 1966 and at the beginning of 1967, for the first time, the winners of the two leagues—Lombardi's Packers and the Kansas City Chiefs—played each other. The game was not close—the Packers won 35–10—and did not fill the capacious Los Angeles Coliseum, where it was played.[88] But it was the inaugural version of what became not only the flagship game of professional football but also, over the decades, the most important annual sporting event in the United States.

Twelve months later, on the last day of 1967, the Packers defeated the Dallas Cowboys for the right to represent the older league in the second Super Bowl, which they also went on to win. What made the game dramatic were the weather conditions.[89] Sunday, December 31, 1967, was a bitterly cold day in Green Bay. The field was frozen: One player likened the game to playing on a stucco wall.[90] The wind-chill drove the temperature on the field down to minus 46 degrees Fahrenheit. An official had his whistle freeze to his lip and in the press box sportswriters' typewriters froze to the ledge on which they were perched.[91] Because the two teams had to battle the elements as well as each other, the contest became a cross between a football game and a polar expedition. To make what came to be known as the "Ice Bowl" even more dramatic, the game was a close one, the outcome decided by a fourth-down touchdown by the Green Bay quarterback, Bart Starr, with sixteen seconds left to play.

In addition to the participation of Vince Lombardi, the three games that ushered in football's golden age had another feature in common, which was the key both to their renown and the rise of the sport's popularity: Each of the three was televised.

The Golden Age

The marriage between television and team sports has proven to be a match made in heaven.

Team sports offer television gripping, suspenseful dramas

that millions of people are eager to watch, enabling television companies to charge high fees to broadcast advertisements during games. And these dramas come to television's proprietors prepackaged—already designed, arranged, and produced. All the television companies have to do is point their cameras at them. For its part, television offers sports teams a way to show their games to millions of people who cannot attend in person and to charge large fees from the television networks for the right to show them.

In the course of the twentieth century television consummated marriages with all three team sports, but the match with football was an especially apt and rewarding one. Football is played during the winter, when cold weather keeps people indoors in many parts of the country, thereby widening the pool of potential viewers. Because it takes time for players to recover from sixty minutes of collisions, a football team, unlike a baseball or basketball team, plays only once a week—the same frequency, as it happens, with which the programs in television comedy and drama series appear. The spacing has made football both a habit and a special event, something that happens often enough to sustain interest and provide continuity but infrequently enough so that each game is important and an event to which the audience looks forward during the days between one and next. The regular season in professional football has sixteen games, in basketball eighty-two, in baseball 162, which means that in its contribution to the outcome of the season, each football game is five times as important as each basketball game and ten times as significant as each baseball game.

Moreover, football offers something in abundance that baseball and basketball do not: violence. Since the earliest times, from gladiatorial contests in ancient Rome to public hangings in early modern England to boxing in the nineteenth and twentieth centuries—not to mention Hollywood movies of the twenty-first—staged events with violence at their core have commanded public attention. For whatever combination of biological and cultural reasons, violence exercises a sufficiently powerful attraction that people will pay to see it. To be sure, football provides a controlled and non-lethal version of it, but violence is what, among other things, the proprietors of television networks and football teams are giving their audiences.

If football is, more than the other two team sports, made for television, television is also made for football. It makes the game easier to watch than it is in person. Because most of the action takes place far from where they are sitting, in the tangle of bodies that many plays produce, it is difficult for the spectator at the game to make out exactly what is happening. Television, with its close-up pictures and its slow-motion replays, can dissect the action and present each slice of it in a way that the naked eye cannot see. Some football stadiums include large mounted screens that show the audience at the game what the people viewing at home can see—a tribute to the benefits that television confers on football.[92]

For this reason, and because many games are held outdoors in cold weather, football is the major American team sport in which the advantages of watching on television are most pronounced. It is also the one in which attendance at the actual game has most to do with the rituals in which the spectators participate—socializing with friends, taking part in organized cheers, drinking—as distinct from the manifest purpose of attendance, which is to watch the play on the field.

Television affected football differently than it did the

other two team sports in another way. It made the defensive players more accessible and therefore more popular. The close scrutiny of play that television made possible raised the level of appreciation for the efforts to prevent scoring, which is half the game of football as it is of baseball and basketball but, for spectators, typically the less interesting half. It did so in combination with two other developments.

One was the emergence of the platoon system. This gave defensive specialists their own distinctive identities. The other development was the evolution of the defensive position of linebacker. The linebacker stations himself between the beefy linemen crouched along the line of scrimmage poised to tackle oncoming ball carriers and the lighter, swifter defensive backs, deployed several yards behind the linemen and with responsibility for defending against passes. The most adept linebackers combine the defining qualities of the other two positions: strength and speed. They smash into opposing ball carriers and sprint after would-be pass-catchers. Occasionally they try to break through the protective wall of blockers surrounding the opposing quarterback and tackle him before he can launch a pass. Versatile, visible, and often formidable, the linebacker became, for the defense, the equivalent of the quarterback and the running back on offense. Linebacker became the glamour position, and its most skillful players earned a measure of celebrity.

The linebacker's rise to a special status in the game was heralded by a television documentary devoted to one of the leading players at the position in the 1950s. It was called *The Violent World of Sam Huff*. As the television technology for singling out and tracking individual players improved, the camera came increasingly to follow the linebacker on his appointed rounds. Hurling himself against blockers and racing after ball carriers and pass receivers all over the field, he resembled a predatory cat—a lion or a cheetah—chasing down its prey in a nature film.

The first professional football game to be televised was played on October 22, 1939.[93] In 1953 the NFL signed a contract with the DuMont television network to broadcast a set number of its games and for the 1958 championship game, carried by the National Broadcasting Company, a then-record 10.8 million homes tuned in to watch. In 1962, prodded by Alvin "Pete" Rozelle, who had succeeded Bert Bell as NFL commissioner, the team owners made the momentous decision to sell the rights to televise their games as a single package and to share the proceeds equally among themselves. This strengthened their bargaining position with the television networks and avoided the extreme disparities in revenues among the teams that produced many of the problems that came to plague major league baseball. From the early 1960s the Sunday telecasts of professional football grew in popularity. Watching them became a regular ritual across the United States. By the 1990s, 100 million people overall comprised the national audience each weekend for the menu of football games.

The season's culminating event, the Super Bowl, played at the end of January, attracted so much attention that, whereas post-season college football games capitalized on an existing national holiday—New Year's Day—the professional championship virtually created a new one: "Super Bowl Sunday." It surpassed New Year's Eve as the most popular occasion for Americans to hold parties in their homes.[94]

In 1970 the union of television and football reached a new level of intimacy. For the first time, games were televised regularly on a weeknight in prime time, which had previously been exclusively the province of programs such as *The Milton Berle Show*, *Gunsmoke*, and *I Love Lucy*.

Monday Night Football joined them. Telecast by the American Broadcasting Company (ABC), it brought another innovation to the television screen. Games had previously been broadcast by two people: a narrator, responsible for describing the action—the "play-by-play"—and a "color" commentator. Roone Arledge, the head of sports programming for ABC, had the idea of putting three men in the broadcast booth. One of them was a standard play-by-play announcer, a role filled from the second season by the former New York Giants player Frank Gifford. The other two, however, did not confine themselves to the low-key analysis of the action in which color commentators had specialized until then.

Don Meredith, also a former player, projected the persona of a folksy, devil-may-care Texan who made it clear that he took neither football nor anything else very seriously. Howard Cosell, a New York lawyer-turned-sportscaster, combined the jaundiced, supercilious outlook on life of the great American journalist of the first half of the twentieth century, H. L. Mencken, with the bombastic self-importance of the Kingfish, a character on the *Amos and Andy* radio program. Given to what seemed to much of his audience to be pompous pronouncements and fond of using longer words than were ordinarily heard on television, Cosell aroused strong feelings: admiration, fascination, and resentment. One national poll found him to be simultaneously the best- and least-liked sportscaster on television.

The game on the field on Monday night sometimes took second place in the telecasts to the spirited interplay in the broadcast booth, which provided the same kind of entertainment as the vaudeville routines of the late nineteenth and

early twentieth centuries and the television situation come-
dies that were descended from them. *Monday Night Football*
in fact resembled the best situation comedy of the 1970s, *The
Mary Tyler Moore Show*, with two strong, offbeat characters
and a more neutral, sympathetic one.*

The popularity of *Monday Night Football* survived the dis-
solution of its original broadcast team. By 2003 it had
achieved the second longest uninterrupted tenure of any
prime-time television program.[95] One of Meredith and
Cosell's successors was John Madden, an equally prominent
figure in the history of sportscasting as the first and most
popular in a series of coaches to switch from guiding a team
on the field to commenting on the game for the television
audience. As a public personality Madden was the opposite
of Cosell. While critics of the former lawyer claimed that he
knew less about football than he pretended—Cosell defiantly
entitled one of the books he wrote *I Never Played the Game*—
Madden, sophisticated about the intricacies of the game after
years on the sidelines and the practice field, presented himself as an average fan enjoying the features of football obvious to everyone.

Beginning in the 1960s the NFL established yet another
vehicle for promoting itself on television. NFL Films assembled half-hour documentaries about the season-long experiences of individual teams and games of special importance—
above all, the Super Bowl. Both were presented as epic dramas, with martial music and a gravel-voiced narrator. They

---

* To draw yet another parallel with an episode from the history of American popular culture, the interplay of the three had something in common with a Marx
Brothers routine, with Cosell as the hyper-articulate Groucho, Meredith as the
relaxed and playful Harpo, and the sometimes flustered and befuddled Gifford as
Margaret Dumont.

resembled the television series of the 1950s that chronicled the American campaigns in the Pacific during World War II called *Victory at Sea*.[96]

While it owed much of its popularity to a twentieth-century innovation, television, football's lofty standing in American popular culture derived as well from its association with a far older practice, one as old as antiquity: gambling. Wagering money on the uncertain outcome of an event is found in so many societies distributed so widely across time and space as to suggest that gambling, like warfare, emanates from human nature itself. Certainly it appeals to personalities, presumably found in all societies, that enjoy or require risk. And gambling also appeals to the even more widespread—perhaps universal—hope of material gain.

Sports offer two additional appeals to gamblers. The outcome of a sporting competition is not—as is, for example, a game of dice—a matter of pure chance. Sports are contests of skill and will. Success in wagering on these contests therefore involves more than luck: It also requires skill in accurately assessing how well-endowed with skill and will the contestants are. Betting on a team can also be a form of vicarious participation in the game. Bettors often wager on the team with which they identify, thereby adding to their emotional identification with that team a financial interest in its success.[97]

Of the three team sports football lends itself most readily to gambling. There are fewer games in each season, which magnifies the importance of each opportunity to win or lose a bet. Another reason for football's special appeal to gamblers is the method used to handicap the game. Gambling is a business, in which profitability depends on roughly the same amount of money being wagered on each possible outcome.

In games of chance such as roulette, this occurs more or less automatically, since statistically each outcome is exactly as likely as all the others. But in sports, where one contestant is often clearly stronger than the other and so usually, but not always, wins, some method of adjustment is needed to yield the distribution of bets without which gambling is not a financially viable proposition for its proprietors.

In boxing and horse racing this is accomplished by setting odds on the victory of each participant. The weaker the contestant, the longer the odds and the bigger the payoff to those who have put their money on that contestant if he, she, or it should win. By the same logic, the stronger the contestant, the shorter the odds and the smaller the payoff. In football, the oddsmakers estimate by how much the stronger team should defeat the weaker one. This number is called the point spread. It reflects the judgment of the person establishing the spread that, while the chances that the stronger team will win the game are greater than the chances that it will lose, the chances that it will win by the amount of the point spread are the same as the chances that it will not—even if it does win the game. To win a bet on the stronger team requires that its margin of victory exceed the point spread. If the favored team wins by less than this number (and also, of course, if it actually loses) it is the bettors on the other team who collect.

Not only does this system make it possible to win a wager on a team that loses the game, but it also helps to maintain suspense, at least among bettors, until the end of the game. Even when the identity of the winner is not in doubt, the question of whether the winner will exceed—"cover"—the point spread often is.[98] Because betting on sports is illegal in most of the United States the amount of money devoted to this purpose is unknown. But the amount is surely a large one, by one estimate $380 billion annually.[99] And the event on which the largest amount of money is bet each year is the professional football championship game, the Super Bowl.[100]

The devotion of the general public to football has matched that of America's gamblers. Beginning in the late 1960s national surveys showed that, of the three team sports, the largest number of people selected football as their favorite one.[101] The audience for the Super Bowl has only confirmed this statistic. In the history of television, the five most-watched programs were all Super Bowl telecasts.[102] In 2003, an estimated 138 million viewers—more than half the country's population—tuned into the contest in the United States.[103] The game succeeded the World Series as a metaphor for a supremely important competitive event: the "Super Bowl" of chess, or of cooking. Its huge audience made the Super Bowl one of the most important annual events in the field of advertising. Air time for commercials cost more than for any other television program—an estimated $2.1 million for a thirty-second unit in 2003. Advertisers often chose the broadcast to unveil new advertising campaigns for their products.[104] To emphasize its elevated status, the NFL officially designated each game with a Roman numeral—the 2004 contest was Super Bowl XXXVIII—in the manner of popes and British monarchs.

The golden age of football coincided with the rise to positions of authority in American society of the generation whose decisive experience was World War II and whose adult lives were lived in the shadow of the Cold War. Just as the experience or the memory of rural life was fresh when baseball held first place in the affections of American sports fans, so for the next generation war, hot and cold, was central. Every American male either served or expected to serve in the institution with multiple affinities with a football team—the armed forces—preparing for, or actually taking part in, the activity—war—that a football game approximates. Football's golden age came during the 1960s and 1970s, the second half of the Cold War, which was a period during which the United States was mobilized for international conflict for a more protracted period than at any other time in the nation's history.

During the golden age of football, the American presidency was held by men who had served as junior officers in World War II and had had direct experience with, and displayed conspicuous enthusiasm for, the game of football. John F. Kennedy, a Navy lieutenant in the Pacific theater, played touch football with members of his large extended family as a way of persuading the public that he was a more vigorous person than his predecessor. Dwight Eisenhower, whom he succeeded, belonged to an older generation. Eisenhower had been the Supreme Allied Commander in Europe when Kennedy had served in the Pacific, and was identified with a less physically taxing sport—golf.*

Richard Nixon, who lost the 1960 presidential election to Kennedy but won the office in 1968, had been a reserve on

---

* In this case the reality was the opposite of the appearance. Kennedy suffered from chronic and debilitating illnesses and in any case had never played organized football, but did enjoy golf. Eisenhower, by contrast, was perhaps the best athlete ever to serve as president. He played football at West Point, where he took part in one of the most celebrated games of the early years of the twentieth century. In 1912 Army was upset by the Carlisle Indian School, coached by "Pop" Warner, the star of which was the Sac and Fox Indian Jim Thorpe. Thorpe later played professional baseball, won the gold medal in the decathlon at the Olympic games, and was voted the greatest American athlete of the first half of the century in several surveys. Wittingham, op. cit., p. 124.

the Whittier (California) College football team and qualifies as the most enthusiastic football fan to occupy the White House. He frequently took time out from his presidential duties to watch games on television[105] and once even suggested a play for use in a game to George Allen, the coach of Washington's professional team, the Redskins. (The play was unsuccessful.)[106] The next president, Gerald Ford, like Kennedy and Nixon, had served as a young naval officer in the Pacific in World War II, but unlike them had had a football career of distinction, at the University of Michigan. And Ronald Reagan, president during most of the 1980s, had also played on his college football team at Eureka College in Illinois and, because of his movie portrayal of George Gipp, was the American chief executive perhaps most closely associated with the sport.

Professional football did not, as did major league baseball, produce a single dominant team. The National Football League had no equivalent of the New York Yankees. Instead, several teams compiled outstandingly successful records during the sport's golden age. The distinction for the best single season belonged to the Miami Dolphins, which in 1972 completed the only unbeaten season in professional football during the golden age of the sport by winning all seventeen of its games, including the Super Bowl. An even more striking achievement was that of the Pittsburgh Steelers, who between 1975 and 1980 won four Super Bowls. Over the span of the sport's golden age, however, from the mid-1960s to the mid-1990s, the most consistently successful teams were two established in the same year, 1960, whose public images were polar opposites: the Dallas Cowboys and the Oakland Raiders.

In the two decades between 1966 and 1986 under the

stewardship of their original coach, Tom Landry, the Cowboys won 208 games, lost 81, and tied 2. They appeared in the playoffs eighteen times, played in five Super Bowls, winning two, played in the conference championship game twelve times, and won thirteen division titles. Later, in the 1990s, under different management, the Dallas franchise won the Super Bowl three additional times.

In American mythology the Dallas mascot, the cowboy, symbolizes rugged individualism and courage. He is a repository of the virtues that the team itself embodied—or so it sought to suggest to the public, styling itself "America's Team." Its dominant figure, Landry, was a native of the Rio Grande Valley in Texas who had served as a pilot in World War II. The Cowboys were the first team to wear white while playing in their own as well as in their opponents' stadiums, thereby creating an enduring association with the color of purity.

The Raiders' signature color, by contrast, was black. And while the Dallas symbol, which adorned its players' helmets, was a lone star like the kind the sheriff wore in the old West, the Oakland Raiders' helmets featured the kind of figure the sheriff was needed to combat—a man wearing an eyepatch with crossed swords behind him: the robber, looter, and plunderer. The Raiders, too, enjoyed considerable success on the field. Between 1968 and 1984 they played in four Super Bowls, winning three. Following the 1973 through 1977 seasons they made five consecutive appearances in the conference championship game, the prelude to the Super Bowl. They did so by operating the team in the tradition of the French Foreign Legion, collecting talented players who, for whatever reason, had failed to get along with the management of other teams. And while the spectators at Dallas home games tended to be affluent and well-behaved corporate citizens, the Raiders' followers arrived at the team's stadium dressed as if for Halloween, as skeletons, witches, and the dark presence of the *Star Wars* movies, Darth Vader.

The Raiders' dominant personality was Al Davis, who coached the team in the early 1960s and then gained financial control of it. If Tom Landry was a version of the stoic lawmen of dozens of Western films, Davis was a Brooklyn-born version of Professor Moriarty, the master criminal of the Sherlock Holmes stories. He developed a reputation for being supremely devious and wholly ruthless. "He'd steal your eyeballs," it was said of him, "and then persuade you that you looked better without them." The coach of an opposing team, convinced that Davis had planted listening devices in the visiting team's locker room at the Oakland stadium, was observed shouting at the ceiling, "F— you, Al Davis, f— you. I know you're up there."[107]

Davis had a powerful influence not only on his own team but on professional football as a whole. In 1966 he became commissioner of the upstart American Football League and launched the bidding war for established NFL players that prompted the older league to agree to a merger. Later, having returned to the helm of the Raiders, he decided to move his team to Los Angeles without the approval of the other owners. When they tried to block him, he sued and won, and in 1982 the Oakland team became the Los Angeles Raiders.

His victory opened the way for other teams to abandon their home bases for cities that offered them more generous financial arrangements. In 1984 the Baltimore Colts moved to Indianapolis. In 1988 the St. Louis Cardinals decamped to Arizona. The Cleveland Browns moved to Baltimore in 1995, and the Houston Oilers to Tennessee in 1997. Meanwhile, in

1995, Davis's Raiders returned to Oakland. All this movement contrasted with the pattern in major league baseball, in which, after 1970, no franchise relocated for more than three decades. Yet the instability did not damage professional football's popularity, in part, to be sure, because the abandoned cities, with the exception of Los Angeles, all ultimately had other teams bestowed upon them, either through the transfer of an existing franchise or the creation of a new one.

Nor did professional football suffer from the kind of poisonous labor relations that did so much damage to baseball. The NFL did experience strikes by its players, in 1982 and 1987. But these were short and infrequent compared with baseball's labor history. The owners and players ultimately reached an agreement according to the terms of which the owners received a cap on total player salaries, while players received a provision for free agency, giving them the right to sell their services to the highest bidder after a fixed number of years in the league, as well as the promise that almost two-thirds of the league's total revenues would be spent on their salaries.

During football's golden age the college game also flourished. It, too, benefited from the sport's marriage to television. Indeed, more college games were ordinarily available for viewing on Saturday than professional contests on Sunday. Although the Saturday audiences were typically smaller, they were large enough that the telecasts of college games had no difficulty in attracting advertising. In the last three decades of the twentieth century, as before, coaches dominated college football. Four of them elevated themselves above their peers by matching the achievement of Stagg and Warner in presiding over a winning game for the three hundredth time.

One was Paul "Bear" Bryant, who began his career in 1945, achieved his greatest success at his alma mater, the University of Alabama, from 1958 to 1982, and retired with 323 victories. Raised in rural poverty in Moro Bottom, Arkansas, he earned his nickname when a man with a bear came to town offering a dollar to anyone who could wrestle the animal for a full minute. The young Bryant took him up on the offer but was ejected from the ring before the required sixty seconds.[108] Bryant was the Lombardi of college football: imposing, imperious, and intimidating. Noted for his exhausting practice sessions, he was able to evoke extraordinary efforts from his players during games.

Joe Paterno, another 300-game winner, was the Amos Alonzo Stagg of late-twentieth-century college football. Arriving at Penn State as a young assistant coach fresh out of college in 1949, he was still there, as head coach, fifty-five years later. Like Stagg, he exemplified the virtues that football's partisans liked to associate with the sport, in Paterno's case by making generous donations to the university's academic programs, especially the library.

A third coach to accumulate three hundred victories was Bobby Bowden, whose success at Florida State University in Tallahassee was part of the ascendance of the players and institutions of that state to the upper echelon of college football. Florida combined the fervor for the game of the American South with the balmy climate—permitting year-round training—of California to produce a steady stream of skillful high school players. Because these players gravitated to in-state institutions—the University of Florida in Gainesville and the University of Miami in addition to Florida State—they turned these three into powerful college teams in the last two decades of the twentieth century.

At the turn of the twenty-first century, the record for the highest victory total by a college coach belonged to Eddie Robinson.[109] In 1941 he was hired to coach football at a predominantly black institution then known as the Louisiana Normal and Industrial Institute. Shortly thereafter it adopted the name of the town in which it was located, and it was as the coach of Grambling College that Robinson compiled 408 victories in 588 games before retiring, after fifty-five seasons, in 1995. A number of his players, and others from the historically black colleges in the South with which Grambling competed, went on to stellar careers in professional football.[110]

While popular during football's golden age, however, college football was not as popular as its professional counterpart. One sign of this was that in the last two decades of the twentieth century a number of elaborate, expensive new stadiums were built for professional teams, but none for college teams.[111] Another was the decline in the strength of the football teams of the military academies. They ceased to be able to recruit the best high school players, as Army, especially, had done in the 1940s and 1950s, because the academies' requirement to serve in the armed forces following graduation all but eliminated the possibility of a career in the professional ranks, to which high school stars had often come to aspire.[112]

The professional game surpassed the college version in national popularity because college players were not as skilled as the older, more mature, more intensively trained professionals. Moreover, no one could play on a college team for more than four years. Having become well known, therefore, college players passed on to the ranks of the professionals, where they could play as long as they were physically able. The college game also offered, on the whole, a less gripping spectacle than the professional version because college teams were less prone to pass the ball in their efforts to score.

For most of the second half of the twentieth century the most successful college teams employed offensive schemes that relied on the run rather than the pass. Oklahoma, the best team of the 1950s, which won forty-seven consecutive games between 1953 and 1957, used the Split-T, in which the quarterback rarely passed the ball. In the 1960s coach John McKay of the University of Southern California popularized the I formation, in which the player at the tail end of the I—the tailback—sometimes carried the ball forty times or more during a single game. McKay's best-known workhorse tailback was O. J. Simpson. When asked whether Simpson wasn't carrying the ball too often, McKay said, "It isn't heavy. And besides, O. J. doesn't belong to a union." In the 1970s, the Universities of Texas, Oklahoma, and Alabama, all collegiate powerhouses, adopted the wishbone offense. It was also known as the "triple option" system—and none of the three options was a pass.[113]

Professional football held greater appeal than the collegiate variety for yet another reason: The teams were more evenly matched. Because of tradition, superior coaching, and above all the resources they devoted to the sport, some universities were able to recruit the best high school players and so fielded teams that were successful year after year, while others, which the superior players usually did not choose to attend, just as consistently lost the majority of their games. Professional football, by contrast, was organized so that no team could monopolize the best players.[114]

Nor, unlike the professionals, did the college game have a

clear, widely accepted system for determining a champion. Beginning in the 1930s the method for deciding college football's best team was a subjective one: polls in which coaches and sportswriters voted that often reached different verdicts. In 1998 the colleges created their own version of the professionals' playoffs, which they called the Bowl Championship Series (BCS).[115] A formula was devised for determining the best two teams and they played each other in one of the four post-season bowl games that were part of the system. But the BCS retained elements of subjectivity. The overall rankings depended in part on the results of different polls, which in turn reflected the opinions of various observers about the relative strengths of college teams. The polls, moreover, did not always agree. In 2004 a team left out of the BCS championship game, the University of Southern California, was voted the best college team in the Associated Press poll of sportswriters instead of the winner of that game, Louisiana State.

The effort to devise a system to produce a collegiate national champion was one example of the way in which, during football's golden age, the professional game established patterns that college football then sought to follow. The major changes in the rules, such as moving the goal posts back and forth between the goal line to the end of the end zone, and the major trends, such as the dominance of the forward pass, came first in the professional game.

The annual draft of college players by the NFL exemplified their relationship. First held in 1936, it provided a method for distributing college players to professional teams in a way that helped to strengthen the weak teams and so make the league as a whole more competitive. Teams select players in the reverse order of their standing in the previous season, with the worst team having the first choice and the best team the last one in each round of selection.

Over the years the draft became a major event on the nation's sports calendar. Football enthusiasts speculated about it for weeks in advance and hashed over the results afterwards. The all-sports television network, ESPN, televised it.[116] It served as a reminder of and an advertisement for football during its offseason, held, as it was, in April, midway between the climax of one season—the Super Bowl—and the beginning of the next—the opening of the professional football training camps in July.

The draft illustrated the symbiotic relationship between college and professional football. The professional teams benefited because players served an apprenticeship in the college game before entering their ranks. And just as television executives arrange their programming schedules so that one program helps to build an audience for the following one, so the best college players earned renown that they carried into their professional careers, thereby sustaining the NFL's popularity. But that popularity served college football as well. The press coverage of exceptional college players often emphasized their professional prospects, illuminating the college game in the reflected glory of the professional version.

Football, collegiate and professional, continued to prosper into the twenty-first century. Attendance at games and television viewership remained robust. In this sense its golden age carried into the twenty-first century. But as with baseball, cultural principles that the sport embodied came into conflict with trends in the wider society. What might be called the cultural contradictions of baseball stem from the fact that the rural, traditional world the game reflects has become ever more distant from the life of almost all Americans, as well as from the fact that a game evoking the past, nostalgically remembered as unchanging, has had to change in order to survive. Similarly, while the beginning of football's golden age coincided with a period when war, with which it has many features in common, preoccupied American society and a broad consensus supported the nation's military efforts, that consensus shattered after the Vietnam War.

The noisy debate that the Vietnam War provoked divided the country, among other ways, along generational lines. The people who had fought in World War II and were responsible for committing the country to fighting in Indochina, the same generation that had presided over the onset of football's golden age, encountered heated criticism from the next generation. The Vietnam War did not seem to many of the successors of the World War II generation noble, worthy, or a vehicle for the expression of the human virtues that champions of football often claim the sport promotes.

Indeed, there took root during the second half of the twentieth century, in the United States and other western societies, an aversion to war in general, a belief that the age-old practice of warfare was both barbarous and unnecessary. And with the rise of "warlessness"[117] came a diminishing willingness to tolerate, let alone admire, violence, even the controlled violence at the core of football. The most explicitly violent sport, boxing, steadily lost popularity in the United States. Moreover, insofar as the direct personal experience of military life cultivated a taste for football, the sport lost one of its sources of appeal with the end of military conscription in the United States. Far fewer members of the Vietnam generation actually served in the armed forces than had been the case with the World War II generation.

The decline in the status of war in American society was accompanied by a devaluation of the norms and the practices that war cultivates and that football fosters as well: discipline, self-sacrifice, the acceptance of hierarchy as a principle of organization, and respect for authority. Their antitheses— spontaneity, self-indulgence, an insistence on equality, and the questioning of authority—became more acceptable and more widespread in American society.[118]

More than once at the end of the twentieth century and the beginning of the twenty-first, a commentator on football wondered whether the great Vince Lombardi could have produced a winning team in the era of sex, drugs, and rock and roll.[119] The techniques he had employed both on and off the field seemed to belong to an era of beliefs and customs that had vanished as completely as the dinosaurs. One man, in particular, however, was able to adapt to the new trends in American society and to become the most successful football coach of the 1980s. His name was Bill Walsh.

In ten years as the head coach of the San Francisco 49ers he won three Super Bowls and assembled and trained most of the players who would win two more under his successor, George Seifert. Walsh grew up in California, played college football at San Jose State south of San Francisco, and spent the first part of his coaching career in the college ranks. He then joined the staff of Paul Brown's Cincinnati Bengals before being hired as the head coach at Stanford University, from which position he ascended to the leadership of the 49ers.

As a coach he had some things in common with his successful predecessors. He was noted for his scrupulous attention to detail in preparing his team to play. He was familiar with military history. Like Rockne and Lombardi before him, he shared his thoughts on how to lead an organization with people from the world of business.[120]

But Walsh's style of managing his players differed from the autocratic methods that Lombardi and other coaches of earlier years had employed. He established a committee of players with which he met to discuss matters involving the team and hired a consultant to advise him on player relations, measures that the pious Stagg, the flamboyant Rockne, the calculating Brown, and the fiery Lombardi are unlikely ever to have contemplated. An episode during the week of the first Super Bowl game in which his team played illustrates Walsh's approach. He arrived at the hotel where the team was staying before the players did and, in order to break the tension surrounding the event, donned the uniform of a bellhop and unloaded several suitcases from the team bus before the players recognized him.[121]

Walsh's distinctive contribution to football was the passing scheme he developed. Dubbed the "West Coast offense" and widely imitated in the professional ranks and ultimately in the college game, it relied on short, precisely timed passes (Walsh timed his passing routes to one-tenth of a second)[122] to advance the ball. The aim of the West Coast offense was not, as had usually been the case with passing, to score touchdowns quickly through long, spectacular plays, but rather to control the ball through a protracted series of short gains, the goal of teams that relied on rushing. Walsh's offense gave the quarterback a wider array of options in passing the ball than had been customary. It therefore required a player in that position who could make split-second decisions as to which among the several potential receivers should be the target of the pass.[123]

Perhaps not entirely coincidentally, at roughly the same time that Walsh was coaching the 49ers, a few miles to the south a new industry was emerging that differed from its industrial predecessors in some of the ways that Walsh's style of football differed from the past approaches to the sport and that, like Walsh's style, was in keeping with the late-twentieth-century changes in American society. The way in which the information technology industry of Silicon Valley functioned emphasized collegiality over hierarchy and flexibility over rigid routine. Its products were light, versatile machines—personal computers—rather than heavy, bulky, powerful ones such as automobiles.

Similarly, the Walsh style of football placed a premium on cooperation, spontaneity, flexibility, and agility. It differed so sharply from the plodding, grinding, rush-oriented style of football that had descended from the methods that Walter Camp had employed as to seem to be part of a different game entirely. And in fact the West Coast offense bore a marked resemblance to another American team sport, which had an affinity for the kind of world in which computers came to be central and the popularity of which surged at the end of the twentieth century. Bill Walsh learned a great deal from Paul Brown, and a term applied to one of Brown's Cleveland teams of the 1950s, which featured a sophisticated passing attack, was even more appropriate for the offense the San Francisco team practiced: "basketball in cleats."

CHAPTER 4

Basketball: The Chemistry of Teamwork

Watch some of these coaches; they're on their feet all night, shouting instructions, and what they're really doing is killing the creativity of their players, taking away the free-spiritedness which makes basketball such a fun game to play and such a fun game to watch. They're beginning to run it like a football game and it really annoys me.

ARNOLD "RED" AUERBACH, *former coach and general manager, the Boston Celtics basketball team*[1]

THE POST-INDUSTRIAL GAME

At the outset of the twenty-first century the industrial revolution was 250 years old and had transformed the world. An ever-growing number of people on the planet lived in cities rather than rural villages and occupied themselves, directly or indirectly, with making things in ever greater profusion or in providing services rather than in growing crops.

In the course of the two and one half centuries since the beginning of this epochal transformation of human life, what people made, how they made them, and how, in general, they lived also changed. These changes were so sweeping that by some accounts they represented not simply the continuation of the age of machines, cities, and economic growth, but something different enough to qualify as a third distinct era in the history of human civilization. In the wake of the traditional, agrarian stage and the industrial period that followed it came, in this view, the post-industrial age. It is the features that distinguish post-industrial society from its agrarian and especially its industrial predecessors—the characteristics that separate the world of satellite television, computers, and the Internet from the world dominated by farms, steel mills, and coal mines—that the third major American team sport, basketball, exemplifies.

In the agrarian age, in addition to human labor, land was the chief ingredient of economic activity. In the industrial world land was supplemented by capital. But in post-industrial society what counts for most economically is neither land nor capital but something more portable and personal: knowledge.[2] Basketball reflects this difference.

Unlike baseball and football players, competitors in a basketball game play with a minimum of equipment. They have no need for the bat that baseball requires and, in contrast to the padded, helmeted, cleated warriors of the football field, their work clothes consist of shorts, a thin sleeveless jersey, and rubber-soled shoes. Like the "knowledge worker" of post-industrial society—the designer, the economist, the psychologist—what the basketball player brings to his enterprise is his own skill.

Basketball also reflects the relationship of post-industrial man to what was for millennia the defining condition of human existence: nature. The farmer of the agrarian world earned his living by collaborating with the forces of nature. Industrial activity was also closely connected to the natural world, powered by minerals extracted from the Earth's crust and devoted to fashioning these naturally occurring materials into products of greater utility to human beings. Post-industrial workers, by contrast, are far removed from the climate and the topography that were so important to their ancestors. They work in buildings where the temperature is controlled. The work they do involves applying their knowledge, not plowing the ground or refashioning wood or metal.

Similarly, official games of basketball take place indoors and unlike baseball and football are not affected by the weather. And while the other two games are played on a natural surface—the field, an expanse of grass and dirt—basketball takes place exclusively on artificial surfaces: almost all informal games on asphalt and formal ones on polished, carefully constructed floors of hardwood. These are called courts, after the playing surface of the older game of tennis, which was originally, in the European game of court tennis, housed indoors.

Basketball embodies another distinctive feature of the post-industrial age: systematic innovation.[3] For almost all of human history useful inventions were rare and came about more or less by accident. But in the twentieth century there began the deliberate pursuit of new products and new techniques to fulfill pre-existing needs. The idea of invention was introduced, and invention in the post-industrial period became a systematic, deliberate, and ongoing process.

That is how basketball came into the world. Baseball and football evolved from folk customs but basketball was deliberately devised for the purpose of occupying the time and the energies of a restless class of fledgling Young Men's Christian Association (YMCA) instructors during the winter months. Unlike the other two team sports, basketball has a founding date—December 1, 1891, when the first game was played— and a founder—James A. Naismith, whose invention of the game, like many an invention in the post-industrial age, came in response to a demand, in this case from his supervi-

sor at the YMCA Training School in Springfield, Massachusetts.

Compared with what industrial workers do on the job,
post-industrial occupations are less rigidly defined and specialized and this, too, is reflected in differences between basketball and the other two team sports, particularly football. A
typical factory worker performs one narrowly circumscribed
task over and over. A typical knowledge worker in a post-
industrial setting, a modern physician-specialist, for example,
or a computer programmer, has wider latitude. He or she
typically undertakes a broader range of tasks.

Like industrial workers, each player on a football team
operates in a particular zone of the football field, carrying
out a clearly defined set of responsibilities. Some throw the
ball, some catch it, others carry it, and many never touch it at
all, blocking on behalf of the player in possession of it or trying to tackle him. Basketball players are also assigned to different positions but, as with post-industrial workers, the
responsibilities that come with these positions are broader,
more fluid, and more flexible than is the case for football
players. Basketball players move all over the court and every
one of them performs each of the basic tasks of the game:
passing, shooting, and rebounding the ball.

The way authority is exercised on basketball teams also
corresponds to the structure of post-industrial organizations
and differs from football teams and industrial enterprises.
The latter are organized in hierarchical fashion. The person
at the top, the coach, the foreman, or, in the military, the
general, issues orders and the subordinates carry them out.
Authority flows vertically and in one direction—from top to
bottom. In post-industrial organizations it also flows hori-

zontally, from side to side. Rather than a pyramid, the structure of authority resembles a network. The component units interact directly with one another and each has greater scope for independent action than is the case in industrial enterprises.[4] Post-industrial organizations are not commanded so much as they are managed, and post-industrial management entails coaxing, persuading, and encouraging instead of (or in addition to) directing.

So it is with basketball in comparison with football, and the reason involves the way that basketball compares with baseball and football on two dimensions common to all three.

One dimension is the temporal pattern of the action in the game. It can be sequential, with one thing happening at a time, followed by a pause, or continuous; with one thing occurring directly after another. Baseball and football are sequential. Basketball, by contrast, is continuous; it flows along like a river. The action in basketball is not entirely uninterrupted: Play stops when the ball goes out of bounds, when a player shoots free throws, when a team calls time out, and between the two halves into which each game is divided. But basketball is more continuous than the other two, and it differs from them in particular in that play does not halt automatically when the teams switch from offense to defense and vice versa.

The second dimension on which team sports vary has to do with participation in the action, which can be individual—one player at a time is involved—or collective—all the members of the team act at the same time. Of the three, baseball proceeds on an individual basis while the action in football and basketball takes place in a collective manner. Thus, baseball is sequential and individual, football is sequential and collective, and basketball is continuous and collective.*

These two dimensions are connected to the structure of authority in baseball, football, and basketball through the matter of coordination. The second dimension bears on the *need* for coordination. Collective games require it because every player is playing the game at the same time and there must be a way to harmonize their actions for optimal effect. In individual games, by contrast, such coordination among different players is not necessary. The other dimension has to do with the *opportunities* for coordination, which are greater in sequential games, in which there are regular periods in which instructions can be given to the team, than in continuous games, which lack such regular occasions for advance planning.

The agent of coordination is the coach, or, in baseball, the manager, who exercises authority in a hierarchical fashion: The players follow his orders. The degree of authority he exercises varies among the three team sports according to where the game is located on these two dimensions. Baseball is a sequential sport, affording the opportunity for hierarchical direction, but because it is also an individual one, there is little need for it. Occasionally a baseball manager will, from his position on the team's bench, signal to the pitcher to deliver a particular pitch or will order—again by signal—a base runner to attempt to steal a base. But in general the

---

* While the fourth combination—continuous and individual—describes individual sports such as boxing and tennis, no major team sport fits this description. The closest approximation of a continuous-individual team sport is a relay race, in which each member of the team covers part of the total distance of the race and then hands the baton that must be carried from the start to the finish to a colleague, who runs the next leg of the race.

leader has less authority in baseball than in the other two team sports, at least in the conduct of the game itself.[5]

Football, being sequential and collective, presents both the need and the opportunity for coordination. That is why it is the coach's game, the one in which hierarchically exercised authority looms largest. Basketball falls between the other two. Because it is collective, coordination is necessary, but because it is continuous, the opportunities for coordination by command are more limited than they are in the sequentially played games of baseball and football.

Coordination in basketball also takes place in another way, spontaneously, in the flow of play, among the players themselves without the intervention of the coach. It is achieved horizontally as well as imposed vertically.[6] This is also the way that post-industrial enterprises act in collective fashion, with the pattern of cooperation often negotiated among the various units rather than imposed by a common superior.

Another term for spontaneous coordination is teamwork, and of the three major American team sports, basketball is the one in which teamwork is the most prominent and most important for a team's success. The capacity of a particular team to practice spontaneous coordination is sometimes called "team chemistry," and it is in basketball that this property matters most.[7] Of the three sports, basketball is the one in which the whole is most often greater than the sum of its parts in the sense that five players adept at spontaneous coordination can defeat five with superior individual skills who are less good at practicing teamwork.

Because the game requires coordination, the basketball coach, the chief coordinator, exercises considerable control. Like the football coach, he has the responsibility for preparing his or her (unlike in football, many basketball coaches, usually of women's teams, are women) players to play. As in football, he or she inculcates the necessary skills in practice sessions dominated by repetitive drills. Like the football coach, the basketball coach designs the offensive and defensive schemes that his or her team employs during games. Like his or her counterpart in football, the basketball coach sometimes orders that the team put into operation a particular play—a preset routine the purpose of which is to score.

Basketball coaches are important enough that, as in football, the team's victories are credited to them. They are important enough that the most successful ones at the college level have remained at the same institutions for decades, compiling hundreds of victories and, like football coaches, in a few cases having the arenas in which their teams play named for them.[8] Basketball coaches, like football coaches, write books and give lectures distilling the secrets of their successes on the court and applying them to other fields of endeavor, notably business.[9]

Still, a basketball coach does not exercise as much authority as a football coach because, since basketball is a continuous game, he or she cannot dictate in advance everything a player does, as a football coach, who presides over a sequentially paced game, is able to do. The coaching staff in both sports, like the general staff of an army, is the brain of the organization. But a basketball team further resembles post-industrial organizations in that decisionmaking power is also decentralized rather than concentrated exclusively in the coaching staff.[10] The need for spontaneous coordination partly shifts the power of decision during a basketball game from the coach to the players.

For this reason, part of the task of the basketball coach is to foster conditions favorable to spontaneous coordination.

In addition to telling the players what to do, the coach must also train them to decide for themselves, on the spur of the moment, under pressure, how to proceed. In this way the basketball coach resembles a group therapist or a management consultant with a psychological bent, working with his or her players to help them work better together.

Basketball corresponds to a final distinctive feature of post-industrial society: gender equality. Important tasks in the agrarian and industrial worlds—working in fields and factories—require physical strength and so favor men (although women have also routinely undertaken them.) For the post-industrial occupations, in which the qualification is knowledge, however, men have no advantages over women. For that and other reasons a trend toward equality between the genders in the workplace marks the post-industrial age.

While women almost never play baseball or football[11] they do play basketball, and have played it since the game was invented. For the first eight decades after basketball began, women played according to different rules. But in the 1970s they adopted the rules that governed the men's game and from that point onward the popularity of women's basketball increased markedly. It became far more widely played and, through television, more widely seen than ever before.

The fact that women play it is one of several ways in which basketball differs from the other two major American team sports. But it also shares several fundamental, defining features with a number of other team games.

The Generic Game

Basketball's objective—to put a round object in a goal—is shared by other sports: ice hockey, field hockey, lacrosse, polo, and water polo. Evidence has been found suggesting that a ball-goal game of some sort was played by pre-European civilizations of Central America.[12] In this sense, basketball is a generic game, and the ball-goal game to which it has the most striking similarities is soccer.

The first basketball game was played with a soccer ball, although over the years the standard basketball came to be somewhat larger. Like basketball, but unlike the other ball-goal games, soccer—the name comes from the third, fourth, and fifth letters of the first word of the game's official name in Britain: association football[13]—requires no special equipment other than the ball. The sticks and mallets that hockey and polo players wield are unnecessary. Nor is it played on a surface unsuitable for ordinary daily activities, as are water polo and ice hockey.

In both basketball and soccer, players must advance the ball toward the goal without carrying it. The normal methods of advance in the two games have the same names: passing and dribbling. So, too, does the attempt to score (a term that the two share with other ball-goal games): shooting. Moreover, the rules of basketball and soccer are designed to minimize the kind of violent contact that is common in ice hockey and endemic to football. Along with these similarities, however, basketball and soccer exhibit marked differences.

Most conspicuously, in basketball the ball is advanced by hand, in soccer mainly by foot.[14] Another difference between the two involves scoring. It is frequent in basketball, rare in soccer. The average basketball team will put the ball in the basket—counting contested field goals and free throws made when time is out—upwards of fifty times per game, and sometimes more. In a typical soccer match each team will score only two or three goals. Often one of the teams and sometimes both will not score at all. (The sparsity of scoring is one reason that soccer lacks what the three major American team sports have in abundance: statistics.)

Because scoring is rare, at the highest levels of play in soccer the two sides are usually tied or separated by a single goal.[15] This gives soccer one of its distinguishing features. Because a single goal often decides the outcome of the game, and because a goal can be scored at any time, soccer is extremely suspenseful. Any moment can be the decisive one. The game has the emotional rhythm of—albeit with greater intensity than—bird-watching: stretches of anxious waiting punctuated by sudden, thrilling, fleeting moments of revelation. A supporter of the English team that scored a goal that proved to be the margin of victory in a tense World Cup match with Argentina described the experience of watching it in this way: "Our throats hurt collectively, our hearts raced and pounded and, after 46 taut minutes—plus moments of unbearable extra time [overtime]—our shoulders and backs ached in the same way. Few spectator sports are more physical than a great game of [soccer]. . . . "[16]

The equivalent circumstance in basketball occurs relatively rarely, only at the very end of the game and only in a game in which the two teams are tied or separated by a point or two—that is, when there is time for only one shot and the success or failure of that single shot will determine the game's outcome.

The striking dissimilarity in the frequency of scoring is related to another difference between the two games. Ties are common in soccer but impossible in basketball, in which, if the score is tied at the end of the regularly allotted time for the game, the two teams play overtime periods until one of these periods ends with one team ahead.*

Basketball differs from soccer, and most of the other ball-goal games as well, in that it lacks a position central to them: the goalkeeper. The soccer goalkeeper patrols and defends his team's goal. He is dressed differently from his teammates in order to distinguish him from them. And he is distinct in that different rules govern what he does on the field. He is allowed to use his hands in ways that his teammates are not. He can, and does, deflect, catch, carry, and throw the ball.

On him rests the heaviest burden that any soccer player bears, the ultimate responsibility for preventing the opposition from scoring. The language of soccer defines the goalkeeper's responsibility as a personal one. When he stops a shot headed for the goal he is credited with a "save." When he fails to do so it is he, not the team as a whole, who is "beaten." It is perhaps for that reason that Albert Camus, the French Nobel laureate in literature who played the position of goalkeeper as a youth growing up in Algeria, once said that he owed to soccer "all that I know most surely about morality and obligation."†

* Perhaps the least satisfactory aspect of soccer is the system for breaking ties at the highest level of the game. An overtime period is played in which the first team to score wins. If, at the end of the period, neither has done so, there follows a contest in penalty kicks, which are awarded during the game itself when an offensive player is interfered with in close proximity to the other team's goal. A penalty kick involves a player from the obstructed team taking a shot at the other's goal at close range, with only the goalkeeper to oppose him. In the post-overtime "shootout" the team that compiles the greater number of successful kicks wins the match. The 1994 world championship was decided in this way, which is akin to deciding a basketball championship by a free-throw shooting contest or awarding a football title on the basis of a competition in kicking field goals.

† Camus was associated with a school of philosophy known as existentialism, according to which life entails the obligation to make choices even when their consequences can be perceived only dimly, if at all. A goalkeeper cannot cover the

Not only does a basketball team include no such position, but the act of knocking away an opponent's shot at the basket on its downward arc is not permitted: It counts as a field goal for the team launching the shot. The name of this forbidden maneuver is goaltending. The reason it is illegal is that for a tall, agile player—and basketball played at the highest level has an abundance of them—what is called goaltending is something that is easy to do. Were it permitted, scoring in basketball would be almost as rare as it is in soccer.

Along with the differences in the rules of the two games, there is an important difference in their global status. Soccer is far and away the most popular sport in the world. It is the favorite team game in most parts of the planet: eastern, western, northern, and southern Europe; Latin America, where baseball is popular in the smaller countries of Central America but not in Mexico and most of the larger countries to the south; Africa and the Middle East; and East Asia, where baseball also has a foothold. Soccer has failed to establish itself in the top tier of team sports only in the Antipodes, where the other games of British origin, rugby and cricket, far surpass it; in South Asia,* where cricket reigns supreme; and in yet another former British possession, North America.[17]

Soccer's world championship, the quadrennial World Cup tournament, qualifies as the most popular sporting event—

continued

entire goal, which is twenty-four-feet wide, and so must often anticipate where a shot will go and move to that part of the goal before he can be sure that he is right. The penalty for incorrect anticipation is frequently a goal allowed.

* Other sports are played in the Asian subcontinent, basketball among them. The author of this book took part in the Indian national junior basketball championship held in Calcutta in January, 1964, playing on a team, composed of four Americans and one Indian, that represented the federal district of Delhi. The team finished second.

perhaps even the most eagerly anticipated and widely followed regular event of any kind—on the planet.[18] In addition
to attracting large audiences, the sport excites powerful pas-
sions. A well-known English manager once said "Some people believe [soccer] is a matter of life and death. I can assure
you, it is much, much more important than that."[19] Games
sometimes trigger riots and one soccer-inspired civil distur-
bance actually led to a 100-hour war between El Salvador
and Honduras in 1969 that left 6,000 people dead and 12,000
wounded. During the 2002 World Cup, violence in which
twenty people were injured broke out between supporters of
the Brazilian and Argentinian teams. The episode occurred
in a village in Bangladesh.[20]

As with American team sports, soccer crosses the boundary separating the realm of mass entertainment from the
smaller province of high culture. Like baseball, it is the subject of writings that explore serious, often literary, subjects.[21]
Like football, it is studied as a window on communities in
which it occupies a position of cultural importance.[22]

Basketball does not have soccer's international cachet.[23]
Unlike soccer, it is centered on one country. The highest
level of basketball competition is to be found in the American professional league and nowhere else. At the apex of soccer, by contrast, stand four different national leagues: the
English, the German, the Italian, and the Spanish. The level
of the players' skills (as well as their salaries) are high in all
four, and the best players move back and forth among them.

Although less popular, basketball is the only team sport
with anything like the breadth of appeal that soccer enjoys.
While a clear second for the distinction of being the world's
foremost sport, it is soccer's sole rival for that title. It spread
rapidly in the decades after it was invented and by the 1930s

its rules had been translated into almost fifty languages.[24] In the last decades of the twentieth century it had closed, although certainly not eliminated, the gap in popularity between the two. In much of the world, especially in Eastern Europe and the countries of the Mediterranean rim—Greece, Turkey, Israel—basketball established itself as the second sport, after soccer (or, in the Caribbean, after cricket). In China, the world's most populous country, it loomed as a rival to soccer for first place in people's affections.

The two sports came to have global appeal for the same set of reasons: they provided comparable attractions for players and spectators. The fact that neither requires elaborate equipment or special conditions makes both relatively easy to play and even easier to practice. Youngsters can develop the basic skills of both games by themselves. They can learn to dribble and shoot both a soccer ball and a basketball all alone, which is not true of baseball and football. They can, and do, play informal games with fewer than the standard complement of players on each side. And they can play without the same fear of injury that shadows other sports. Soccer and basketball players do suffer injuries from all the running, jumping, twisting, and turning that they do, but their injuries are neither as frequent nor as serious as are the ones incurred by those who play the games—football and to a lesser extent rugby—in which violent collisions are routine.

Soccer and basketball attract spectators in large numbers because, like other continuous-collective games, they offer ongoing rather than punctuated action. Something is almost always happening, unlike in baseball and football. George Will once observed that two of the characteristic vices of American life beset football: violence and committee meetings. Basketball is relatively free of both and soccer is even freer: It is played more continuously, with fewer interruptions, than is basketball, which makes it more compelling to spectators but less attractive to the television industry, which favors pauses in the action into which commercial messages can be inserted.

Soccer and basketball appeal to spectators as well because, compared with other sports, they are far more comprehensible. Their rules are relatively simple and straightforward: The offense attempts to put the ball in the goal, the defense seeks to prevent this but may not adopt the tactics of direct physical restraint—blocking, holding, and tackling—that football players employ. The task of the defender in basketball resembles the role of the woman in ballroom dancing: staying parallel to the player with the ball while moving from side to side and backward. Moreover, the action of a basketball game or a soccer match is easier to follow than that of the other team sports, which is yet another reason for their popularity. A baseball, like a cricket ball, a hockey puck, and the balls used in field hockey and lacrosse, is smaller than a basketball and so more difficult for spectators to see. In football and rugby the ball often disappears in the tangle of bodies that is characteristic of the sport. In basketball and soccer it is always visible.

Not only how well they see the action but also what the spectators see when they watch soccer and basketball helps to account for the large audiences the sports attract. In both games spectators see episodes of spontaneous coordination, players devising and implementing schemes for achieving the aim of scoring. They see, that is, acts of creation. If architecture is, as is sometimes said, music set in concrete, then soccer and basketball may be said to be creativity embodied in team sports.

In both games the chief creator, the one who envisions the scheme and sets its implementation in motion, is the player responsible for distributing the ball to teammates who can put it in the goal. In soccer this is often the midfielder. In basketball it is the point guard. Both are adept at keeping track of the movements of the other players and delivering the ball at just the right time and in just the right place to enable a teammate to score.

Soccer and basketball have also reached a level of global popularity unmatched by other team sports because of an esthetic property they share that the others lack in the same measure. The players, and the play, are graceful. It is for this reason, as well as for the creativity that they generate, that soccer is known as "the beautiful game." The physical attribute that counts for most in soccer and basketball is not the power and speed that are on display in football, or the hand-eye coordination that baseball players must have. It is agility.[25]

Soccer and basketball are played partly in the air. Basketball players routinely spring off the floor to launch shots at the basket and soar toward it to snatch missed shots as they bound off the rim or the backboard. In soccer, players often leap upward to intercept a kicked ball with their heads in order to control it or tap it to a teammate or, even more dramatically, to redirect it into the goal itself for a score. Soccer and basketball are therefore the team sports that most vividly evoke a basic human fantasy: to leave the ground and fly through the air like a bird. At such moments players in both sports turn into ballet dancers in jerseys and shorts, soaring and pirouetting with the combination of explosive power and delicacy that marks that art form. And because the capacity to leap high and remain in the air for an unusually long time[26] is a prized ability on the court as in ballet, basketball is a game depicted by Degas played by figures designed by Giacometti.

At the outset of the twenty-first century soccer had occupied the rarefied niche in global mass culture for which its particular features qualified it for the better part of one hundred years. The broad appeal of basketball was more recent. Compared with soccer, indeed compared with the other two major American team sports, basketball was a latecomer to mass popularity. And unlike soccer, the form basketball took as the new century began had changed considerably over the course of the preceding one.

THE LATECOMER

In the winter of 1891 Luther Gulick, the head of a training school for YMCA instructors in Springfield, Massachusetts, ordered one of his faculty members, a thirty-year-old Canadian named James Naismith, to find an outlet for the considerable energies of his rambunctious students. Naismith devised and posted thirteen rules for a new game and on or about December 1, 1891, the first game of what would become the third major American team sport was played by the eighteen students in Naismith's class, nine on each side. (The number was reduced to five in 1897.) It was an indoor game because the harsh Massachusetts winter climate did not lend itself to outdoor play.

Several of the original rules—the proscription against carrying the ball and the limits on physical contact among the players, for instance—would endure, as would the game's object: to toss a ball into a goal suspended above the playing surface.[27] The balcony in the room in which the first game was played was located ten feet above the floor, and so ten feet became the standard height of the goal. Naismith asked for two boxes to serve as the goals but the building's janitor could find only two one-bushel peach baskets to nail to the balcony. The game therefore became known as basketball.[28]

Like football, basketball took root in institutions of education—in high schools and on college campuses.[29] The first five-on-a-side college game took place in January 1896, between a YMCA team representing the University of Iowa and a team from the University of Chicago supervised by Amos Alonzo Stagg, who had been an associate of Naismith's at the Springfield YMCA school. In 1898 Naismith himself became the head basketball coach, as well as athletic director, chapel director, and a member (indeed the only member) of the department of physical education at the University of Kansas.[30] But the game of basketball evolved as it did in spite of him.

Naismith envisioned basketball as a form of recreation, the aim of which was to promote good health and sportsmanship. As the Kansas basketball coach he did not direct the team from the sidelines. Indeed, he did not always attend its games and when he did he sometimes served as the referee. Ironically, he is the only head basketball coach in the history of that university to have finished his career with a losing record.[31]

The man who made the largest contribution to shaping the way the game came to be played and especially the way it came to be organized in American institutions of higher education was Naismith's successor as the Kansas basketball coach, Forrest "Phog" Allen.[32] Naismith himself called Allen "the father of modern basketball coaching," and it was Allen who did most to change the game from a leisure time activity and a form of healthy exercise to a well-organized enterprise with an overriding goal—the winning of games.

Like Stagg with football, Allen made coaching basketball a full-time occupation with the responsibility for the rigorous training of the players in the techniques of the game and the design of offensive and defensive schemes. When he retired, after thirty-nine seasons, he had compiled 746 victories, at that time more than any other college coach. And he produced disciples who also made major contributions to the college game.

One of his players, who graduated in 1928, Adolph Rupp, went on to serve as the head coach at the University of Kentucky from 1930 to 1972. When he retired he had exceeded Allen's victory total, ending with 876. A reserve player on Allen's 1952 national championship team, Dean Smith, became the head coach at the University of North Carolina from 1962 to 1997, and at the end of his tenure there he had surpassed Rupp with 879 career victories. Like Rupp, Smith made the university at which he coached one of the powerhouses of the college game.

In the course of the twentieth century, basketball, like football, became a widely attended and extensively televised form of mass entertainment.[33] College teams competed in the same regionally based conferences that had been established for football, and the sport gave rise to the same abuses that football produced: paying—or overpaying—players and exempting them from the academic requirements other students had to meet.[34] If anything, the abuses were more pervasive in basketball. Small schools that could not afford 100 scholarships for a football team did provide support for fifteen basketball players, thus increasing the number of schools that sought to compete at the highest level. And with the much smaller teams for basketball, a single player can do more than in football to make a team successful. The temptation to break the rules to secure the services of an outstanding performer is therefore all the greater.

As with baseball and football, the way basketball was played changed considerably over the years. In 1896 the value of a field goal was set at two points, and the following year five was established as the number of players per team on the court. A few years after the initial game, backboards on which the baskets were mounted were introduced, to prevent errant shots from landing among the spectators.

Along the same lines a rule was established in 1913 awarding the ball, when it went out of bounds, to the team other than the one that had last touched it on the court, in order to prevent the scramble among players to retrieve it that had occurred previously. One early method for keeping the ball within the confines of the playing area was to surround the court with wire mesh, turning it into a kind of cage. Long after the practice was discontinued, in the late 1920s, basketball players continued to be known as "cagers."

Naismith's original rules had defined "shouldering, holding, pushing, tripping, [and] striking in any way the person of an opponent" as fouls[35] and provided for a referee to decide when one had been committed. In 1895 an unimpeded shot at the basket—a free throw—was awarded in some circumstances to the team that had been fouled. The line from which the free throw is launched was moved from twenty feet from the basket to fifteen feet in 1895, and beginning with the 1908–1909 season a player's fifth personal foul during a game disqualified him from further play.

Naismith's original rules said nothing about dribbling the ball. He had envisioned passing as the means of advancing it.

But those rules did not prohibit dribbling and it soon came into common use. In 1927 several coaches tried to restrict it by limiting each player to a single bounce of the ball per possession, but the effort was defeated and dribbling came to pervade the game.

In 1932–1933 a rule was adopted requiring the team in possession of the ball to advance it beyond the mid-court line within ten seconds of putting it in play. Five years later came the elimination of the rule, which dated from the origin of the game, mandating that after each successful shot the ball be tossed up between a player from each team, each of whom then tried to tap it to a teammate—a practice known as the center jump. Thereafter, each time a field goal was made the team allowing it received possession of the ball under its own basket.

These rule changes had the effect of making basketball a faster-paced, more freely flowing game than the one James Naismith had invented. It also became a higher-scoring game than it had been, in no small part as the result of a new technique of shooting the ball. The principal offensive approach in the early decades of the twentieth century involved intricate patterns of movement by the five players in an effort to free one of them for an unimpeded, close-in shot at the basket. He or she would bounce the ball off the backboard and into the goal—a lay-up—or fling the ball with both hands from a stationary position at longer range—the two-handed set shot.

In the mid-1930s a new way of scoring appeared. Its pioneer was a player at Stanford University named Angelo "Hank" Luisetti. He held the ball in the palm of one hand and launched it toward the basket with the other, and did so while moving rather than standing still. The new technique proved as revolutionary for basketball as the home run had been for baseball and the forward pass for football. Like them, it was a visually impressive feat that made scoring more common.

The game that established Luisetti's reputation and brought the possibilities of one-handed shooting to national attention, the equivalent for this technique of the 1913 Notre Dame–Army football game for the forward pass, took place on December 30, 1936, in New York. Stanford defeated Long Island University, which had won its forty-three previous consecutive games, by a score of 45 to 31, with Luisetti scoring fifteen points in his then-novel style. On New Year's Day, 1938, he became the first player to score fifty points in a college game, a significant and rare achievement even seven decades later.[36]

Over those decades the one-handed shot, usually launched while the player is in the air and therefore known as the jump shot, became by far the most popular method of attempting to score. It proved easier to score in this way than by the older techniques and for this reason, and because the end of the center jump after each successful shot made more time available for shooting, basketball became a higher-scoring game than it had been during its first four decades.

In the next decade, the 1940s, another major change in the game occurred. For the first time, very tall players made their mark on it. Height has obvious advantages in a game in which the object is to put a ball in a goal located ten feet above the floor. But for basketball's first half century the occasional very tall players tended to be clumsy and lacking in the skills the game requires. In the mid-1940s, however, two agile giants emerged in the ranks of college players. Bob Kurland of Oklahoma A&M (later called Oklahoma State) and George Mikan of DePaul University, in Chicago, each stood almost seven feet tall. Each was able to dominate the games in which he played by standing near the basket, receiving the ball from his teammates, and using his unusual combination of height, strength, and quickness to score.

To reduce the considerable advantages that players such as Kurland and Mikan enjoyed, the lane extending from underneath the basket to the free throw line, within which no offensive player could remain for more than three seconds at a time, was widened, so that the tallest players could not loiter close to the basket, and the proscription against goaltending was adopted, so that these players could not swat away incoming shots at will.

From its origins in the last decade of the nineteenth century as a game played at a deliberate pace and featuring highly choreographed movement, frequent passes, and very little scoring, basketball became, by the second half of the twentieth century, a faster game, one played more in the air, and one in which scoring was more prolific. It was transformed from a minuet into a ballet, which increased its appeal to spectators. Still, basketball remained, in its early decades and indeed for much of the twentieth century, a far less prominent part of American popular culture than were baseball or football. Although played throughout the country, interest in basketball tended to be local rather than national in scope. The sport had no equivalent of baseball's World Series or football's college bowl games.

In the 1930s basketball raised its national profile by capturing the fancy of New York City, America's largest metropolis and its newspaper and radio center. In 1934 a sportswriter turned impresario named Ned Irish had the idea of booking two college games on the same night in New

York's largest indoor arena, Madison Square Garden. These "doubleheaders" became popular—the first one, on December 29, 1934, attracted 16,000 spectators—spurring an interest in basketball that was reinforced by the strength of the local college programs. Long Island University, St. John's University, and New York University all fielded successful teams. New York became the basketball capital of the world. In 1938, Irish put into practice another idea: a postseason tournament to determine the best team in college basketball. He invited four colleges to send their teams to Madison Square Garden and the National Invitation Tournament (NIT) was born.

Two subsequent developments, however, deprived New York of its place at the center of the world of basketball. One was a series of gambling scandals that came to light in 1951, involving thirty-two players from seven college teams, four of them located in the New York area.[37] Betting on basketball, as on football, involves a point spread. Players on the offending teams were found to have contrived to keep the margin of victory below the point spread, a practice known as point shaving, thereby rewarding gamblers who, armed with the foreknowledge of what the players would do, had bet on the opposing teams. Because several of the offending teams were located in New York and some of the gamblers lived there, the city came to be associated with corruption and scandal in basketball and so lost its place as the sport's showcase.

The other development that undermined New York's status as the basketball capital was the creation in 1939, by the governing body of college athletics, the National Collegiate Athletic Association, of a postseason championship playoff to rival the NIT.[38] Because the NCAA could and did compel the best college teams to participate in the tournament that it sponsored, which was played all over the country, it soon surpassed the NIT in importance.[39]

In the second half of the twentieth century the NCAA tournament grew in popularity and by the century's end it rivaled baseball's World Series and football's Super Bowl as a national event. The championship game came to be the most important basketball contest of the year and several of these games became landmarks in the history of the sport. The first of them took place in 1957, when the University of North Carolina completed a season without a single loss by defeating Kansas in triple overtime, 55 to 54.

Because the game was exciting and closely contested, it had an effect comparable to that of the Baltimore–New York National Football League championship game of the following year in attracting national attention for the sport— although the impact of the basketball game was not as powerful because, unlike the football championship, it was not nationally televised. The 1957 contest marked the first national championship for the league to which North Carolina belonged, the Atlantic Coast Conference, which had been founded only three years earlier, and in which, unlike the older conferences of the Midwest—the Big Ten—and of the deep South—the Southeastern Conference—basketball rather than football came to be the most important team sport. Many of the players on the North Carolina roster, and the team's coach, Frank McGuire, came from the New York area. With the scandal-induced devaluation of New York basketball, many of the ablest players from the New York area migrated south to play college basketball.

By the mid-1950s, therefore, college basketball commanded the attention of a modest national audience. And by that time so, too, did a professional version of the game.

Players began to be paid for playing basketball almost as soon as the game was invented. In the following decades, squads of skilled players traveled the country, playing local teams. In the same period leagues of professional teams were formed, which typically survived for a few years before going out of business.[40]

In the late 1930s the National Basketball League (NBL) was established in a number of Midwestern cities and in 1946 a new, rival professional league was formed, called the Basketball Association of America (BAA). Its founders owned ice hockey arenas along the eastern seaboard and wanted a regular attraction for the buildings on the evenings when their hockey teams were not playing. They appointed as the first president of the BAA the owner of the New Haven arena, Maurice Podoloff, who, at the time he was chosen, had never actually seen a basketball game. Podoloff instituted a draft, comparable to the one that the National Football League employed, to distribute college players among the teams in the league and organized a postseason playoff system to decide the league championship. He managed to lure the strongest franchises of the NBL into the BAA, triggering a merger of the two leagues for the 1949–1950 season. The new league was named the National Basketball Association (NBA).

The NBA survived where other professional basketball leagues had perished because it secured the services of a star. George Mikan, of the Minneapolis Lakers, accomplished for professional basketball in the late 1940s and early 1950s what Red Grange had done for professional football in the 1920s: He had acquired a broad enough reputation in college that substantial numbers of people were willing to pay to see the professional games in which he played, to the benefit of the entire league.[41]

Even with Mikan, however, in the early 1950s the NBA had difficulty attracting spectators because of the style of play that had developed. Teams in the lead toward the end of games took to holding the ball—stalling—rather than trying to score. In response, the trailing team would commit frequent and sometimes violent fouls, hoping that the ensuing free throws would be missed and it could then get control of the ball and score. These tactics made the game both boring and brutal, an unfortunate combination for an enterprise that sought to provide entertainment.

The league's solution to the problem, adopted in the 1954–1955 season, was a rule requiring each team to launch a shot at the basket within twenty-four seconds of taking possession of the ball. Clocks ticking off twenty-four seconds were prominently placed around the court so that players could keep track of the time remaining to shoot.[42] The result reprised the impact, two decades earlier, of the one-handed shot: the twenty-four-second rule made the game faster, with more scoring, and so more appealing to a wider audience. The rule gave basketball a way to force the action, to prevent stalling tactics from rendering play a tedious exercise, and to ensure that each side in the game gets multiple opportunities to score.

Thus, by the middle of the twentieth century, both college basketball, divided as it was among the same conferences as in football, and the professional game, with the NBA having attained the status in the sport of the American and National Leagues in baseball and the NFL in football, had assumed the form they would maintain to the end of the century and beyond. And in the third quarter of that century both produced what the New York Yankees had become in baseball: a single, dominant team. By far the most successful college basketball team during this period represented the University of California at Los Angeles (UCLA), while the Boston Celtics dominated professional basketball.

In the twelve seasons between 1963–1964 and 1974–1975 UCLA won the national championship ten times. Its teams won twenty-eight consecutive games in the single-elimination NCAA tournament and between 1971 and 1974 won eighty-eight consecutive games overall. No college program before or since enjoyed such success. The key to that success, the one continuous feature of the team over its twelve-year reign, was the coach, John Wooden.

Wooden exercised the kind of all-encompassing authority that football coaches normally wield. His practice sessions were timed to the minute. He instructed his players on every facet of the game, telling them not only how to pass, shoot, and defend on the court but even how to put on the socks they wore while practicing and playing. He enforced a strict code of dress and appearance, which forbade facial hair. Once his best player, Bill Walton, announced that he had begun to grow a beard. "Go right ahead, Bill," Wooden told him. "I wish you well and the team will miss you." Walton shaved.

The style of play Wooden favored emphasized quick players who applied defensive pressure to the opposing team. UCLA's success stemmed not only from Wooden's skill as a coach, however—considerable though that was—but also from his ability to convince the most talented high school players to attend the school. In basketball, as in football, while the collegiate draft, the method of distributing college players to professional franchises, proceeds according to rules that favor the least successful teams, allocating high school players to the colleges is more of a free-for-all. As is not the case in the professional ranks, the best teams have the opportunity to recruit the best new players.

UCLA was able to attract good players in part because many of them lived nearby. Walton, for example, came from San Diego, 124 miles south of the UCLA campus. But the college's basketball supremacy also rested on its success in attracting a few highly skilled players from far away. The linchpin of Wooden's first championship team, Walt Hazzard, came from Philadelphia. Perhaps his greatest player, Lew Alcindor, whose UCLA teams won three consecutive national championships and compiled an overall record of 88–2 (and who subsequently converted to Islam and changed his name to Kareem Abdul-Jabbar), was a New Yorker.

UCLA's success on the court attracted these and other talented players who, like most athletes, wanted to play for a winning team. Alcindor was perhaps the most sought-after recruit in the history of high school basketball, and in announcing his decision to attend UCLA he said, "I have always been captivated by California." The school had a special appeal to African-Americans such as Alcindor and Hazzard because Jackie Robinson had been a student there—and had excelled in basketball as well as baseball and football.[43] But like many other colleges, UCLA also attracted talented basketball players by offering them inducements that NCAA rules prohibited. After Wooden retired, reports surfaced of illegal gifts to players from businessmen who supported the basketball program. For these transgressions, the UCLA basketball program incurred NCAA-imposed penalties.[44]

In professional basketball the Boston Celtics matched what UCLA achieved in the college game. In the thirteen years between the 1956–1957 and the 1968–1969 seasons they won the NBA championship eleven times, eight of them consecutively between 1958–1959 and 1965–1966. The franchise won twice more in the 1970s and again three times in the 1980s.

The major figure in the Celtics' success, the one person associated with all sixteen championship teams, was Arnold "Red" Auerbach, who coached the first nine, served as the general manager, responsible for selecting the players, for another six and president of the organization for one. Auerbach was born and raised in Brooklyn and attended the George Washington University, in Washington, D.C., where he played basketball. Although his previous coaching experience was at the high school level, after World War II he persuaded the owner of the newly founded Washington Capitols of the BAA to hire him to coach the team in the league's inaugural season of 1946–1947. In 1950 he moved to the Celtics.

In the world of basketball Auerbach projected a personality the common term for which is "fiery."[45] Like his fellow Brooklynite Al Davis in football, he became a controversial figure. Intensely competitive, shrewd, and even by his own description occasionally devious, as with Davis Auerbach's rivals accused him of underhanded and unfair tactics.

The visiting team's locker room at the Celtics' home arena, the Boston Garden, if not bugged as Davis's rivals suspected the comparable facility in the Oakland Raiders' stadium of being, was a dank, dark, and dirty place, kept that way by Auerbach, his opponents believed, to annoy and demoralize the visiting team even before it took the court.[46] As a coach, Auerbach had the habit of lighting a cigar when he was confident a Celtics' victory was assured, which was regarded (and probably intended) as a way of taunting the soon-to-be defeated team and its supporters.

Auerbach wielded considerable authority over the Celtics.

He, like Wooden of UCLA, decreed a dress code for his team. Yet his definition of his job differed from that of football coaches and many college basketball coaches. He did not attempt to exercise anything like the same degree of on-court control. Football coaches and many basketball coaches design a large number of set plays for their teams to implement. Auerbach had very few and, unlike football coaches, he did not constantly issue orders from the sidelines, nor did he have a high regard for basketball coaches who did. At crucial moments in games he routinely asked his players what approach they recommended, a habit that "Bear" Bryant and Vince Lombardi, Auerbach's peers in football, never acquired.

Because professional basketball players are older, more mature, and more experienced than their college counterparts, Auerbach had less need than a college coach, let alone a football coach, to coordinate the team by issuing commands. And because the continuous character of basketball, combined with the twenty-four-second rule, makes offensive sequences more rapid in the professional game, it is more difficult for a professional coach than for someone presiding over a college team or a football team of any kind to issue such commands effectively. Professional basketball came to rely more heavily than the college game, and far more heavily than football, on spontaneous coordination. As a result, Auerbach went to great lengths to create conditions conducive to it. He was careful to tell each player what he was expected to do for the team and to select players who would play harmoniously with one another.

He worked actively to foster harmony as well. He arranged for the team to travel abroad together in the off-season. The ostensible purpose of these trips was to spread knowledge of the game of basketball but a by-product was forging personal relationships among players that would contribute to their ability to coordinate themselves on the court. The Celtics' players came to know each other well for another reason: They played together for a long time. Auerbach kept the team's roster remarkably stable. During the thirteen years of the first eleven championships he made only a single trade of one player for another, a period in which the typical NBA team made dozens.*

Although he spurned the micromanagement of his team on the court, Auerbach did make several major contributions to the way basketball is played. He pioneered what came to be the most popular distribution of roles among the five players on a team. By mid-century almost every team employed a center, who stationed himself near the basket, two forwards, who flanked him, and two guards, usually shorter and more agile than the other three, who operated farther away from the basket and so formed the team's back-court. Auerbach assigned one forward responsibility for scoring while the other, the power forward, concentrated on rebounding.

Similarly, one of his guards concerned himself principally with scoring while the other, the point guard, assumed responsibility for controlling the ball most of the time and distributing it to the scorers. The first and best known of the

---

* The other professional coach to win nine championships, Phil Jackson, had a radically different background from Auerbach's. The son of a Pentecostal minister in North Dakota and raised in a religiously strict household, he played for the New York Knickerbockers in the 1960s and 1970s and rebelled against the strictures of his upbringing, gaining a reputation as a free spirit. But his approach to coaching resembled Auerbach's in that he emphasized fostering harmony among team members as much as, if not more than, designing patterns for them to follow on the court.

Celtics' point guards was Bob Cousy, who introduced the technique of changing direction suddenly by dribbling the ball behind his back and whose flair for deception and imaginative passing earned the nickname "Houdini."

Auerbach actually invented another position, the "sixth man." He kept one of his five best players out of the game at its start, sending him in to play after several minutes had elapsed. Inserting a skilled player as the opposing team was beginning to tire gave the Celtics a competitive advantage: Their efficiency increased as the opponent's decreased. It also conferred a psychological advantage by lowering the other team's morale, just as fresh reinforcements for one side in the midst of a battle can discourage the opposing soldiers.[47]

Auerbach also established a trend in basketball by using the fast-break style of offense, which he had learned from his own college coach, Bill Reinhart. To launch a fast break, one of the team's frontcourt players, the center or one of the forwards, snatches an opponent's missed shot and quickly passes it to one of the guards. Receiving this outlet pass, the guard advances the ball toward the opponent's goal as quickly as possible. Simultaneously, his teammates race toward it as fast as they can, hoping to arrive before the defenders. If they succeed, the ball can be passed to one of them whom no opponent is defending, giving him an unobstructed and easy-to-make shot at the basket.

The fast break has no real equivalent in baseball and football because unlike them, basketball is a continuous game, with no mandatory pause in the action marking the transition between offense and defense for each team.[48] But the philosophy underlying the fast break is a familiar one. It reproduces the logic on which many running plays in football, and the standard flanking maneuver in warfare, are based: achieving the goal—a victory on the battlefield, a score in football and basketball—by outnumbering the opponent at a particular spot. As in warfare and football, the success of the maneuver in basketball depends on the speed with which troops and players arrive at the designated point.

The key to success in the fast break is a player who can be relied upon to seize the rebound from the other team's missed shots and send the ball swiftly upcourt. In 1956 Auerbach added such a player to the Celtics. As the team's center he led it to its first eleven championships and, in the process, had as powerful an effect on the game as Hank Luisetti had had two decades previously.

Bill Russell was born in Louisiana and moved with his family as a youngster to Oakland, California. An eager but not particularly skillful basketball player in high school, his abilities on the court blossomed at a small Catholic college across the San Francisco Bay from Oakland, the University of San Francisco. He led the school to two NCAA championships in 1954–1955 and 1955–1956, during which time his team won fifty-five consecutive games. After playing for the gold medal–winning United States basketball team in the 1956 Olympic Games in Melbourne, he joined the Celtics. The team proceeded to win the first of its eleven championships in thirteen years. For the last two of them, in 1967–1968 and 1968–1969, Russell served as the Celtics' coach as well as its most important player.

No other individual in the history of American team sports has compiled such a record: fourteen championships (including the Olympics) in fifteen years. And no basketball player has had a greater impact on how the game was played during his career. For its record of success, Russell's career in basketball bears comparison to Babe Ruth's in baseball. Yet Russell never achieved anything like the national (or international) acclaim that Ruth enjoyed, nor did his legacy loom as large in basketball as did Ruth's in baseball in the decades after he retired from the game. For this there are several reasons.

One is that, in Russell's time as a player, basketball was not as popular a form of American entertainment as was baseball in the 1920s. Basketball was not even the most popular winter team sport in Boston. The local professional ice hockey team, the Boston Bruins, attracted more spectators than Russell's Celtics, which rarely filled the arena where they both played, the Boston Garden.[49]

Russell's personality also limited the public acclaim he received. He did not court popularity, insisting on conducting his life in ways that made sense to him no matter what others thought. He refused, for example, to sign autographs on the grounds that a player's obligation to the sporting public involved exerting himself to the utmost during the games he played and that it concluded when the games ended.[50] Moreover, his career spanned the civil rights era, when the country was preoccupied with, and divided over, racial issues, and Russell made no attempt to conceal the outrage he felt at the discrimination to which he and other African-Americans were subject.

Just as important a constraint on his reputation both during and after his playing career was the fact that he specialized in the least glamorous, although not the least important, facets of the game. He made an indispensable contribution to the Celtics' most reliable method of scoring. Without his stellar rebounding, the fast break could not begin. But by the time it ended, with an easy basket at the other end of the court, he was far from the center of the spectators' attention.

His greatest contribution to the Celtics' success came as a defensive player. But in basketball, as in baseball and football, preventing the other team from scoring attracts less popular attention and admiration than—although it is just as important to the outcome of the game as—scoring itself. As a defender, Russell made more extensive and adept use than any player before or since of the technique of blocking shots. Intercepting an opponent's shot after he has launched it toward the basket is relatively infrequent in basketball because the effort to do so can have three adverse consequences for the defending team. The would-be shot blocker can foul the shooter, who is then awarded free throws. He can be judged by the referee to have committed a goaltending violation by intercepting the ball on the downward part of its arc, which results in two points being awarded to the team whose player has attempted the shot. Or he can escape both these pitfalls but deflect the shot out of bounds, in which case the other team retains possession of it.

Russell perfected the art of blocking shots so as to avoid all three. By his quickness, leaping ability, and close study of the styles of play of opposing players, he was able to block shots in such a way that he or one of his teammates could snatch it, and often then initiate a fast break that ended with the Celtics scoring. Russell successfully blocking a shot made for a visually arresting scene as he shot up off the floor like a coiled snake striking and tipped the ball to a teammate.[51] But the most important impact of his mastery of this technique was not visible. For the *possibility* that Russell would block a shot had a pervasive effect on the opposing team's offensive maneuvers.[52] Opposing players rushed their shots, or hesitated to shoot at all, or launched shots from a greater distance than they would have preferred—avoiding the Russellpatrolled area near the basket, where scoring was easiest—all because of the chance that the Celtics' center would otherwise rise up to swat the shot away.

These evasive tactics limited the number of shots he actually blocked, but at the cost of opposing teams' offensive efficiency. In order to have fewer shots blocked they made fewer baskets, which worked to the advantage of the Celtics. But the effect Russell had on opposing teams could not be readily quantified, or even detected, as Babe Ruth's exploits could be and were. Ruth's contributions to the Yankees' victories involved what he himself did, Russell's to the Celtics involved what his actions prevented other players from doing.

During his playing days Russell was best known beyond the small circle of basketball aficionados less for the decisive but subtle ways in which he lifted his team to a position of dominance in the NBA than for his decade-long rivalry with an opposing center of great talent, Wilt Chamberlain. Because it is a continuous sport, with players making the transition from offense to defense without interruption, and because players are often matched against each other in both phases of the game, basketball lends itself to personal rivalries, in the fashion of individual sports such as tennis and boxing, as baseball and football do not.*

Chamberlain, whose Kansas team lost the triple-overtime NCAA championship game in 1957, was basketball's most

---

* Baseball does consist of a series of duels between pitcher and batter, but each individual duel recurs at most four or five times per game, whereas in basketball the duels can be continuous. Moreover, the baseball duels are not symmetrical. Batters do not have the opportunity to pitch to the opposing team's pitcher, except in the case of the team's pitcher, and then only in the National League. Similarly, in football an offensive lineman may frequently be assigned to block a particular defensive player, but the reverse is never true. Because of the system of platooning, the rival players never switch roles, with the offensive player playing on defense and vice versa, as is the case in basketball.

prodigious scorer and a mighty rebounder as well. He once recorded an average of fifty points per game over the course of an entire NBA season (no other player ever averaged as many as forty) and in the year he did so—1961–1962—he tallied one hundred points in a single game.[53]

Chamberlain twice led his team to the league championship but, although he was bigger and stronger than Russell (as well as every other player) and consistently outscored him in their ongoing duel, which covered a total of ninety-four games over ten years, the Celtics won more games and many more championships. Four times Russell's team opposed Chamberlain's in the deciding game of a best-of-seven playoff. The Celtics won all four.

In the history of basketball, therefore, the Boston Garden, where Russell and the Celtics played, and Pauley Pavilion, UCLA's home court, housed the most successful teams. But the beating heart of the game, the places where it was played with the greatest intensity, the communities where it mattered most, were located elsewhere. The two principal hotbeds of basketball were connected to the sport's dynastic teams through their major figures. For these were the places—in one case one of the fifty states of the United States, and in the other, a type of neighborhood found throughout the country but especially in the Northeast—from which UCLA's Wooden and the Celtics' Auerbach and Russell came.

THE GRASS ROOTS

Among the fifty states Indiana falls near the middle by most criteria—size, population, and location, for example. In one respect, however, it leads the nation: enthusiasm for basketball among its citizens. Basketball, as an Indianapolis newspaper said in an editorial in 1955, "occupies a particularly lofty place in the Hoosier scheme of things. It is far more than a boys' sport—in fact, it is just about the most important thing there is."[54] Basketball's originator, James Naismith, said, in 1939, that "basketball really had its origin in Indiana, which remains today the center of the sport."[55]

Basketball was introduced to Indiana in 1893 by the Reverend Nicholas McKay, a Presbyterian minister who was general secretary of the YMCA in Crawfordsville, in the central part of the state, and who had learned the game in Springfield, Massachusetts, from Naismith himself. The sport put down roots all over the state almost immediately.

The two major universities in Indiana each enjoyed a period of national prominence under the leadership of a highly successful coach. Purdue University's heyday spanned the years 1917 to 1946, when Ward "Piggy" Lambert, an early exponent of the fast break, supervised the team. One of his star players was John Wooden. Indiana University occupied a place in the upper ranks of college teams under the tutelage of Bob Knight, who presided over the basketball program from 1973 to 2000, winning eleven Big Ten titles and three national championships.[56] But the state's passion for the game manifested itself most vividly in its enthusiasm for high school basketball.

High school teams became the focus of their community's attention and, when successful, sources of local pride. Indiana schoolboys grew up aspiring to play for these teams and they devoted many hours to developing the basketball skills, especially the technique of accurate long-range shooting, for which Indiana-bred players came to be noted.[57] Towns across the state treated outstanding high school players as heroes, sometimes posting signs at the city limits proudly informing travelers that they were entering the place the player called home. Entire communities routinely attended high school games. So popular did Indiana high school basketball become that fifteen of the sixteen largest high school gymnasiums in the United States were built in the state, as well as twenty-nine of the thirty-five high school arenas seating 5,000 or more spectators.[58] The gymnasiums often had seating capacities that exceeded the total population of the towns in which they were located.

Basketball's special status in Indiana had several sources. Especially in the first half of the twentieth century the state consisted largely of farming communities and small towns, whose high schools were too small to have football teams. The harsh climate made it preferable to hold winter entertainment indoors. Basketball thus suited the local conditions, and college and, especially, high school basketball gained a particularly wide following because, unlike other Midwestern states such as Ohio, Illinois, and Michigan, Indiana had no professional team to compete for the attention and loyalty of its sports-following public.

The most important ingredient in Indiana's preoccupation with high school basketball was the state's high school championship tournament. First held in 1911, it differed from the state-wide competitions in all but two of the other states in that every high school in Indiana, from the largest to the smallest, participated. Because the tournament proceeded in stages stretching over a full month, with a progressively widening geographic scope, in the early rounds neighboring schools were always pitted against each other, creating fierce and enduring rivalries.[59] And because every high school participated, the tournament provided David-versus-Goliath confrontations, with teams representing small, rural high schools playing opponents from schools with far larger enrollments. In the most famous of all Indiana high school basketball games, an event on which the 1986 film *Hoosiers* was based, tiny Milan High School defeated the much larger Muncie Central High School to win the 1954 state championship on a last-second basket by its best offensive player, Bobby Plump. The smaller school had a total enrollment of 161—seventy-three of them boys—making it one-tenth the size of its rival. The Muncie Central gymnasium had room for seven times the population of Milan.[60]

The tournament championship game became an annual event that captured the attention of the entire state. It was played in the field house of Butler University in Indianapolis, which was built expressly for this purpose in 1928 and, at the time of its construction, was the largest arena devoted strictly to basketball in the world.[61]

In the history of the Indiana state high school tournament two players in particular enjoyed great success and went on to even greater achievements and renown in the wider worlds of college and professional basketball. One was John Wooden, who led his team to the championship game in three consecutive years from 1925 to 1927. Wooden's team represented Martinsville, population 4,800, a typical version of the small Indiana town in which basketball flourished.[62] The other tournament star was Oscar Robertson, who led his team to state championships in 1955 and 1956 and went on to become one of the best of all college and professional players. Robertson came not from a small town but from Indianapolis, from the other kind of place that served as the incubator of basketball talent in the United States—the inner part of a large city.

Basketball became the most popular sport in the crowded neighborhoods of America's largest urban areas because space was invariably at a premium and basketball requires less space to play than do baseball and football. Growing up in Brooklyn, Red Auerbach remembered, "Everywhere you looked, all you saw was concrete, so there was no football, no baseball, and hardly any track there. Basketball was our game. ... "[63]

In the twentieth century successive waves of immigrants inhabited these neighborhoods and took up basketball as they did.* In the sport's early decades Jews figured prominently. Four of the five starting players on the St. John's University "Wonder Five" of the 1929–1931 seasons were Jewish.[64] So were major promoters of the sport such as Eddie Gottlieb, who in 1918 organized a successful team for the South Philadelphia Hebrew Association that was known as the SPHAs and later owned the Philadelphia franchise in the NBA for which Wilt Chamberlain played in his epic 1961–1962 season. So, too, were Auerbach and another successful coach of his era, William "Red" Holzman, who grew up in New York City and, after a career as a player, led the New York Knickerbockers to two NBA championships in the 1970s.

Urban Catholics also contributed to the sport, among them Bob Cousy and the brothers Dick and Al McGuire, prominent players, executives, and coaches who, like Cousy, came from the borough of Queens in New York City. In New York the Catholic Youth Organization sponsored basketball

---

* These were the same groups whose votes gave the Democratic Party an advantage over the Republicans in national politics in the middle third of the twentieth century, leading to the observation that basketball was the sport of Franklin D. Roosevelt's New Deal coalition. Walter LaFeber, *Michael Jordan and the New Global Capitalism*, Second Edition (New York: W. W. Norton, 2002), p. 37.

programs in which youngsters refined their skills and
Catholic high schools fielded some of the best teams in the
city. (Lew Alcindor attended one of them, Power Memorial.)
At the college level, a number of Catholic schools sponsored
major basketball programs. Although none of them maintained a Division I football team, at one time or other the
basketball teams representing the University of San Francisco, Loyola and DePaul Universities of Chicago, Marquette
of Milwaukee, Georgetown of Washington, D.C., and
LaSalle and Villanova of Philadelphia all won the national
championship.

During World War II the great internal migration of
African-Americans from the deep South to the inner cities of
the North began and the new residents of these urban neighborhoods also embraced basketball. In the early postwar
decades they came to dominate the sport. As with football,
journalists selected All-American basketball teams, which
included the best players from around the country for a particular year. In 1948 the consensus All-American team was all
white. Ten years later the five best collegiate players all were
black.[65] The best black players emerged from the heart of
America's cities. Between 1956 and 1960 four of the greatest
of all basketball players entered the professional ranks. Each
had begun his career in an inner city high school in which all
or almost all of his fellow students were also black: Bill Russell at McClymonds in Oakland; Elgin Baylor of the Minneapolis and later the Los Angeles Lakers at Spingarn in
Washington, D.C.; Wilt Chamberlain at Overbrook in
Philadelphia; and Oscar Robertson at Crispus Attucks in
Indianapolis.

The first African-American player entered the NBA in
1950 and by the 1980s four out of every five starting players

in the league were black.[66] But the moment that most closely corresponded to Jackie Robinson's debut in major league baseball, one that dramatically demonstrated the prominent role of African-Americans in basketball, came in 1966, in the second NCAA championship game (after the 1957 contest) of national importance. In that game a team from Texas Western University, a college in El Paso with no national reputation that fielded five black players in its starting lineup, defeated a team representing the most glamorous basketball program of all, the University of Kentucky, coached by the most famous and successful coach of his time, Adolph Rupp, whose team was all white.

As in the state of Indiana, in America's inner cities in the second half of the twentieth century basketball served social purposes that transcended recreation. To young men growing up in these neighborhoods basketball was more than a game. It functioned as a focus of social life for the community. Just as residents of Indiana's towns turned out for the local high school games, so people in the inner cities gathered at the playgrounds, with their asphalt courts, to watch the impromptu games that were played there and, in greater numbers, to attend the summer tournaments staged at these courts. For some youngsters the playground was as important a locus of social life as the family, the school, or the church.[67] Like their largely white counterparts in Indiana, young inner city blacks became obsessed with the game and played it throughout the year. Basketball meant more to them than to their suburban counterparts, so they practiced more intensively and played longer hours than people of the same age who lived elsewhere. In this way, they became the best players and so came to dominate the sport.[68]

In addition to the companionship that playground games

provided, the local prestige that accrued to the most accomplished players, and the pure enjoyment of playing, basketball offered inner-city young men an opportunity for social mobility.[69] They could aspire to lift themselves out of the poverty in which many of them lived by means of a career in professional basketball.

Basketball players who learned the game on inner-city playgrounds tended to develop a distinctive style of play. They adopted an individual approach to scoring rather than relying on teammates, becoming more adept at dribbling and maneuvering themselves close to the basket by bumping, feinting, twisting, and spinning while dribbling than at passing or at shooting from long range. They developed characteristic individual routines and strategems—moves—for sliding around the defender to gain a clear shot at the basket. Their approach emphasized, in particular, the ability to leap high and handle the ball deftly, shifting it from one hand to the other while airborne. And players from the inner city worked at completing their airborne pirouettes by dunking the ball—bringing it to a point above the cylinder of the hoop and dropping it through the rim for a basket.

In its original sense a dunk is a downward movement, often submerging something (or someone) in liquid. A common usage refers to dipping a piece of cake, often a doughnut, in coffee or milk.[70] Dunking of that kind is a casual, modest, unremarkable act. A dunk in basketball is usually far more dramatic and forceful. The NBA's dunking contest, staged at its midseason all-star game—with the player judged to have performed the most difficult version of the maneuver declared the winner—is called the slam-dunk competition, to convey a sense of the sheer forcefulness involved. A dunk is often intended as a gesture of power, defiance, and supremacy. It is, in the playground style, the basketball equivalent of the home run in baseball. Occasionally a player has performed a dunk of such power in an indoor game that it has shattered the glass backboard on which the basket was mounted.

The playground style, with the acrobatic, thunderous dunk as its highest achievement, came to be associated with African-American players, since it was they who lived in the nation's inner cities. To this association there have been notable exceptions. Bill Russell's style of play had nothing to do with individual flamboyance on offense. Nor did that of Oscar Robertson, perhaps the best all-around player in the history of the game. In the second half of the twentieth century the mark of versatility in a basketball game came to be called the "triple-double," the achievement by a single player of totals in double figures in the three discrete categories of scoring, rebounding, and assists. In the latter years of the century this feat was rarely accomplished: The best players managed it only a handful of times in a given season. But in 1961–1962 Oscar Robertson *averaged* a triple double—30.5 points, 12.5 rebounds, and 11.4 assists—over the course of the entire season, and he did so with understated efficiency. His basketball repertoire did not include the spectacular dunk.

In the college ranks, Georgetown University, which in 1983 became the first team to win the national championship with a black head coach, John Thompson, and which included a number of inner-city players on its roster, succeeded through tenacious defense, the product of teamwork and determination, rather than flamboyant offense. And the player in the last third of the twentieth century who displayed the flashy techniques of playground basketball most conspicuously, Pete Maravich, who led the nation in scoring for three consecutive years as a college player at Louisiana State University and continued his prolific offensive performances in the professional ranks, was white.

Still, a style of play emphasizing a particular set of individual skills did evolve on the inner-city playgrounds, from which it spread to college and professional basketball. One reason for the birth and development of the playground style, regularly cited in the several books written about inner city basketball,[71] is that it represents a form of self-expression for people who, because of the straitened circumstances of their lives, have few other outlets for it. It is a way of establishing a personal identity, winning respect and admiration, and succeeding in the eyes of the world.[72]

In this sense, playground basketball can be compared to jazz music, much of which originated in the same stratum of American society and takes the same form: individual improvisation within a fixed structure, spontaneous variations on a preset motif. The rhythm and basic melody of a piece of music are in this sense the equivalent of the rules of basketball. Jazz, like basketball, has served as an avenue of self-expression and individual self-assertion for people for whom other avenues were blocked. And just as the leading jazz musicians have inspired others, so too did the virtuoso basketball players. Elgin Baylor, for example, or the skilled ball-handler and shooter from the Philadelphia playgrounds who played for the Baltimore NBA franchise and on a New York Knickerbocker championship team as well, Earl "The Pearl" Monroe served as the Louis Armstrongs and Miles Davises for subsequent generations of basketball players.

But the form that playground basketball took had causes other than the social status of those who played it. One was the age and gender of the players. Young males are prone to preening, strutting, and otherwise calling attention to themselves. At the root of this behavior lies not culture but hormones. Inner-city basketball, it has been said, "is a game for young athletes without cars or allowances."[73] Without the opportunity to drive fast automobiles or outfit themselves in garish, expensive wardrobes, young men in the inner cities channel the chemically driven impulses that produce such patterns of conduct into the way they play basketball.

These same youngsters do not spend their time developing their aptitudes for long-range shooting because, unlike their counterparts in the small towns of Indiana, they almost never have a court to themselves on which to practice: City playgrounds are always crowded. Nor do they always own their own basketballs. Perfecting shooting skills is also difficult for them because the balls with which they do play are often misshapen and the rims at which they shoot bent out of alignment, both the result of overuse.

Finally, inner-city players do not cultivate the arts of teamwork because their year-round informal games lack coaches to foster it, because those games match ad hoc collections of players rather than permanently established teams that play and practice together continuously, and because, since the standard procedure on the playground is for the winning ad hoc team to remain on the court to play the next game while the losing players retire to the sidelines, to increase his chances of being selected for one of the teams a player must display the skill most directly relevant to winning the game: the ability to score.

In the second half of the twentieth century, players from the inner cities of the United States, the vast majority of them African-American, made monumental contributions to basketball. The game as it developed would have been far poorer in every way without them. The contribution of basketball to the lives of African-Americans during that period, however, was less self-evidently a happy one. Because the dream of individual glory and social mobility through prowess in basketball has such power, over the decades hundreds of thousands, probably millions, of young men in the inner cities devoted themselves to mastering the game, allocating a very large proportion of their waking hours to it. But only a tiny fraction of them fulfilled that dream.

By one calculation, the odds of an African-American male between the ages of twenty and twenty-nine earning a living in the NBA were 135,800 to 1.[74] Basketball is an example of a more general phenomenon, the "winner-take-all" market, in which the distribution of income is radically unequal. The most skillful people are enormously well compensated but most earn virtually nothing.[75] Acting in films is another example. The incomes of the most successful actors are among the highest in the world. But in one typical year only 12 percent of the members of the actors' union were actually paid for appearing in a film and of those who were paid, 90 percent received less than $5,000.[76]

Winner-take-all markets are typically overcrowded. The prospect of great riches attracts far more people to these fields than will ever become wealthy in them. These people are attracted because, as Adam Smith noted, "The overweening conceit which the greater part of men have of their own abilities is an ancient evil remarked by the philosophers and moralists of all ages.... The chance of gain is by every man more or less overvalued, and the chance of loss is by most men under-valued. ..."[77] Basketball is no exception. In some such fields of endeavor—investment banking or the law, for example—the skills a person acquires in the hope of gaining the highest rewards will assist him or her in other occupations. But this is not true for basketball: A hard-won repertoire of playground moves will not help its possessor to earn a living outside the sport. For the purpose of preparing for a productive adult career, almost all of the inner-city youngsters who spent their days and nights on playgrounds playing basketball were therefore wasting their time.

Still, a few supremely talented players have scaled the heights of the world of basketball and become both famous and rich. At the end of the 1970s two in particular—each, as it happened, from one of the zones of greatest enthusiasm for the game—rose to the top of the sport. Larry Bird, from the small southern Indiana town of French Lick, and Earvin "Magic" Johnson, from the city of East Lansing in Michigan, began a rivalry to which only the one between Bill Russell and Wilt Chamberlain compares in intensity and importance. That rivalry, and the skills the two players brought to it, inaugurated basketball's golden age.

The Golden Age

Larry Bird and Magic Johnson led their college teams, Indiana State and Michigan State respectively, to the final game of the 1979 NCAA tournament. So broad was the national interest the two players had inspired during that season that the championship game, won by Michigan State, became the most-watched college basketball game ever played[78] and as such counts, along with the 1957 and 1966 contests, as the third of the three historically important versions of the college championship. The next year they joined the two most celebrated and successful professional teams and continued their rivalry for a decade. With Bird as their leading player, the Boston Celtics won three more championships. Johnson became a member of the only team to rival the Celtics' record of accomplishment, the Los Angeles Lakers.

Over the years, as many of basketball's outstanding performers played for the Lakers as for the Celtics.[79] Elgin Baylor, the first professional master of the playground style, Jerry West, a sharp-shooting guard from West Virginia who built several championship teams as a Laker executive and whose silhouette dribbling a basketball the NBA adopted as its official logo, and Kobe Bryant, a prolific scorer who went directly from high school to the professional ranks, all played for the Lakers.

Of the five most notable centers in the history of the league, four of them—Bill Russell was the fifth—played for the franchise. George Mikan led the team to its first five championships in the late 1940s and early 1950s[80] when it was located in Minneapolis—hence the name, incongruously transferred along with the team in 1960 to Los Angeles, a city set in a region blessed with mountains, desert, and a seacoast but no significant lakes. In 1972 the team won its first championship in Los Angeles, setting an NBA record with thirty-three consecutive victories, with Wilt Chamberlain at center. Kareem Abdul-Jabbar teamed with Johnson to bring the team five more titles in the 1980s and the bulky (340 pounds), powerful, but also agile Shaquille O'Neal combined with Bryant to win the first three NBA championships of the twenty-first century.

Bird and Johnson did not sustain quite as intense a personal rivalry as did Russell and Chamberlain. Their teams did not play each other as often and when the two were on the court at the same time, unlike Russell and Chamberlain, neither normally had direct responsibility for defending against the other. But each was the central figure on one of the two teams that dominated professional basketball when they played: In every one of the nine years between 1980, when they entered the league, and 1988, one or the other of the two teams played in the championship series and in eight of those years, one of them won it.[81] Moreover, each of the two was preoccupied with, and measured himself against, the other.[82]

The personalities of the two players differed. Bird was shy and stoic, a man of few words or visible emotions and apparently interested only in basketball. Johnson, by contrast, was ebullient, garrulous, and comfortable with members of the press, whom Bird avoided. After his playing career ended the former Laker became a media personality himself as well as a businessman with a variety of lucrative interests.

Their styles of play, however, were similar and although neither deployed the acrobatic individual maneuvers nurtured on urban playgrounds, similarly compelling. Both were versatile. Although tall—Bird stood six feet nine inches, Johnson six feet eight—each possessed skills usually found in much shorter players. Bird, like other graduates of Indiana high schools, could shoot accurately from long range. Johnson had responsibility for controlling and distributing the basketball on offense, meaning that he combined the size (and some of the abilities: he was a formidable rebounder) of Bill Russell with the ball-handling talents of Bob Cousy—a combination unimaginable in previous decades.

Both players excelled at the art of passing, which is the essence of what is distinctive about basketball: spontaneous coordination. Each contributed mightily to his team's capacity for teamwork, and it was the individual virtuosity of each in concert with the capacity to catalyze effective cooperation among his teammates that elevated the two to a level of popularity that no basketball player had previously enjoyed.[83]

That popularity, in turn, lifted the professional game out of the doldrums into which it had fallen in the 1970s.[84] That decade had seen the return of New York City to the center of the world of basketball with the two championships won by the Knickerbockers, in 1970 and 1973, based on an exceptionally high level of teamwork. Those New York teams included the future United States senator and consummate team player Bill Bradley. But the expansion in the number of teams in the NBA, following the example of major league baseball and professional football and augmented by a merger, in 1976, with a rival league, the American Basketball Association, which added four new franchises to the NBA, decreased professional basketball's popularity. Expansion diluted the talent in the league, creating teams that failed to attract local followings of any size or enthusiasm. Because half the teams qualified for the postseason playoffs, the league's regular season became less important, and this also reduced interest. So, too, did the skyrocketing salaries—the result of the same shift in bargaining power between owners and players that had taken place in baseball—that were paid to players who did not always appear to be exerting themselves on the court and several of whom turned out to be using illegal narcotics.

The nadir of the NBA's standing with the American public came with the final game of the 1980 championship series. A spectacular performance by Magic Johnson secured the championship for Los Angeles over a formidable Philadelphia team that included the most acrobatic player of his era, Julius "Doctor J" Erving. The CBS network owned the rights to televise NBA games, having acquired them the previous year for a far smaller fee than professional football commanded.[85] The audiences the games attracted were disappointingly small.[86] The Los Angeles–Philadelphia game occurred in the middle of a period in which the size of a network's audience determined the advertising fees it could charge the following year. So the network decided not to telecast it when it was played. Instead, a tape of the game was shown in much of the country late at night—a decision that would be unthinkable for the World Series or the Super Bowl.

From that low point, basketball, both college and professional, launched a steep upward ascent in the affections of Americans, and not only Americans. It gained popularity from the performances of Bird and Johnson,[87] but the sport also capitalized on broader trends in American society.

The decade of the 1980s, the era of Bird and Johnson and of basketball's rise to a popular and important place in American mass culture, was also the time when the generation of Americans born in the ten years after World War II began to occupy positions of importance in American society. The formative experiences of this "Baby Boom" generation, the largest numerically in the history of the country, differed from those of their predecessors in ways that predisposed them to embrace basketball. Unlike their grandparents, they had no connection with the traditional, rural frontier period of American (or European) history that baseball evokes. World War II had not marked their lives as it had those of their parents. The Vietnam War, a far less popular conflict and one in which far fewer of the age cohort of eligible males had actually taken part, had shaped their attitudes toward the activity with which football has such a pronounced affinity.

More than previous American generations, moreover, the Baby Boomers sought to distinguish themselves from their predecessors, and this streak of rebelliousness made basketball, the favorite sport of neither of the two preceding generations, all the more attractive. It was appealing to Baby Boomers as well because they had a wider assortment of forms of entertainment from which to choose than their parents and grandparents had had and they gravitated to a sport that provided continuous action.

Basketball appealed to Baby Boomers as well because they were familiar with, and comfortable in, the post-industrial world that the game reflects. Many of them were accustomed to working in cooperative rather than hierarchical fashion. The rise of the Baby Boom generation to the upper tier of American society also coincided with the revolution in information technology, which fostered the creation of networks of all kinds throughout the society—the Internet being the most prominent example—and accelerated the trend by which knowledge rather than manual strength or skill became the basis of productive work, a development that basketball more than baseball or football came to incorporate. Perhaps not coincidentally, two men who made fortunes at an early age in information technology then bought professional basketball franchises: Mark Cuban, who sold his company to Yahoo, purchased the Dallas Mavericks, and Paul Allen, of Microsoft, became the owner of the Portland Trail Blazers.*

The first American president from the Baby Boom gener-

---

* Allen also owned the Seattle professional football franchise. Ted Leonsis, another high-tech multimillionaire, became part-owner of the Washington NBA franchise. And Howard Shultz, the owner of the Seattle Supersonics of the NBA, made his fortune in a business associated with the Baby Boom generation: He founded the Starbucks chain of coffee houses.

ation, Bill Clinton, displayed an interest in basketball, especially when his home-state Arkansas team won the national collegiate championship in 1994. Indeed, the rise of the Baby Boomers to positions of political authority, cultural influence, and economic power in American society coincided with, and helped to launch, a surge in the popularity of college as well as professional basketball.

After John Wooden retired as the UCLA coach following his tenth championship, in 1975, no other team approached the record that he and the school had compiled. Only once in the next three decades did a college win two consecutive NCAA tournaments.[88] Like professional football in the 1990s, college basketball entered an era of competitive parity in which many teams had a legitimate chance to win the championship each year. And like professional football, college basketball changed its rules in ways that favored the offense.

In the 1985–1986 season the college game followed the professionals in adopting a shot clock, speeding up its pace. At first, teams had forty-five seconds to shoot after gaining possession of the ball. Before the 1993–1994 season the time limit was reduced to thirty-five seconds. College basketball borrowed another professional innovation, introducing in the 1985–1986 season the three-point shot, which had originated in the American Basketball Association. A successful shot launched beyond an arc nineteen feet nine inches from the basket came to count for three rather than merely two points[89] and it became increasingly popular to attempt such a shot.[90] Besides increasing scoring, the three-point field goal reinforced parity. It gave teams with shorter, smaller, slower players who could not jump as high as their opponents the opportunity to compensate for these disadvantages with skill at long-range shooting.

As with football, a new medium of communication—or more properly a new form of an established medium—helped to propel basketball into its golden age. The transmission of television signals through cables rather than over the airwaves made possible a proliferation of separate channels. Because there came to be so many of them, some of the new channels specialized in a single subject: news, fashion, classic movies, food—and sports. The first all-sports television channel, ESPN (Entertainment and Sports Programming Network) appeared in 1979 and soon made college basketball a staple of its offerings.

As the third of the nation's three major team sports, basketball was more readily and cheaply available for telecasting than the other two. The longer-established and wealthier networks had invested more heavily in baseball and football. Greater exposure via cable television did more to enhance basketball's standing around the country than would have been the case with the other two because, as the third of the three in popularity, basketball's opportunities for expanding its audience were greater.

College basketball proved particularly well suited to cable television because most games were played at night and during the winter, when television had fewer alternative forms of entertainment with which to compete than at other times of the day and year. ESPN duplicated for the entire country what the promoter Ned Irish had brought to New York five decades earlier. Indeed, the network improved on the college doubleheaders that he had staged by adding a third game, at 11:30 P.M. eastern time, to the two that began at 7 and 9 respectively.

College basketball games on ESPN, like telecasts of professional football on Monday nights, gave the country a distinctive and unlikely new television personality. Like Howard Cosell, Dick Vitale did not conform to the traditional image of a sportscaster. He was not handsome,[91] bland, young, or a former athlete. But unlike Cosell, he had coached the sport he broadcast, at the high school, college, and professional levels. And while Cosell set himself up as a critic of football, Vitale functioned on the air as a booster of his sport, even a kind of cheerleader, especially for coaches, every one of whom, by his account, seemed to be a paragon of sagacity on the court and a tower of integrity off it.

Both Cosell and Vitale distinguished themselves by their use of language. Cosell deployed longer, more abstract, more ornate words than other sportscasters were accustomed to using and than most viewers were accustomed to hearing. Vitale invented his own slang by coining a series of terms for different aspects of the game with which he peppered his on-air commentary, usually delivered at the decibel level of a bark: A "diaper dandy," for example, was a precocious first-year college player; a "PTP-er"—a prime time player—was a star.

The wider access to games played all over the country that viewers received with their subscriptions to local cable services, and Vitale's hyperactive celebration of them, helped to promote interest in college basketball in the 1980s. But the innovation that did the most to enhance its national popularity involved the procedure for determining the national champion.

In 1985, having begun with eight teams and then, over the years, expanded to sixteen, thirty-two, and forty-eight, the NCAA decided to include sixty-four teams in its championship tournament.[92] The expansion transformed the tournament, turning it into an event of national significance, on a par with baseball's World Series and football's Super Bowl. Like the professional baseball and football championships, the college basketball tournament acquired a name that connoted not only the games themselves but a national festival at a particular time of year: "March Madness."[93]

It began on the last day of the regular season, a day known as Selection Sunday, with the announcement of the qualifying teams, their allocation among four separate regional competitions, and their rankings—seedings—within these regions, as in a tennis tournament, in the order of the selection committee's assessment of their abilities. Newspapers printed these four brackets the following day and people all over the country filled them out, choosing the teams they expected to win each of the sixty-three games scheduled to be played. Many entered office pools, with the person correctly predicting the most number of games collecting the jackpot. As an occasion for betting, March Madness came to be second only to the Super Bowl.

The competition on the last weekend of the competition, in effect a four-team tournament, came to be known as the Final Four. The media converged on the city where it was to take place (which varied from year to year) as it did on the site of the Super Bowl and on the two cities where the World Series was played. The championship game took place on a Monday night during prime time and invariably attracted one of the largest television audiences of the year. So popular did March Madness become that in 2003 CBS paid $6 billion for the right to telecast the tournament for eleven years.

The organization of the competition contributed to its popularity. Because it unfolded over several weeks, interest and suspense built steadily, as in the multi-week professional football playoff culminating in the Super Bowl. With so many teams included, the tournament appealed to people all over the country because teams from every section took part. Everyone had a local, or at least regional, team to follow. In this respect the expanded NCAA tournament resembled the Indiana state high school championship, which, because every school in the state entered, captured the interest of the entire state.

The collegiate championship resembled the Indiana tournament in another respect, which also made it compelling. Each year some games, mainly in the opening stages of the competition, pitted a small school with a team of modest achievements and expectations, against a far more powerful one. As in Indiana, the David-versus-Goliath motif was an integral part of the event.[94] In the first round in each of the four regions the highest-rated team played the one judged by the selection committee to be the weakest, the second seed opposed the team seeded fifteenth, and so on. Dramatic upsets were rare. In the first eighteen years after the adoption of the sixty-four-team format no sixteenth seed ever defeated a team seeded first, although a couple came close. But fifteenth seeds did on four occasions win a game against second seeds, and every year in the first two rounds a number of lower-seeded teams defeated their higher-rated opponents.

Although obscure, unheralded teams sometimes won early games in the tournament, none won the tournament itself after its expansion to sixty-four teams. The national champion was invariably one of the sport's Goliaths. But this did not mean that each of the sixty-three teams that failed to win each year therefore considered its season to have ended in failure. As in baseball, with its individual statistical achievements, and college football, with its annual "rivalry" games, the tournament offered ways for the teams taking part to achieve success even without winning the final game.

A comparison with a marathon race is illuminating, for such a race usually has three categories of runners: those for whom simply finishing is a major achievement; those who have already completed marathons and are seeking to do so more quickly than they have in the past; and those who aim to be the first to cross the finish line. Similarly, the NCAA tournament offers three different goals, appropriate to teams with different levels of skills. For some, the weakest—small schools with modest basketball programs whose games never appear on ESPN—simply earning an invitation to what came to be known as the "Big Dance" counted as a notable achievement. For others, winning a game or two surpassed the expectations generally held for them and made the tournament a successful experience. The most powerful teams aspired to win the four games necessary to become one of the Final Four and then the two additional games needed to secure the championship.

Professional basketball also prospered in the 1980s and 1990s, in no small part due to the efforts of David Stern, who became commissioner of the NBA in 1984, having joined the league as its counsel in 1978. Like Kenesaw Mountain Landis, the first commissioner of baseball who paved the way for its emergence as the nation's favorite sport by guaranteeing the game's integrity, and Pete Rozelle, who launched football into its era of supreme popularity by presiding over a relationship with television that enriched the NFL's teams while maintaining a competitive balance among them, Stern helped to inaugurate basketball's golden age. He did so by recognizing the relevance for the sport of, and then capitalizing on, two broad social trends: globalization, and the promotion of individual stars.

In the last two decades of the twentieth century, the age-old but often very slow process of worldwide economic integration accelerated. As part of this trend, professional basketball began to export its product, telecasting games more and more widely. In 1996 the championship series was broadcast to 175 countries in two dozen languages. By the year 2002, the league's all-star game reached 210 different countries in forty-one languages.[95] In some of these countries the championship series drew an even higher percentage of the total television audience than it did in the United States.[96] Merchandise bearing the logos of NBA teams—basketballs, articles of clothing, caps, key chains, and the like—could be found not only in the United States, where the league opened a store on one of the nation's most famous commercial streets, Fifth Avenue in Manhattan, but all over the world as well. Forty percent of those gaining access to the official NBA Internet Web site did so from outside the United States.[97]

While exporting its games through television, the NBA began to import some of its players. In 1983–1984 it had only eight players from seven countries outside the United States. By 2003, sixty-eight players from thirty-six different countries had earned places on NBA rosters.[98] Major league baseball had, by percentage, a heavier representation of players from outside North America—close to 25 percent as compared with 15[99]—but almost all came from Latin America and the majority of these from Central America. (Beginning in the 1990s a few Japanese and Koreans came to North America to play professional baseball.) The NBA had a more diverse international representation. Most of the non-American players came from Europe—east, west, and south—but Mexico, Argentina, Brazil, Turkey, Africa, and China also contributed to the league's teams.

In the process of extending the NBA's reach beyond North America, two landmark events, a decade apart, stand out. In 1992 in Barcelona, Spain, the Olympic basketball competition, which had begun in 1936 in Berlin with Naismith present, admitted professionals for the first time. The United States sent a squad composed of the NBA's best players, nicknamed the "Dream Team," which not only overwhelmed all its opponents but proved to be the most popular attraction at the Olympic Games. The Olympics had a global television audience rivaled only by soccer's World Cup. An estimated 600 million people around the world watched the final game of the competition.[100] In 2002, seven-foot-five-inch Yao Ming from Shanghai joined the Houston Rockets, triggering a dramatic increase in interest in American professional basketball, measured by television coverage and the sale of merchandise, in China. As in other countries, as China grew wealthier the expansion of leisure time created an increased interest in sports, and basketball had the chance to become that country's most popular game.

Basketball's rising popularity came from the intrinsic appeal it shared with soccer—the simplicity of the rules, the fast pace of the game, the grace of the players—in combination with the broader ingredients of globalization. In the last two centuries, periods of rapid global economic integration have occurred because of advances in technology and related developments in politics. In the second half of the nineteenth century, for example, the flow of trade and the movement of capital across national borders both increased substantially in volume. What made this possible was the invention and diffusion of the steamship, the railroad, and the telegraph, in conjunction with the expansion of British naval power, economic prowess, and political control, which served to foster and protect commercial activity across much of the planet.

Similarly, at the end of the twentieth century, the globalization of basketball drew on a technical innovation—television broadcasting by satellite, making possible the transmission of games all over the world—and a political event—the collapse of Communism in Europe, which freed players from that part of the world to join the American professional league. The international pool of players that became available made basketball a more intensely competitive and interesting sport—with many non-Americans possessing the skills, especially long-distance shooting, associated with players from Indiana—and the expanding reservoir of overseas spectators brightened the financial prospects of the professional teams.

The NBA's rising popularity both at home and abroad had another source: the emphasis the league placed on promoting its best players. Basketball became a game of stars.[101]

In every team sport some players are better than others and the best receive disproportionate attention. But basketball has a more pronounced tendency than the others to produce stars. It has fewer players, so each one can have a larger overall impact on his or her team's fortunes than players in baseball and football. Unlike the most important baseball and football players—the pitcher and the quarterback—everyone on a basketball team has a major role in both its offensive and defensive efforts (and unlike a pitcher, plays in every game).

A basketball player can be in the middle of the action for a larger proportion of the game and, while his or her individual contribution to the outcome cannot be isolated and assessed with the same precision that baseball permits, he or she can have, or at least can seem to have, a greater effect on the outcome than a baseball or football player.

Stars emerge more readily from basketball, as well,

because it is a more intimate game than the other two. Most of the spectators sit close to the players, whom they can see more clearly because basketball uniforms—shorts and a jersey—do not envelop them as baseball and football uniforms and headgear do. This makes it easier to read the players' emotions on the court during the course of a game and thus get a sense of their distinctive personalities. Fans identify more readily with basketball players because they feel they know the athletes better than they do those in the other two team sports.

The NBA's strategy of building up its best players in the eyes of the public also stemmed from David Stern's recognition that basketball, as a consumer product, had to compete with other forms of mass entertainment. He also recognized that well-known brands have an advantage in commercial competition. In baseball and football the team is the brand. The way basketball is played made it possible to adopt a different marketing strategy and assign that role to individual players. This is what professional basketball did in the 1980s and 1990s. In that period, by far its most popular brand, the most celebrated basketball player in the history of the game and one of the most famous athletes—probably, indeed, one of the most famous human beings—in the history of the world was Michael Jordan.

Jordan first came to national attention as a six-foot-five-inch college freshman in 1982, when he made a last-second shot to win the championship game of the NCAA tournament for the University of North Carolina.[102] In the 1984–1985 season he moved from North Carolina to the Chicago Bulls of the NBA, where his career followed a pattern worthy of the heroes of epic literature: an arduous rise to the peak of success, a steep fall from grace, and then a recovery and a scaling of the heights of basketball for yet a second time.

Jordan established himself almost immediately as the most potent offensive player in all of professional basketball, but during his first six years in the NBA his teams did not manage to win the championship. The Bulls' chief rivals, the Detroit Pistons, paid tribute to his prowess by devising a special system to defend against him that became known as the "Jordan rules." Then he achieved a breakthrough, winning three consecutive league titles between 1992 and 1994. There followed the fall. An association with gamblers with criminal connections came to light, his father was brutally murdered in a robbery, and he quit basketball for a career in professional baseball but failed in his efforts to reach the major leagues. Giving up baseball, he returned to the Bulls and led them to three more consecutive championships before retiring for a second time following the 1997–1998 season.[103]

Jordan's popularity rested above all on his triumphs on the court. No professional team since Bill Russell's Celtics had compiled a better record—six titles in eight years. (The Bulls played without Jordan for all of the first non-winning year and most of the second.) And while Russell's contributions, immense though they were, were subtle, Jordan's were obvious. He was the leading scorer, the man with the ball in his hands more often than any other player. Just as important for the renown he achieved was his mesmerizing, balletic style of play, leaping high, soaring toward the basket, and dunking the ball emphatically, a combination of regal self-assurance and Baryshnikov-like aerodynamic grace that earned him the nickname "His Airness."

Like Babe Ruth in the 1920s, Jordan became the most

celebrated athlete of his time, someone whose fame spread beyond the boundaries of his sport and penetrated the wider culture.[104] A distinguished historian, Walter LaFeber, and an eminent journalist, David Halberstam, both well known for their works on history, politics, and economics, each wrote a book about Michael Jordan that used his career to shed light on wider subjects.[105]

The television ratings for NBA games testified to Jordan's popularity and its effect on the viewing habits of the American public. In 1993, when his team won its third title, the audience for the championship series exceeded the one attracted that year by baseball's much older and better established World Series, a development that would have been unthinkable a decade earlier. The next year, when he was not playing in it, the ratings for the championship series of the playoffs fell by a third: almost ten million fewer people watched. But when Jordan returned to basketball at the tail end of the regular season in 1995 his first game earned the highest ratings achieved by any basketball game on the NBC network over the previous five years.[106] During the first year of his return, the cable television station TBS found that games in which his Bulls played attracted 50 percent more viewers than games in which they did not.[107]

Further evidence of Jordan's popularity came from the range of commercial products to which, like Babe Ruth before him, he lent his name: men's cologne, cereal, sunglasses, and long-distance telephone service, to name only some of them. His endorsements, combined with his basketball salary, made him an extremely wealthy man. In 1997, he earned an estimated $100 million.[108] His feats on the basketball court made others rich as well. In 1984, when he joined the team, the Chicago Bulls had an estimated value of $18.7

million. By 1997 it had reached $190 million.[109] In the summer of 1998 *Fortune* magazine estimated the total income that Michael Jordan had had a major part in generating for basketball and the companies whose products he endorsed at $10 billion.[110]

Jordan's Midas touch stemmed from a celebrity that went far beyond the borders of the United States. Like Babe Ruth, he was routinely mobbed by adoring fans at the hotels at which he stayed, but for Jordan these hotels were located not only in Los Angeles and New York but also in Paris.[111] LaFeber records the experience of a young American in China in 1997:

> While stranded by winter weather in west Sichuan, a long fifteen hundred miles from Beijing, he encountered a group of Tibetans bound for their capital, Lhasa. The Tibetans ... had never strayed far from their native village. They had apparently not seen anything like his camera. As they shared with him bites of meat from the raw, bloody rib cage of an unspecified animal, retrieved from their rucksacks, the group began to discuss things American. Just how, one of the Tibetans asked the young American, was Michael Jordan doing?[112]

At the height of his career Jordan was described in ways that made liberal use of superlatives: "The greatest ever to play" basketball;[113] "the greatest athlete ... in any sport;"[114] and the ultimate accolade, "Michael Jordan plays basketball better than anyone else in the world does anything else."[115] One of the earliest, most arresting, and perhaps most flattering of these tributes came from Larry Bird. In Jordan's second professional season, 1985–1986, a broken bone in his foot kept him out of action for most of his team's games but he insisted on returning to play at the end of the season and helped the Bulls win enough games to qualify for the playoffs against the mighty Celtics, then on their way to another championship. In the second game of the series, in Boston, Jordan put on a remarkable individual display, scoring sixty-three points in a game that extended to two overtime periods before the Celtics finally won. Afterwards Bird said of his rival's performance, "That was God disguised as Michael Jordan."

No other single person made as large a contribution to basketball in its golden age and no other player had a statue of himself erected outside the arena at which he played his home games. Yet Jordan's performances on the court also contributed to the emergence of a contradiction in basketball similar to those that beset the other two major American team sports.

At the end of the twentieth century the conflict in basketball was between the teamwork that, as a continuous-collective game, it fostered, on the one hand, and its increasing emphasis on individual virtuosity on the other. The quintessential team game become the one most conspicuously featuring individualism, which trends both on and off the court during the sport's golden age encouraged.

Not the least of these trends was the prominence of Michael Jordan himself. The most widely noticed individual statistic in basketball is scoring. Jordan led the league in scoring ten times. By contrast, in none of the Boston Celtics' championship seasons was a member of that team the scoring champion.[116] Jordan's approach to the game emphasized individualism. Although he came from a medium-sized southern city (Wilmington, North Carolina) not a northern metropolis, from a middle class rather than from an impoverished background, although he became an accurate middle-range shooter, and although he had learned to be an effective team player on offense and a skilled defender as well under the tutelage of coach Dean Smith at North Carolina, Michael Jordan embodied the playground style, with its stream of moves designed to gain position for a close-in shot or a dunk.

He was not a selfish player. His tactics optimized his team's chances of winning. And other teams imitated them. It became standard practice for four players to go to one side of the court on offense and stand idle, thereby "clearing out" the other side for the most skillful scorer to maneuver by himself, without any participation by his teammates, for a shot. Spontaneous coordination among all five team members dwindled in importance.[117]

ESPN's nightly sports news program, *SportsCenter*, routinely showed the most spectacular individual scoring plays, especially dunks, demonstrating to players and fans alike that this style offered the royal road to celebrity.[118]

During basketball's golden age players' salaries rose sharply. The highest salaries went to the biggest stars, and the biggest stars were the highest and most flamboyant scorers.[119] In Bill Russell's era, Red Auerbach promised the Celtic players that he would never cite individual statistics in salary negotiations with them. To be sure, the circumstances prevailing then disfavored the players. Salaries were modest and most of the leverage in the negotiations belonged to management. Still, Auerbach was able to foster team harmony, and thereby reinforce the conditions conducive to effective spontaneous coordination, by rewarding defensive skills, rebounding, and other underappreciated or unmeasurable facets of the game. By the Jordan era a player's salary, which was negotiated by his agent rather than by the player himself, depended far more on his individual achievements, and this, combined with the huge increases in the amounts of money available, led to immense disparities in salaries within teams. The highest paid player could earn fifty or more times the salary of the lowest paid. Cooperation becomes difficult among people so radically unequal in a category so important to all of them.

One particular development during the sport's golden age symbolized the rise of individualism: the importance of basketball shoes. These became for basketball what caps were for baseball and jackets for football: an article of clothing closely identified with the sport that those who followed it were fond of wearing. While baseball caps and football jackets bore the names of teams, however, basketball shoes were identified with individual players, with Nike's "Air Jordan" model becoming, not surprisingly, the most popular brand of all.[120]

The original name for the kind of footgear basketball players wear comes from the first sport for which they were worn and in which the best competitors were first paid by particular companies to wear their products: tennis shoes. When Michael Jordan signed his first contract with Nike, which called for a shoe bearing his name, the general manager of the Bulls accused his agent of "turning him into a tennis player."[121] It was a shrewd observation and it underscored a wider pattern, one that brought team sports back to the beginnings of human competition.

For most of recorded history the formally organized, systematically recorded, and extensively watched games were all individual contests such as tennis. As an organized activity, team sports barely existed. That changed over the course of the twentieth century, as first baseball, then football, and finally basketball embedded themselves at the center of American popular culture. But by the end of that century American sports had come full circle. The most team-like of the three, because the one giving greatest emphasis to spontaneous coordination—that is, teamwork—was increasingly devoted, like tennis and the other popular pre-twentieth-century competitions, to the performance not of several people working together but to a single person performing alone: not, that is, to the team, but to the individual.

Conclusion: The Future of Sports

The twentieth century in the United States was the sports century. Over its course baseball, football, and basketball were transformed from minor pastimes to major national institutions. What does the twenty-first century hold in store for them?

It is unlikely that any will disappear entirely. But it is possible that baseball, football, and basketball will become less important. This would not be an unprecedented development. In the course of the twentieth century the novel, boxing, and live theater all lost some of the cultural cachet they had once enjoyed. And at the outset of the twenty-first century each of the three major team sports confronted its own particular set of challenges.

Of the three, the problems facing baseball were the most

serious. Baseball had lost its one-time position as the only team sport with national popularity. The world of tradition that baseball evokes, already passing at the dawn of the twentieth century, had receded even farther into the historical distance by the beginning of the twenty-first. The impression the sport conveys, and on which its appeal partly rests, of a timeless rural world means that any change, even if it is necessary for baseball's popularity and prosperity, is bound to seem disruptive and unwarranted. And the game's leisurely pace, which is in keeping with the rhythm of the traditional world, was at odds with the more frenetic rhythm of life and norms of entertainment to which citizens of the twenty-first century are accustomed.

At the grass-roots level, as well as at the professional one, signs of ill health in baseball were visible as the new millennium began. Fewer American teenagers were devoting their summers to playing the game. In part this was due to the multiplication of other organized activities available during the long holiday from school. But it was due as well to the attractions of other sports: By some accounts more young American males were participating in soccer than in baseball. At the same time, the audience for major league baseball was significantly older than for the other two major team sports, which did not bode well for its future, and the television ratings for the World Series declined by a total of 50 percent between 1992 and 2002.[1]

The American and National Leagues suffered from competitive imbalance, with some teams having little chance to reach postseason play, let alone to win the World Series. The imbalance stemmed from the uneven distribution of revenues, itself largely the result of geography. Teams that played in the largest metropolitan areas could earn enormous sums from the sale of the rights to televise their games. Small market teams could not.[2] Baseball had become an example not of meritocracy but of plutocracy.* By its own account the financial position of major league baseball was a dismal one. In 2001 the major league commissioner tried to eliminate two teams, and the following year the Montreal Expos franchise went into a kind of receivership and was taken over by the league itself.

Still, baseball was not necessarily destined to be, like the phonograph or the dial telephone, something that flourished in the twentieth century but disappeared in the twenty-first. Along with its problems, the oldest of the three major American team sports had reserves of strength and staying power. The total annual attendance for all professional baseball games far exceeded those for football and basketball. To be sure, this was a function of the fact that there were more leagues, teams, and games in baseball than in the other two but it was still a sign of vitality. And four times as many baseball as football cards were sold annually.[3] Moreover, baseball had been coping with some of its problems—competition from other sports, the conflict between the promise of changelessness and the need for change—for half a century. Indeed, baseball had found a way to take advantage of its association with the past by building new, comfortable, technologically up-to-date parks that nonetheless, by their design, gave spectators a sense of having traveled back in time to an earlier period in American history.

---

* By some measures professional basketball was competitively less evenly balanced than baseball. But because all NBA teams operated under a salary cap, the imbalance stemmed from differing levels of skill in choosing players (as well as luck in having the opportunity, through the draft, to choose them) and so did not offend the spirit of merit-based competition, as baseball did. Andrew Zimbalist, *May The Best Team Win: Baseball Economics and Public Policy* (Washington, D.C.: Brookings Institution Press, 2003), p. 39.

The game's emphasis on individual achievement gave it a permanent and effective method for producing heroic figures, whose deeds, because of the importance of statistics in baseball, can be precisely measured and attributed to one individual. Baseball also had become, by the dawn of the twenty-first century, the sport with the greatest representation of players from Latin America. Since Hispanics comprise the fastest-growing group in the population of the United States, they could serve as an expanding reservoir not only of baseball players and but also of baseball fans.[4]

As for the finances of the major leagues, although a number of teams were clearly in economic distress, it was also true that between 1995 and 2001 total revenues had grown at an average annual rate of 17 percent. The gloomy picture of its economic health that the baseball authorities presented seemed intended to exaggerate the sport's difficulties through the use of techniques of creative—and deceptive—accounting. The reports of baseball's imminent financial collapse—which came from organized baseball itself—were greatly exaggerated.

At the end of the twentieth century, football's vital signs were healthier than were baseball's. The professional teams turned annual profits, or at least broke even, the value of the franchises increased steadily, and the seats for almost every game were filled. Major college teams also played before crowds as large as 100,000 and, like their professional counterparts, received high fees for the rights to televise their games. Except for the smallest of them, which lacked the necessary manpower, high schools around the country fielded football teams and in some places, notably Pennsylvania, Ohio, and Texas, the teams' Friday night games were as important to the life of the community as was high school basketball in Indiana.

Football did, however, have an Achilles heel: the growing social aversion to the essence of the game—violence. The declining tolerance for violence in the last decades of the twentieth century coincided with, and was probably linked to, the rise in the status of women. Women are less likely than men to engage in violent behavior but are just as likely to be the victims of violence. Tellingly, of the three major American team sports, football is the only one that lacks a version widely played by girls and women. Women's basketball operates under the same rules as the men's game, and women's softball, an increasingly popular game at the outset of the twenty-first century, is similar, although not identical, to baseball.

The second half of the twentieth century witnessed a sharp decline in the standing of the most organized and historically the most socially legitimate form of violence: warfare. In the early years of that century President Theodore Roosevelt routinely praised war as an activity drawing on and stimulating admirable individual and social qualities. No twenty-first-century American president would speak as enthusiastically about war as he did.[5]

Yet in early-twenty-first-century America violence, while the object of widespread and mounting disapproval, had scarcely disappeared. People still paid to see it in Hollywood-made films. The United States continued, however reluctantly, to wage wars and the men and women who did the fighting continued to be honored by their fellow citizens.

Moreover, the decreasing acceptability of violence of all kinds—organized and spontaneous, domestic and international—might actually serve to enhance the popularity of football, which stands out as a legitimate outlet for conduct that, however discredited it has become, has been found in virtually all human societies at almost every stage of human history. The football field has the potential to be in the twenty-first century what the zoo became in the twentieth: a place where something once common but now rare is on display.

The philosopher and psychologist William James called, at the beginning of the twentieth century, for the development of a "moral equivalent of war," by which he meant an enterprise that incorporated the desirable features of armed conflict, such as courage, discipline, and camaraderie, without the destruction that war brings. At the outset of the next century, football could be seen as a candidate to fulfill his prescription.

Like the two older team sports, basketball confronted, as the new millennium began, its own internal contradiction, between the teamwork that the rules of the game foster, on the one hand, and the increasing tendency toward a style of play that emphasizes individual virtuosity on the other. The rise of individualism in basketball diminished what is distinctive about the game and tied the commercial fortunes of professional basketball to a handful of outstanding players, whose retirements therefore adversely affected its popularity.

Like baseball and football, however, basketball possessed some impressive sources of vitality. The college version of the sport, in some ways more popular than the professional game, depended less on individual stars. Nor did the tendency of the most promising high school players to skip college altogether and move directly to the professional ranks noticeably reduce national interest in college basketball, and especially in its March championship tournament.

Moreover, basketball had some advantages that the other two sports lacked. Unlike football, it had a considerable appeal beyond the borders of the United States. Unlike base-ball, the character of the game was in tune with the salient features of the post-industrial world of the twenty-first cen-tury. And it was accessible to the female half of the popula-tion in a way that baseball and football were not. Women had the same opportunities as men to play basketball.

As well as their individual difficulties, all three team sports confronted a common challenge stemming from a major change in the way the mass media, especially newspa-pers, presented sports and sports figures to the public. The range of subjects on which it was considered legitimate to report broadened considerably to include the conduct of ath-letes outside the arenas in which they played, and that con-duct often did not reflect well on them.

Indeed, so badly did some baseball, football, and basket-ball players turn out to behave in their personal lives that parts of the sports pages came to resemble the police blotter. Reports of athletes charged with, and often convicted of, shoplifting, drunk driving, abusive conduct toward women, the possession of illegal narcotics and firearms, fraud, and the failure to pay child support became routine.[6] Nor was the misconduct that the press recounted confined to these crimes. It included as well rape, spousal abuse, assault, armed robbery, and even murder.[7]

The change in the media's treatment of the off-the-field lives of athletes followed the same pattern as the coverage of political figures, where the practice of discretion also gave way to full disclosure. It began with the publication, in 1970, of the book *Ball Four*[8] by Jim Bouton, a major league pitcher who revealed unflattering personal details about his team-mates on the New York Yankees earlier in his career. The commissioner of baseball tried to persuade the author to recant what he had written but Bouton refused,[9] and thereafter the private lives of athletes, about which sportswriters had known but never conveyed to the public, ceased to be off limits for publication and broadcasting.[10]

Whether the baseball, football, and basketball players of the last decade of the twentieth century engaged in embarrassing, disreputable, and illegal conduct more often than their counterparts in the earlier years of the century was difficult to say. The early baseball players were certainly not all paragons of virtue. But the frequency with which episodes of misconduct came to public attention in the later period made it seem that sports was less an escape from the troubles of American society than a mirror of them. Members of the Portland Trail Blazers professional basketball team had so many encounters with law enforcement authorities that the local press took to referring to them as the "Jail Blazers."[11]

Yet the exposure of what sometimes seemed to be an epidemic of misconduct did not appear to decrease the popularity of any of the three team sports. Nor did it interfere with one of the offshoots of sports: the production of heroes.[12] Successful athletes continued to be paid to testify to the virtues of consumer products, although the revelation of an adverse encounter with the law seldom proved helpful in obtaining or retaining endorsement contracts: The Hertz car rental company decided that it could dispense with O. J. Simpson's services after he was indicted for murder.[13]

The public evidently felt capable of distinguishing between those athletes who were worthy of admiration and those who, by virtue of crimes, misdemeanors, or generally obnoxious conduct, were not. It also apparently felt comfortable with the distinction between what these men did as baseball, football, and basketball players, which was of general interest, and how they behaved out of uniform, which ordinarily was not. Athletes served as models for those virtues that they exhibited while playing, and not for others. To make the point in a different context, Picasso was neither an admirable husband nor a model father but this did not diminish the public admiration for or the financial value of his art.

The popularity, and thus the cultural prominence, of baseball, football, and basketball faced another challenge at the outset of the twenty-first century from something distinctly new: chemical compounds, particularly steroids, taken by athletes to increase their size, strength, speed, and endurance.

Each of the three professional leagues compiled a list of proscribed performance-enhancing drugs, each designed a system for detecting the use of these forbidden substances by players, and each imposed penalties on those caught using them.[14] Because scientific research is likely to continue to generate new performance-enhancing drugs, however, and because the incentives for superior performances by athletes will surely remain formidable, baseball, football, and basketball in the twenty-first century are destined to inspire an ongoing competition between the development of new chemical compounds and ever more sophisticated techniques for concealing their use on the one hand and progress in devising tests for detecting them on the other.

The use, or the public perception of the widespread use, of such drugs in team sports risks depriving athletes of one of the sources of their appeal: their authenticity. Such a perception would undermine the spectators' confidence that the players are in fact responsible for doing, unaided, what they appear to be doing. The players would risk falling into the same category as movie actors whose most difficult on-screen feats are usually performed by others. The games might cease to be regarded as tests of the athletes' own will and skill and come to be seen as contests in which victory goes to the team with the most ingenious pharmacologist.

With its emphasis on individual achievements, baseball is particularly vulnerable to such a loss of credibility. Just as a home run hit with an artificially fortified bat—with cork inserted into its center—is disallowed, so a home run record achieved by an artificially fortified batter might well seem equally illegitimate. And in fact Mark McGwire and Barry Bonds, the two players who broke the single-season home run record in 1998 and 2001, were each suspected of steroid use.[15] Yet like the reports of individual misconduct, the revelations about athletes' use of performance-enhancing drugs did not noticeably reduce the popularity of baseball, football, or basketball, perhaps because so many Americans themselves relied upon medications in their daily lives.

Team sports' prospects for remaining important in the national life of the United States in the twenty-first century are bright not only because the two general threats to their popularity—the players' off-the-field misconduct and their use of drugs to improve performance on it—have not disenchanted the public, but also because the features of American society that have made them popular seem likely to persist well into the future.

In a world in which knowledge plays an ever-greater economic role, schooling will remain important, and schools will need outlets for the high levels of energy that students bring to them. Team sports are likely to continue to serve as such outlets, which will mean that virtually every American will be introduced to baseball, football, and basketball at an early age, and many will surely develop attachments to the games that will last a lifetime.

After leaving school twenty-first-century Americans will continue to find employment on farms and in factories, office buildings, and work sites scattered around the country and the world that are linked together by computers to form virtual offices. This will perpetuate the traditional, industrial, and post-industrial conditions that baseball, football, and basketball respectively evoke. Since fewer people will work on farms and in factories, and more in offices, the number of Americans who will earn their living through physical, as distinct from mental, exertion will continue to decrease. This will make baseball, basketball, and football players, who belong to the dwindling cadre of physical laborers, ever more unusual, interesting, and to many, heroic.

The work that Americans will do, chiefly in offices, in the twenty-first century will be increasingly specialized, and they will work as part of collective efforts involving large and far-flung networks of people. Such work depends for its success on the existence of impersonal, universally applied rules and the extensive practice of cooperation; this will sustain the cultural resonance of baseball, football, and basketball, which embody both.

Both within and outside the workplace twenty-first-century Americans, like all peoples at all times, will find themselves buffeted by incomprehensible forces and events. Like their forbears they will sometimes experience life as arbitrary and capricious. This, too, will perpetuate one of the social functions of team sports, which provide not an explanation of life's vicissitudes but rather an escape from them, an island of coherence and transparency in a world that is often confusing and opaque.

Assuming that the pattern of the past century prevails, Americans can expect to become increasingly affluent and thus have more leisure time. This in turn will expand the demand, which team sports help to fill, for entertainment. Under these circumstances it is also to be expected that other forms of entertainment will compete with sports to satisfy this demand. In the face of such competition in the last century, baseball, football, and basketball displayed the capacity to adapt in ways that sustained their popularity.

Each of the three changed its rules to encourage higher scoring, in order to make the games more compelling spectacles. And they all capitalized on one of the century's most conspicuous technological trends: the development of new forms of communication. The advent of mass-circulation newspapers, magazines, radio, television—both through the airwaves and via cable—and the Internet all broadened the appeal of team sports. At the outset of the twenty-first century these two patterns of adaptation were still in evidence. The combination of computer technology with the hand-eye coordination required by the game of pinball produced a new and extremely popular form of recreation, video games,[16] among the most popular of which were ones that simulated baseball, football, and basketball.

In the twenty-first century, finally, the United States will continue to be a nation composed of people of different races, practicing different religions, who have come, or whose ancestors came, from different countries. In the future as in the past, America's diversity will create the need for methods of promoting social solidarity, of which team sports provide three in particular. College teams and professional franchises are sources of local patriotism, serving as focal points of loyalty on the part of local residents of different occupations and

backgrounds. The three sports' major championships are festivals in which the whole country takes part. By the end of the
twentieth century the most popular of them, the Super Bowl,
had become, according to one close observer of communal
activities, "the best ritual we have in the United States.... It's
the one thing that everyone watches, and everyone knows
everyone else is watching. It's a forum. It's a common knowledge generator."[17] And the most successful teams, groups
selected purely on merit and drawn from different regions,
different age groups (when the coaches are included), and different ethnic and racial backgrounds who cooperate for the
successful achievement of a common goal, symbolize one of
the highest American social ideals, which is expressed in the
national motto *e pluribus unum*.

What, therefore, does the twenty-first century hold for
American team sports? "Never make predictions," Yogi
Berra once cautioned, "especially about the future." Fore-
casts about the world at the beginning of the twenty-second
century would seem to be especially hazardous, for the present century is likely to see sweeping and rapid transforma-
tions, many of them unexpected. Yet it does seem as safe as it
is possible to be in such matters to assert that at the end of
the twenty-first century, for all the changes that will
undoubtedly have taken place, the United States will continue to be a country in which the three team sports thrive
and Americans will continue to be a people for whom baseball, football, and basketball are a source of complex, rich,
and intensely felt meaning.

Epilogue to the
Paperback Edition

In the last quarter of the year 2004, four events in the world of sports captured the attention of the American public as a whole. They spilled over from the sports pages of the nation's newspapers, which are devoted to the results of the games people play and watch, and into the news sections, which are reserved for matters of wider interest. In addition to their wider social significance, each of the four—the results of the baseball World Series, a scandal involving the use of performance-enhancing drugs, a controversy about the method for determining the champion of college football, and a fight at a professional basketball game—showed the ongoing relevance of the histories and cultural meanings of baseball, football, and basketball.

The Quest

The victory of the Boston Red Sox in the 2004 World Series was noteworthy for the way it was achieved; it featured both individual and team heroics.

The team's star pitcher, Curt Schilling, tore a tendon in his ankle, which a surgeon stapled in place between games to enable him to play. It came loose during two games, causing blood to ooze from the wound and turning his white baseball sock a bright red. Schilling persevered, and won both games.

The team as a whole performed an epic feat in the League Championship Series against the New York Yankees, losing the first three games and then rallying to win four in a row. In the more than one hundred years that the baseball championship had been held, no team had ever recovered from a deficit of three games to win four; indeed none had rallied from such a deficit to win even three. What the Red Sox did was therefore not only heroic, it was unprecedented. On the morning after they had vanquished the Yankees, *The New York Daily News* ran an appropriate headline: "Hell Freezes Over."

The fact that it was the Boston team that won the World Series in 2004 had a larger significance, which stemmed from the importance to baseball of its own past. As readers of this book will know, it is the sport most tied to the past and most conscious of its own history; and in that history the failure of the Red Sox to win the championship was, until October, 2004, one of the longest-running and best-known stories. Their most recent triumph had come in 1918, a moment so far in the past that people who could actually remember it were almost as rare as veterans of World War I, which ended a few weeks later, on November 11, 1918.

The two Chicago baseball teams, the White Sox and the Cubs, had experienced longer championship droughts, 87 and 94 years respectively, but unlike them the Red Sox had come agonizingly close to this goal on several occasions only to fall short. In 1946, 1967, 1975, and 1986, they reached the seventh and deciding game of the World Series but lost it each time. The triumph in 2004 therefore had an epic quality: it was tantamount to the fulfillment, after decades of frustration and disappointment, of a quest.

All observers of baseball experienced a measure of satisfaction at the Red Sox victory, but the emotions of their legions of fans were considerably stronger than that.[1] The feeling of its fans for this particular team are the strongest in all of professional sports.[2] A passionate attachment to the Red Sox is woven into the fabric of life throughout New England. It has been passed from one generation to the next. Generations of Red Sox fans harbored the hope of living long enough to see them win the World Series. When this finally happened, descendants of people who had died before their hope could be realized marked the occasion by placing team memorabilia on their relatives' grave sites.[3] The extraordinary connection the people of New England feel to their baseball team has its roots in three features of the game and the region.

First, the association of baseball with history has a particular resonance in New England because the region has so much history, and the people living there are more aware of it than is the case anywhere else in the United States. Second, the saga of the Red Sox embodies one of the principal themes in the history of the region and its largest city: the rivalry with New York. Bostonians call their city "the hub of the universe"—shortened to "the hub" for newspaper headlines—and if not the universe it certainly counted as the economic and cultural capital of the United States in the early decades of the republic, only to lose that distinction to the seaport the Dutch had founded 215 miles to the south.

Similarly, the Red Sox' most bitter disappointments came at the hands of teams from New York. In 1978 they lost a one-game playoff to the Yankees for the American League eastern division championship on a home run by the previously undistinguished New York shortstop, into whose name the Red Sox faithful, as a sign of their disgust and dismay, forever after inserted an obscene gerund: Bucky ("Bleeping") Dent. In 1986 the Red Sox lost a World Series they had seemed poised to win when their first baseman, Bill Buckner, allowed an easily catchable ground ball to trickle through his legs.[4] And in the League Championship Series the year before Boston staged its remarkable comeback, the Yankees won the seventh and deciding game on an extra-inning home run by another infielder of modest batting achievements, Aaron Boone.

The team's long decades of affliction began, of course, in 1919 with the sale of its star player, Babe Ruth, to the same Yankees, inaugurating the 86-year period in which the Yankees won 27 world championships and the Red Sox none. Some Boston supporters came to believe that a malign spell had been cast on the team as punishment for this terrible error: the 2004 victory finally lifted the "curse of the Bambino."[5]

A third reason for the deep attachment of the people of New England to their baseball team is the weather. The region has harsh winters, during which its residents naturally look forward to the spring. The symbol of spring and the herald of summer is the beginning of the baseball season.

Baseball, and the Red Sox, are associated in the New England mind with deliverance from cold, snow, and ice.

The 2004 World Series marked the end of the team's long quest but not of the sentiment that had grown up around it. Because their fans' loyalty had such a broad and deep basis, the achievement of the goal for which so many had hoped for so long was not likely to weaken the grip of the Red Sox on the affections of the people of New England. The bond between the team and its fans that the long years of failure had nurtured was strong enough to survive anything—even success.

The Scandal

If the high point of the 2004 baseball season came with the Red Sox' World Series victory, the low moment occurred several weeks later when leaked testimony from a grand jury investigating the illegal distribution of performance-enhancing drugs, including steroids, revealed that three notable Major League players, Jason Giambi, Gary Sheffield and Barry Bonds, had used such substances. (Sheffield and Bonds denied, implausibly, knowing that what they had used were steroids.)

The news did not come as a complete surprise. Rumors of steroid use had shadowed baseball for several years. One player, Ken Caminiti, had publicly admitted using them and had asserted that many others did as well. When setting a single-season record for home runs by hitting 70 in 1998, Mark McGwire had regularly ingested a steroid-like compound, which was not, at the time, prohibited in baseball. And suspicions of steroid use had been raised by dramatic changes over the years in the physical appearances of some players, including Bonds, who had become stockier and more muscular than a regular regimen of weight-lifting alone would normally have produced.[6]

Still, the confirmation of those suspicions did come as something of a shock and undercut one of the fundamental appeals of all sports, not only baseball: their authenticity.[7] Unlike actors in a scripted drama, especially on film, athletes really do what spectators see them do. John Wayne was not a war hero (let alone a cowboy in the Old West) and Arnold Schwarzenegger did not in fact perform the feats that audiences saw him carry out on the screen in the "Terminator" movies. But Barry Bonds actually did hit 73 home runs in the 2001 baseball season, surpassing McGwire's total of three years before, and seemed to do it solely on the basis of his own skill, strength, reflexes, and guile. The news that he had employed performance-enhancing drugs to help him at bat made his achievement seem less authentic. Steroids were the equivalent of the stunt doubles and camera tricks that made Wayne and Schwarzenegger appear heroic.

Steroid use called into question not only one of the reasons for the popularity of all sports, but a distinctive feature of baseball as well: its individual records. The importance of these records stems from two defining characteristics of the sport. It is, more than football or basketball, the individual's game in that responsibility for everything that happens on the field can be assigned to one player alone. In addition, baseball has changed less in the twentieth century than the other two, making it sensible to compare the accomplishments of contemporary players with those of their predecessors in a way that it is not for football and basketball.

In the pursuit of a baseball record a twenty-first century player is competing against someone who played in the past, a competition that, because the game has changed so little, can be seen as a fair one. In this light the McGwire and Bonds home run records are tainted because the players whose achievements they surpassed—Roger Maris, who hit 61 in 1961, and Babe Ruth, who hit 60 in 1927—did not avail themselves of chemical supplements to improve their performances. Bonds' pursuit of Henry Aaron's record for total home runs over the course of a career, 755, seemed similarly unfair.[8]

When Roger Maris surpassed Babe Ruth's single season home run total in a season that was eight games longer—162 to 154—than Ruth's had been, it was suggested that his feat be entered into baseball's official record book accompanied by an asterisk, to denote the different circumstances in which it had been accomplished.[9] Whether Bonds' achievements will be listed in a way that indicates that they are tainted, or eliminated altogether, remains to be decided,[10] but he himself suffered a fall from grace that brought to mind the fate of a star of an earlier era, Joseph "Shoeless Joe" Jackson. Like Bonds a superior left-handed batter, Jackson was caught up in the scheme of several of his Chicago White Sox teammates to fix the 1919 World Series by losing deliberately to the opposing Cincinnati Reds.[11] The news of his involvement inspired a comment from a young fan that entered the lexicon of American speech as a statement of pained disillusion: "Say it ain't so, Joe."

Jackson was banned from baseball for life. Bonds did not face so severe a sanction because his transgression was less serious. He had committed what qualifies in sports as a venial sin: cheating to win. Jackson, by contrast, through his association with a misdeed that violates the basic premise of all sports—that they are spontaneous performances in which the competitors are trying to produce a different, indeed, the opposite outcome—was implicated in the equivalent of a mortal sin: cheating to lose.

THE CONTROVERSY

At the end of 2004 college football experienced a controversy over the system for determining the national champion known as the Bowl Championship Series, or BCS. The system designated the two best of the 117 teams in Division I-A, composed of the schools playing football at the highest level, which then played each other for the championship. The University of Southern California (USC), located in Los Angeles, and the University of Oklahoma in Norman, each of which had completed its season without losing a game, were chosen for this game. Left out, however, was Auburn University of Alabama, also undefeated and the champion of the powerful Southeastern Conference, and thus having a strong claim to play in the final game.[12]

Because the formula for determining the finalists involved some computations, a number of critics of the system cited it as an example of the dangers of substituting computers for human judgment. In fact, however, the system, and the problem it created, arose from a conflict, and a compromise, between two powerful forces: principles at the heart of all competitive sports, on the one hand, and the traditions of college football on the other.

All the other major American team sports—professional baseball, college and professional basketball, and the professional version of football—have long had systems for determining a single champion each year. In each one, all teams play a fixed number of games in what is known as the regular season and the most successful of them take part in a post-season tournament that yields a single winner. This conforms to the defining logic of sports: a game is a contest with a clear result decided on the field by two teams competing on equal terms—each has no score at the outset and the rules apply equally to both. As with individual games, so with the sequence of games known as the season: it, too, should produce a clear winner by the same methods.

College football lacked such a system for determining a champion because it was established in the days before commercial air travel and racial integration made it feasible on a national basis. For decades sportswriters and coaches ranked the country's best teams in national polls, and the leading team (or teams: there has always been more than one poll) at the end of the season was proclaimed the national champion.

The category of colleges with less ambitious football programs than the most accomplished ones—known as Division I-AA[13]—does employ the familiar method for determining the best team each year. After the regular season the best sixteen teams are selected and they take part in a tournament in the four weeks between Thanksgiving and Christmas, with the winner of the final game declared the I-AA champion.[14] The Division I-A schools could adopt this method but have not done so because it would conflict with one of the sport's hallowed traditions.

With its initial game having been played in 1874,[15] college football is almost as old as baseball, and although the game itself has changed markedly since its beginnings, over the course of a century and a quarter it has accumulated a number of traditions that have enhanced and solidified its popularity. Perhaps the most powerful of them is the series of long-standing annual rivalries between neighboring schools—Yale and Harvard, Texas and Oklahoma, California and Stanford—that usually come at the end of the season and invariably attract large audiences of students and alumni.[16]

Another tradition, and the one that a genuine playoff would threaten, is the array of year-end bowl games, matching two invited teams that have performed well during the regular season. The oldest of them, the Rose Bowl in Pasadena, California, was first played in 1902. The Sugar Bowl in New Orleans and the Orange Bowl in Miami began in 1935, the Cotton Bowl in Dallas in 1937.

The bowl games became important civic rituals in the cities where they were staged, the centerpiece of New Year's festivities that came to include elaborate (and in several cases nationally televised) parades as well. They became as much a part of the celebration of the New Year as the drinking of eggnog and the singing of "Auld Lang Syne." The older bowls established ties with major football conferences. The Rose Bowl matched the champion of the Pacific Coast against the winner of the Big Ten in the Midwest, the Orange Bowl invited the best team in the Big Eight (later the Big Twelve) from the great plains, the Sugar Bowl played host to the Southeastern Conference champion. It came to be the goal of the football players and coaches of the schools in these conferences to earn a trip to the designated bowl games, and when they did it was an occasion for their supporters to travel to a glamorous and, in the middle of winter, a warm-weather city, to celebrate the New Year. By the 2004 season, moreover, a grand total of 28 bowl games were staged, meaning that 56 teams—almost half of all those playing football in Division I-A—could earn a postseason reward.

The bowl system, as it has evolved, is incompatible with a

genuine playoff in college football. The bowl games could not be played at roughly the same time, and the older ones, if they were incorporated into the playoff structure, could not all be played on or near New Year's Day. The establishment of a playoff system would almost certainly lead to the end of the system of bowl games.

The BCS was devised in 1998 as a compromise between the growing demands for a clear method for determining the best college football team in the country, on the one hand, and the need to preserve the bowl system, with the weight of tradition and the multiple constituencies behind it, on the other. It involves six major conferences and four bowls—the Rose, Orange, and Sugar Bowls and the Fiesta Bowl, played in Tempe, Arizona. A system of assessment that includes the results of several independent polls and computations of the strength of a team's schedule—that is, how strong its opponents are—produces a ranking of the best college teams. The top two play for the national championship in one of the four designated bowl games: the honor of staging the ultimate contest rotates annually among the four. The other three bowls select their teams from among the champions of the participating conferences and the non-champions that rank highest in the BCS ratings.

In the 2004 season the BCS yielded the worst of both worlds. It could not produce an unambiguously deserving national champion because only two teams could play in the championship game and there were three teams plainly worthy of inclusion. In this sense the championship was not decided on the field. Nor, however, did the system serve the interests of tradition.

In 2004 the University of California at Berkeley, an institution noted more for the number of its Nobel laureates than for the prowess of its football team, seemed headed for the Rose Bowl for the first time since the 1958 season—the longest streak of non-participation of any Pacific Coast team. While not the champion of its conference, the Berkeley team won all but one of its games and for almost the entire season stood high enough in the BCS rankings to qualify for the game in Pasadena, maintaining a narrow lead over another once-beaten team, the University of Texas at Austin. In the last week of the season, however, a few sportswriters in one poll, and several coaches in another, changed the way they had voted in previous weeks, putting California lower and Texas higher, to reverse the two schools' BCS positions and send Texas to the Rose Bowl.

The outcome aroused suspicions of favoritism and bad faith in the voting because several of the writers who changed their votes were based in Texas.[17] (The coaches' poll refused to reveal how individual coaches had voted.) By playing in the Rose Bowl, moreover, Texas and its conference, the Big Twelve, earned considerably more money—$4.5 million—than they would otherwise have done, and by being relegated to a less lucrative postseason game California and its conference earned that much less.

Because it fully satisfied no one, as a solution to the problem of determining a college football championship the BCS seemed shaky. The way a similar conflict between the need for a definitive outcome and a long-established feature of football was resolved for individual games suggests the eventual likelihood of a different solution.

For most of football's history tied games were common. If the score was even at the conclusion of sixty minutes of play, the game ended in a tie. Because it violated one of the basic purposes of all sports, however—the determination of a clear winner—this rule caused increasing discontent, and ultimately the college and professional games devised systems for breaking ties—the college system ensuring that no game could end in a tie, the professional version making ties much rarer than before although not impossible. If the same pattern prevails where the outcome of the yearly sequence of games—the season—is concerned, eventually tradition, in this case the bowl games, will give way to a playoff system that will produce an unquestionably worthy national champion.

THE BRAWL

The lowest moment in all of American sports in 2004 occurred on the evening of November 19 at a professional basketball game between the Detroit Pistons and the Indiana Pacers at the Pistons' home arena in a Detroit suburb, when a fight broke out. Fights among players do occur in baseball, football, and basketball games, and in ice hockey are sufficiently common almost to qualify as part of the game. This one, however, differed from routine in-game imbroglios in that it involved players and spectators fighting each other.

Spectator sports share with scripted drama on stage and on screen a convention known as the fourth wall—the invisible barrier that separates the performers from the audience. A playwright or screenwriter will occasionally pierce the fourth wall for dramatic effect by having a character address the audience rather than his or her fellow actors. The brawl in Detroit shattered that barrier completely, which made the episode both startling and troubling.

It began when an Indiana player, Ron Artest, committed a hard foul against a Detroit opponent, Ben Wallace. Wallace shoved Artest and players from each team rushed on to the court in anticipation of further blows between them. While the officials separated the opposing teams, Artest retired to the sidelines and lay down on the long table at which the people keeping official track of the game sit. A spectator then threw a cup of beer at Artest who instantly leaped into the stands to exact revenge. Several of his teammates followed him, and in seconds players were flailing away at fans, and vice-versa, both in the stands and on the court. As a result, the Commissioner of the National Basketball Association, David Stern, suspended five players from their teams for varying lengths of time—Artest was banished for the rest of the season. The local prosecutor filed charges against five Indiana players as well as against five spectators, all of them for misdemeanor assault and battery except one, who had thrown a chair in the melee and was charged with felonious assault.

The brawl provoked angry and rueful commentary about the progressive deterioration of social behavior in American sports and in the wider society as well.[18] This kind of violence was not entirely without precedent. In his storied career as an NBA coach from the late 1940s to the late 1960s, Arnold "Red" Auerbach was involved on four different occasions in altercations with fans that led to lawsuits against him.[19] In even earlier days, in the 1920s, basketball courts were surrounded by mesh fences—cages—partly to keep the ball from flying into the stands but also to separate the spectators from the players.

If not necessarily worse than fights in basketball's previous eras, however, this one became far more notorious because it was shown over and over on television in the days after it occurred. It was repeated so often, on local news programs across the country and on national sports and news channels, that it would have been difficult for anyone in the United States with a television not to become aware of it. By this repetition the fight, like the scream of the unsuccessful candidate Howard Dean after the Iowa presidential caucuses the previous February, became imprinted on the national consciousness. The following day football players for intrastate rivals Clemson and the University of South Carolina got into a fight before their game began and the Clemson coach blamed what happened on the televised pictures of the episode in Detroit, which his players had seen.[20]

The basketball brawl brought to mind the fights that are common at and in connection with soccer matches in Europe, especially in Great Britain, but the motives differed. Soccer violence ordinarily involves fans, not players, and tends to be, in the broadest sense, political. Soccer hooligans fight, in their own minds, on behalf of their teams, their neighborhoods, their cities and, when abroad, their countries—the kinds of collective identities with which politics is concerned. The violence in Detroit had personal motives, which in turn were fostered by several of the features of the way basketball is staged and promoted.

Basketball is played in a more intimate setting than are baseball or football. Games take place indoors: everyone is gathered together in a single large room. Sitting closer to the players than in the other sports, the spectators can see them more clearly and even talk to them. Interaction with the players is therefore easier and violent interaction, if scarcely natural, at least seems more feasible because basketball players are not only closer, they are less forbidding than the athletes in the other two major team sports. Baseball players have at their disposal clubs, in the form of bats, and wear spiked shoes. Football players are clad in a kind of body armor. (Moreover, if a spectator is so angry at a football player as to wish to hit him, he or she need only wait for the next play on the field, when an opposing player will do exactly that.) Basketball players appear vulnerable, by contrast, because they play their game dressed, in effect, in their underwear.

If the opportunities for personal interaction with basketball players are greater than in the other two sports, so, too, are the incentives: basketball encourages—for better and, on that evening in a suburb of Detroit, for worse—a greater sense of personal connection between the fans and individual players. This is so because of the intimacy of the setting in which the game is played and because, since there are only five players on a basketball team, each one is more important and more noticeable than his counterparts playing baseball or football. The felt sense of a personal connection with players stems also from the way that professional basketball chose to market itself beginning in the 1980s, emphasizing not its teams, as did Major League Baseball and the National Football League, but rather its best players.[21]

When Michael Jordan emerged as the league's most spectacular and successful player, and an international celebrity, the NBA made him central to the way it presented itself to the world. While it initially contributed to a sharp rise in the game's popularity, this emphasis became a liability when Jordan retired from competition and it proved difficult to replace him as the sun king of basketball. It also contributed to an esthetically unappealing style of play that favored individual virtuosity over the teamwork that is integral to the game. To the extent that this fixation on individual players also helped to foster not only admiration on the part of fans, but also animosity toward them of the kind that was on display in Detroit, the November 19, 2004 brawl counted as yet a third unanticipated and unwanted consequence of the legacy of basketball's brightest star.

Whatever it may have owed to Michael Jordan, the Detroit brawl, along with the triumph of the Red Sox, the steroid scandal, and the BCS controversy demonstrated the enduring relevance of the nation's most popular team sports to issues and themes beyond the games themselves. They showed that, in addition to entertaining millions of people across the country and beyond its borders, baseball, football, and basketball give expression to values, traditions, hopes and fears that are central to American life.

NOTES

Introduction

1. "What I Don't Know," *The New York Observer*, March 4, 2002, p.15.
2. Quoted in Ved Mehta, *Fly and the Fly-Bottle* (Baltimore: Penguin Books, 1965), p. 135.

CHAPTER I

A Variety of Religious Experience

1. Mike Wise, "The Wild, Wild West, and Basketball Too," *The New York Times*, May 11, 2002, p. B18.
2. Phil Barber, "Super Bowl Commercials," in Bob Carroll, Michael Gershman, David Neft, John Thorn, *Total Football: The Official Encyclopedia of the National Football League* (New York: HarperCollins, 1999), p. 515; Stefan Fatsis, "NBC Sports Maps A Future Without the Big Leagues," *The Wall Street Journal*, January 31, 2003, p. A1.
3. "Chicago Rules," *The Wall Street Journal*, October 3, 2003, p. W15.
4. By one estimate the total amount of money spent in the United States in 1999 on all sports—individual as well as team—was $213 billion, more than twice the size of the American auto industry and seven times the size of the movie industry. Sportsbusinessjournal.com, January 8, 2004.
5. The pattern of participation in team sports has the shape of a pyramid, with primary and secondary schools forming its base. On their numer-

ous fields are played many games, involving many people. As the level of skill rises, the number of players declines. At the summit of professional expertise there are few teams and therefore few players. The number of spectators for these contests follows the reverse pattern: very few at each of the many school-sponsored contests, tens of thousands for each of the games involving the most skilled professionals, with millions more watching at home via television.

6. An association between religion and sports is suggested in Michael Novak, *The Joy of Sports* (New York: Basic Books, 1976), p. xi.

7. On the association of religious ritual and play see Johan Huizinga, *Homo Ludens: A Study of the Play Element in Culture* (Boston: Beacon Press, 1955), especially pp. 20, 31.

8. The terminology of sports underscores this distinction. The opposite of work is play and play is a word closely associated with baseball, basketball, and football. Team members are players; to take part in a game is to play in it.

9. Edgar Allan Poe's story "The Murders in the Rue Morgue," often deemed the father of the mystery story, was published in 1841. Jacques Barzun, "Detection and the Literary Art," in Barzun, editor, *The Delights of Detection* (New York: Criterion Books, 1961), p. 12.

10. Quoted in Novak, op. cit., p. 182.

11. *ESPN The Magazine*, February 4, 2002, p. 36.

12. The main purchasers of these packages are youngsters, who chew the gum and collect and trade the cards with others. In the last decades of the twentieth century old and rare cards, mainly depicting baseball players from the early years of the century, became valuable collectibles and sold for very high prices.

13. The practice is not confined to Christianity. The most sacred object to Muslims in the Indian province of Kashmir is what they believe to be a hair from the beard of the Prophet Mohammad.

14. The process for admission to the National Baseball Hall of Fame bears a resemblance to the procedure for attaining sainthood. A period of five years must pass from the time of retirement in the first case, death in the second, for it to begin. Admission to both select companies is ultimately by election.

15. A scene from the 1930 Marx Brothers movie *Monkey Business* captures this feature of modern life. Confronted by an angry man who accuses him of consorting with the man's wife, Groucho vehemently denies the charge. "But I saw her with you," the man insists, to which Groucho replies: "Who are you going to believe: me or your own eyes?"

16. This approach is prominently associated with the anthropologist Clifford Geertz. See, for example, "Thick Description: Toward an Inter-

pretive Theory of Culture," and "Deep Play: Notes on a Balinese Cockfight," in Geertz, op. cit.

17. Tocqueville's seminal book, *Democracy in America*, is available in a number of translations and editions, for example the one by Harvey C. Mansfield and Delba Winthrop (Chicago: The University of Chicago Press, 2000).

18. "Some 7,000 people were supposed to be living off the game, including manufacturers of rackets and balls, teachers, custodians of the courts, and professional performers and hustlers." Richard Mandell, *Sports: A Cultural History* (New York: Columbia University Press, 1984), p. 130. See also Jacques Barzun, *From Dawn to Decadence: 500 Years of Western Cultural Life* (New York: HarperCollins, 2000), p. 187.

19. Mandell, op. cit., p. 39.

20. On this general point see David Cannadine, *Ornamentalism* (New York: Oxford University Press, 2002).

21. The earliest baseball uniforms were alike in every way. It was only in the 1920s that each player was assigned a different number to adorn the back of his jersey. The player's last name was added in the 1960s.

22. Athletic achievement can confer visible signs of status off the field. A well-established custom in American secondary schools and universities is for members of the school's teams to wear jackets or sweaters with the first initial of the school's name embroidered on it, denoting that the person has played well, or at least often, enough to earn a "letter."

23. The older principle of ascription does persist, sometimes in odd corners of the society. In dog shows, for example, animals are judged by how closely they conform to the ideal of their particular type, which is largely a matter of breeding—of the genes with which each dog happens to be endowed. In the human realm many companies are owned by families, with the leadership handed down to family members.

24. Disqualification from the contest can also result from the official's judgment that the player being ejected has deliberately tried to injure a member of the opposing team.

25. See Niall Ferguson, *Empire: The Rise and Decline of the British World Order and the Lessons for Global Power* (New York: Basic Books, 2002), p. xxv.

26. Another organizational feature of professional sports promotes equality of opportunity: the schedule of games. In baseball, football, and basketball each team has the same number of games in its own arena and in those of other teams. Playing at home is advantageous in all three.

27. Sportsbusinessjournal.com, January 12, 2004.

28. Bill Buford, *Among the Thugs* (New York: W. W. Norton, 1992), pp. 169–172.

29. Phil Ball, "Mucho Morbo," *The Observer* (London), April 21, 2002.

30. On the way that European soccer competition expresses local rivalries and resentments see Tim Parks, "Soccer: A Matter of Love and Hate," *The New York Review of Books*, July 18, 2002.

31. See, for example, a book about high school basketball in Oakland, California: Tim Keown, *Skyline: One Season, One Team, One City* (New York: Macmillan, 1994), pp. 63–65.

32. "The [Washington] Redskins [professional football team] are one safe topic of conversation in this town. It doesn't matter if you're Republican or Democrat, black or white. People in this town follow the Redskins." Tim Wendel, "A Coach Embraced As Hopes Are Lifted," *The New York Times*, January 9, 2004, p. C15.

CHAPTER 2

Baseball: The Remembrance of Things Past

1. New York: Scribner, 1997, p. 171.

2. George F. Will, *Men at Work: The Craft of Baseball* (New York: Macmillan, 1990), p.5.

3. Between 1989 and 2001 sixteen baseball-only facilities were built for major league teams. Andrew Zimbalist, *May the Best Team Win: Baseball Economics and Public Policy* (Washington, D.C.: Brookings Institution Press, 2003), p. 123.

4. This is foul territory, where a batted ball that touches the ground is out of play and counts as a strike on the batter who hits it, but if caught without touching the ground puts the batter out, just as if the ball had been caught in the air between the foul lines—that is, in fair territory.

5. This is so because a pitcher can make the ball curve. A curve ball thrown by a righthanded pitcher to a righthanded batter can look, when it leaves the pitcher's hand, as if it is going to hit the batter, then swerve away to cross the plate within the strike zone. Only the most skilled and determined batter can, under such circumstances, avoid flinching and proceed to hit the ball squarely; and not even the best hitters can do this all the time. The same is true for a lefthanded pitcher and a lefthanded batter.

While a curve ball from a righthanded pitcher in effect sneaks up behind a righthanded batter, to a lefthanded batter it starts out well away from him and then moves toward him, giving him a good view of it and, so it seems, more time to gauge its trajectory and hit the ball.

6. The tactic of deploying batters so as to make for dissimilarity, which dates from the early twentieth century, is known as platooning. It is difficult to employ throughout a game because, unlike football and basketball, baseball does not allow free substitution. If a lefthanded pitcher is sent into the game to substitute for a righthanded one, the righthander cannot return to the contest. This is true, of course, for batters as well. All this means that a valued skill in a batter is the ability to hit from either side of the plate. (A righthanded batter actually stands to the left of home plate, a lefthander to the right.) Although virtually everyone is born favoring one hand or the other, players can be trained to become "switch-hitters." The same skill for pitching is too difficult to master, however: Major league baseball has never had a true switch-pitcher.

7. Just as rare as lefthanded-throwing infielders are lefthanded-throwing catchers. For a catcher the handicap is more modest; but because of the shortage of lefthanders in general and the value of a lefthanded pitcher, lefthanders who can throw hard are steered into pitching. Bill James, *The New Bill James Historical Baseball Abstract* (New York: The Free Press, 2001), p. 41.

8. Despite the overriding importance of the pitcher, over the course of an entire season the contribution of the different members of a baseball team to its success is probably more nearly equal than it is for the other two team sports. The contribution of the offense and the defense are by definition equally important. Since in the major leagues, 12 percent of the runs given up by pitchers are unearned—due to mistakes by fielders, not safe hits by batters—pitching may be said to make up one half of the 88 percent that remains, or 44 percent of a team's success. If a team has five starting pitchers, each will be responsible for approximately 9 percent of a team's accomplishments. But starting pitchers seldom pitch the full nine innings of a game. Taking six innings as the average for the tenure of a starting pitcher, each contributes two-thirds of 9 percent, or 6 percent.

   On the offensive side, there are eight non-pitching regular players. They must, by rule, bat sequentially; none can bat twice before all have batted once. Each therefore contributes to the team's success and failure one-eighth of 44 percent, or—by an admittedly crude calculus—about the same as the starting pitchers: 6 percent.

9. Another non-standard feature of baseball, which sets it apart from football and basketball, is worth noting. Scoring is not uniform. In football, every touchdown counts for six points; in basketball every field goal counts for two or, if the shot is launched beyond a certain

distance, three points. But a play in baseball on which a team scores can bring in one, two, three, or even four runs, depending on circumstances.

10. Geoffrey Ward and Ken Burns, *Baseball: An Illustrated History* (New York: Knopf, 1994), p. 45.

11. "The eye-hand-body coordination required for throwing stones and javelins accurately (and aiming arrows as well) was another human physiological peculiarity, as important for ancient hunters as their sweat glands and long-distance-running capabilities." J. R. McNeill and William McNeill, *The Human Web: A Bird's-Eye View of World History* (New York: W. W. Norton, 2003), p. 16.

12. James Glanz, "The Crack of the Bat: Acoustics Takes on the Sound of Baseball," *The New York Times*, "Science Times," June 26, 2001, p. D1.

13. "You get a star hitter, he hits .300; that means he failed seven out of 10 times. And if you're a [football] quarterback and you make 30 percent of your passes, or you're a basketball player and you make 30 percent of your shots, you're probably not going to be very successful. So this game is built on that premise of failure...." Mike Hargrove, manager of the Baltimore Orioles, quoted in *The Washington Post Magazine*, September 16, 2001, p. 10.

14. Quoted in Roger Angell, "Introduction: Hard Lines," in Ward and Burns, op. cit., p. xxiii.

15. "One time Al Simmons [an accomplished hitter from the mid-1920s to the mid-1940s] was in a terrible slump, couldn't buy a hit for a week or more. After going oh-for-four [no hits in four at-bats] he stumbled out of the shower in a funk and, not really thinking about what he was doing, put on his hat.... The next day, Simmons had four hits. You can imagine what happened then: Simmons began getting dressed after the game every day by putting his hat on first. And, as he got hot and stayed hot, this spread to the rest of the team." James, op. cit., p. 656. See also p. 573.

16. Evidence of the sport's connection with the past is the fact that baseball memorabilia—the artifacts of games and players of the past—have become collectors' items, sometimes sold for very high prices.

17. *Baseball As America: Seeing Ourselves Through Our National Game* (Washington, D.C.: National Geographic, 2002), p. 246.

18. Football coaches try to do so. After each game they go over film of it, grading each player's performance on each play. But these grades, unlike baseball statistics, are subjective, private, and unofficial.

19. A batted ball on which the hitter reaches base that the fielder has, in the judgment of the official scorer, no reasonable chance of handling, counts, of course, as a safe hit for the batter.

20. Some dedicated baseball fans have embarked on a search through archives of old newspapers to fill in gaps in the record of all major league games played between 1901 and 1983, after which complete records do exist. Stefan Fatsis, "Batty? A Man Tries To Log Every Play Made in Baseball," *The Wall Street Journal*, April 24, 2002, p. A1.

21. "At first glance, baseball in Japan appears to be the same game played in the U.S.—but isn't. The Japanese view of life stressing group identity, cooperation, respect for age, seniority and 'face' has permeated almost every aspect of the sport." Robert Whiting, *The Chrysanthemum and the Bat* (New York: Dodd, Mead, 1977). Quoted in William Kelly, "Baseball in Japan: The National Pastime Beyond National Character," in *Baseball As America*, pp. 47–48.

22. "A batter's experience at the plate can be unpleasant. The first chapter of Leonard Koppett's *A Thinking Man's Guide to Baseball*, published in 1967, opens with a one-word paragraph: 'Fear.' Koppett continues, 'Fear is the fundamental factor in hitting.' The fear is instinctive and reasonable." Will, op.cit., p. 176.

23. By one count, there were eight deaths between 1901 and 1984 and one or two serious injuries—bad enough to damage severely the player's career—per year during that time. Bill James, *The Bill James Baseball Abstract, 1985* (New York: Macmillan, 1985), pp. 137–138.

24. Random House dictionary, quoted in Daniel Okrent, "You, Too, Can Be a General Manager!" in *Baseball As America*, p. 166. On the operation of Rotisserie leagues see Sam Walker, "Crunch Time in Fantasy Land," *The Wall Street Journal*, September 27, 2002, p. W4. At the outset of the twenty-first century "fantasy leagues" for professional football, organized along similar lines, had also become popular.

25. Their various contributions can be separated, thanks to the concept of the earned run.

26. Bill James, quoted in Will, op. cit., p. 245.

27. Nicholas Dawidoff, "Introduction," to Dawidoff, editor, *Baseball: A Literary Anthology* (New York: The Library of America, 2002), p. 6; Edward Wong, "Baseball's Disputed Origin is Traced Back, Back, Back," *The New York Times*, July 8, 2001, p. A1; Richard J. Tofel, "The 'Innocuous Conspiracy' of Baseball's Birth," *The Wall Street Journal*, July 19, 2001, p. A20.

28. Those who confessed were banned from baseball for life. The fixing of major league baseball games did not begin in 1919. Rumors of players purposely playing badly in exchange for payments from gamblers were common before 1920, and in retrospect some of these rumors came to seem well founded. G. Edward White, *Creating the National Pastime: Baseball Transforms Itself, 1903–1953* (Princeton, New Jersey: Prince-

ton University Press, 1996), pp. 89–93; James, *Historical Abstract*, pp. 136, 466.

29. This and other details of Ruth's life are drawn from Robert Creamer, *Babe: The Legend Comes to Life* (New York: Simon and Schuster, 1974).

30. Ibid., p. 289.

31. Ibid., p. 251.

32. New York: Norton, 1954.

33. The major Yankee achievements tended to be in offensive rather than defensive categories. For instance, the generally accepted standard for outstanding career accomplishment among pitchers is 300 victories. In the twentieth century thirteen pitchers achieved it. (Seven others earned all or most of their 300 victories in the nineteenth century.) None of the thirteen spent the bulk of his career with the Yankees. Allen Barra, "300-Victory Club Becoming Tougher to Join," *The New York Times*, May 26, 2003, p. D2.

34. In the previous decade in the Rogers and Hammerstein musical *South Pacific*, American sailors on a Pacific island had paid ironic tribute to a local woman by singing, "Her skin is tender as DiMaggio's glove."

35. *Baseball As America*, p. 289.

36. James, *Historical Abstract*, p. 370.

37. In 2003 both the Red Sox and the Cubs almost—but not quite—reached the championship competition. Each lost the League Championship Series, making the World Series itself, which pitted the Florida Marlins against the Yankees, an anticlimax for millions of baseball fans.

38. Philip Roth, "My Baseball Years," in *Baseball As America*, p. 94.

39. The letter, typed on White House stationery and dated January 15, 1942, is reprinted in *Baseball As America*, p. 61.

40. The first recorded use of the term is in 1856. Ward and Burns, op. cit., p. 6.

41. *The Random House Dictionary of the English Language*, Second Edition Unabridged (New York: Random House, 1987), p. 1,419.

42. The historian Frederick Jackson Turner's essay announcing the closing of the frontier, and thus the end of a defining chapter in America's national life, was published in 1890.

43. When a baseball game is postponed because of rain the ticket stub admits the bearer to the rescheduled game.

44. "Baseball is a fat Victorian novel, replete with colorful minor characters and discursive subplots, into which a fan can disappear for months; football is a series of quick-cutting TV cop shows." Bob Thompson, "Diamond Dilemma," *The Washington Post Magazine*, August 31, 2003, p. 16.

45. On Lardner see Jonathan Yardley, *Ring: A Biography of Ring Lardner* (New York: Random House, 1977).

46. Roger Angell, *Late Innings: A Baseball Companion* (New York: Simon and Schuster, 1982), p. 286.

47. Ibid., p. 282.

48. It happened also to be the first book typeset entirely by computer, and thus a preview of the pervasive role that that machine would come to play in late-twentieth-century life, including in the analysis of baseball statistics. James, *Historical Abstract*, p. 268.

49. Not all members of this society practiced sabermetrics. Most, in fact, were amateur historians, not scientific analysts, of baseball.

50. On this subject see also James, *Historical Abstract*, pp. 349–350, and Ben McGrath, "There's No Such Thing as a Clutch Hitter," Slate.com, October 4, 2001.

51. Jules Tygiel, *Past Time: Baseball as History* (New York: Oxford University Press, 2000), pp. 208–209; Michael Lewis, *Moneyball* (New York: W. W. Norton, 2003), Chapter 4.

52. James himself made the point more forcefully: "a great part of the sport's traditional knowledge is ridiculous hokum." *The Bill James Baseball Abstract, 1986* (New York: Ballantine, 1986), p. 46.

53. John Thorn, Peter Palmer, and David Reuther, *The Hidden Game of Baseball: A Revolutionary Approach to Baseball and Its Statistics* (New York: Doubleday, 1984).

54. White, op. cit., p. 88.

55. Beane and his approach to baseball is the subject of Lewis, op. cit.

56. Tyler Kepner, "Red Sox Have the Thinking Fan's Writer on Their Side," *The New York Times*, November 28, 2002, p. C13; Tom Verducci, "A New Bean Counter," *Sports Illustrated*, November 18, 2002, p. 30; Ben McGrath, "The Professor of Baseball," *The New Yorker*, July 14 and 21, 2003. The 2003 Red Sox were good enough to reach the American League Championship Series but lost there, in seven games, to the Yankees.

57. Prior efforts to end segregation in baseball had foundered, in part on the opposition of Commissioner Kenesaw Mountain Landis, who died in 1944. Ward and Burns, op. cit., p. 283. Baseball was integrated for a brief time in the nineteenth century. See Jules Tygiel, *Baseball's Greatest Experiment: Jackie Robinson and His Legacy* Expanded Edition. (New York: Oxford University Press, 1997, Chapter 2.

58. Steven Riess, "Baseball and Ethnicity," in *Baseball As America*, p. 89. The story of Jackie Robinson's path to the major leagues and the consequences of his debut is told in Tygiel, op. cit.

59. White, op. cit., p. 263.

60. The numbers come from John Donovan, "A new game face," cnnsi.com, July 11, 2003.

61. White, op. cit., pp. 156–157.

62. He told the story of being outraged when an African-American member of the baseball team he coached at Ohio Wesleyan University in 1903 was refused admission to a hotel in Kentucky, and dated his determination to fight against segregation to that episode. Ward and Burns, op. cit., pp. 128–129.

63. White, op. cit., pp. 68–69.

64. Quoted in Roger Kahn, "We Never Called Them Bums," in *Baseball As America*, p. 160.

65. On the Dodgers and Brooklyn see Michael Shapiro, *The Last Good Season: Brooklyn, the Dodgers, and Their Final Pennant Race Together* (New York: Doubleday, 2003).

66. John Helyar, *Lords of the Realm: The Real History of Baseball* (New York: Villard Books, 1994), pp. 134–135.

67. Ward and Burns, op. cit., p. 432.

68. The principal pitching records predate not only World War II but World War I—before, that is, the "lively ball era." Almost all of Cy Young's 511 victories were earned in the nineteenth century, and Dutch Leonard compiled a 0.96 earned run average in 1914.

69. Cited in Will, op. cit., p. 316. See also Andrew Zimbalist, "Competitive Balance in Major League Baseball," *The Milken Institute Review*, First Quarter, 2001, pp. 57–58.

70. Creamer, op.cit., p. 226. The National League home run champion hit fifteen.

71. Forces of decompression were also at work. Because there were more teams, a higher percentage of the total population played in the major leagues, creating a wider distribution of talent and a larger gap between the best and the worst players. Along with the changes in the strike zones, the bats used, and the physical conditioning of the players (perhaps including the use of performance-enhancing drugs), this helps to account for the superior offensive performances of the late 1990s. Zimbalist, op. cit., pp. 6–8.

72. Allen Barra, "Are We Seeing the Best Player Ever?" *The Wall Street Journal*, October 4, 2002, p. W4.

73. James, *Historical Abstract*, pp. 306–309.

74. Idid., pp. 318–322.

75. Not coincidentally, this was also a period when the Yankees dominated baseball. Zimbalist, op. cit., p. 51.

76. White, op. cit., pp. 166, 214–216. Broadcasting games on radio and ultimately television became a major source of revenue for the major

league teams. Another example of baseball's reflexive and not always far-sighted conservatism is the response of the New York Yankees' General Manager George Weiss to the suggestion, in the 1950s, that the team designate one of its home games as "cap day," at which a free Yankee cap would be given to all paying customers. "Do you think I want every kid in this city walking around with a Yankee cap?" he said. Only a few years later cap day was a standard event for every team, Major League caps were widely sold throughout the country, and it was the fondest dream of every baseball executive to have "every kid" in his city wearing his team's cap. John Helyar, *Lords of the Realm: The Real History of Baseball* (New York: Villard Books, 1994), p. 67.

77. Ward and Burns, op. cit., p. 386.

78. Will, op. cit., p. 60.

79. In the World Series and interleague play the rule of the league to which the home team belonged prevailed. In American League parks the designated hitter was used by both teams; in National League parks the pitcher for both teams had to take a regular turn at bat.

80. This was one of the reasons that the frequency of batters hit by pitches rose over the last two decades of the twentieth century. It was not the only reason, since hit batsmen increased in the designated hitter–less National League as well as the American League. Steve Hirdt, "Ins and Outs," *ESPN The Magazine*, June 10, 2002, p. 40.

81. In 2004, after twenty years of pitching in the American League, Clemens reversed his previously announced decision to retire from baseball and signed a contract to pitch for the Houston Astros in the designated–hitter–less National League.

82. Craig M. Vogel, "What Wood You Rather Use?" in *Baseball As America*, p. 261. By the twenty-first century metal bats were made of alloys and other high-tech materials. Bill Pennington, "Going Against the Grain," *The New York Times*, April 2, 2003, p. A25.

83. Stefan Fatsis, "Battle of the Bats," *The Wall Street Journal*, February 22, 2002, p. W4. In 2003 a number of Massachusetts high schools banned the use of aluminum bats and reverted to wood. Pennington, op. cit., p. A21.

84. White, op. cit., pp. 77–81; Andrew Zimbalist, "The Peculiar Business of Baseball," in *Baseball As America*, pp. 187–188.

85. In fact the arbitrator ruled that the reserve clause applied for only one year beyond the life of the contract and was not, as it had previously been interpreted as being, renewable indefinitely. This gave every player the right to free agency one year after his contract expired.

86. Cited in Thomas Boswell, "Baseball Released From Its Labor Incarceration," *The Washington Post*, September 1, 2002, p. D7.

87. In 2002 Rodriguez's salary, $22 million, exceeded the entire payroll of a rival American League team, the Tampa Bay Devil Rays. "Baseball Economics: 1 Man More than 25," *The Washington Post*, April 4, 2003, p. D7.

88. In 2002 the two teams that contested the World Series, the San Francisco Giants and the Anaheim Angels, were both in the top half but not the top quartile of major league payrolls. Zimbalist, *May The Best Team Win*, p. 43. And in the 2003 World Series the Florida Marlins, with a payroll of $57 million, defeated the New York Yankees, the player salaries of which totaled more than $180 million.

89. The figures are from Zimbalist, "Competitive Balance," p. 55, who writes that the "correlation between team payrolls and team won/loss percentages was statistically significant at a 99 percent probability level in every year between 1995 and 2000 (and in no year between 1985 and 1994)." Ibid., p. 58. For a dissenting view, that major league baseball did *not* suffer from competitive imbalance, see Allen Barra, "A Piece of the Pennant," Slate.com, September 26, 2003.

90. The figures are cited in George Will, "Baseball's Disparities," *The Washington Post*, August 11, 2002, p. B7. In July 2003, the affluent Yankees and a penny-pinching rival American League team, the Cleveland Indians, played a game in which the annual salaries of the nine New York starting players totaled $83.2 million and those of the nine Cleveland starters was $3 million. Dave Sheinin, "Decision Time Now, Judgement Day Later," *The Washington Post*, July 27, 2003, p. E8.

91. Will, op. cit., p. 323.

92. "When asked [in 2001] by the Gallup poll their favorite sport to watch, only 12% of Americans said baseball, behind basketball and well behind football; this percentage is down two-thirds from 40 years ago." Albert R. Hunt, "A Great Game With Big Problems," *The Wall Street Journal*, August 30, 2001, p. A13.

CHAPTER 3

Football: The Spectacle of Violence

1. Peter King, "King's Corner," *Sports Illustrated*, October 21, 2002, p. 85.

2. Only rarely have football games been cancelled: when fog was so thick that the players could not see the ball, for instance, or in anticipation of a severe hurricane.

3. The name was inspired by a popular song of the era as well as by the color of their uniforms.

4. Football players did sometimes have individual nicknames. The great collegiate player of the 1920s, Harold "Red" Grange, was dubbed the "Galloping Ghost." And a few baseball teams earned collective names. The New York Yankees since the Ruth era have been known as the "Bronx Bombers."

5. In 2003 major league baseball began using high-precision cameras to evaluate umpires' consistency and accuracy in calling balls and strikes. Although the system did not directly affect the games themselves, true to the spirit of baseball it evoked protests against the infringement of machines on human judgment. Tom Verducci, "Man vs. Machine," *Sports Illustrated*, June 9, 2003, p. 17.

6. John Sayle Watterson, *College Football: History, Spectacle, Controversy* (Baltimore: The Johns Hopkins University Press, 2000), p. 20.

7. Camp also suggested that the field be marked by horizontal lines every five yards (later changed to every ten yards), which, one observer noted, gave it the appearance of a gridiron, a utensil consisting of parallel metal bars on which meat is broiled. The term caught on, and well into the twentieth century football players were known as "gridders." Ibid., p. 20.

8. Football records are less meaningful as well because much of what contributes to on-field success is not captured by statistics. In 2002 one prominent sportswriter offered his list of the best quarterbacks in the history of professional football. The player rankings consisted of the sum of the rankings in twelve different categories. But six of those were subjective, not statistical—"game management," for instance, and "toughness." Paul Zimmerman, "The U Ratings," *Sports Illustrated*, September 23, 2002, pp. 68–98.

9. Here, too, football corresponds to a trend in industrial society. "Industrial society, unlike the commercial, craft and agrarian societies which it replaces, does not need the past. Its intellectual and emotional orientation is toward change rather than conservation ... The new methods, new processes, new forms of living of scientific and industrial society have no sanction in the past and no roots in it." J. H. Plumb, *The Death of the Past* (London: Pelican Books, 1973), p. 14.

10. From the techniques of armed conflict come, directly or indirectly, many of the world's individual sports: boxing, wrestling, fencing, archery, and horse racing. In one of his routines the comedian George Carlin drew attention to the parallels between football and war, and offered an extended comparison of football and baseball.

11. Because violent encounters are regular, indeed integral features of football but not of baseball or basketball, football is sometimes distinguished from them (and lumped together with boxing) as a "contact

sport." About this term a football coach once scornfully remarked: "Football isn't a contact sport. Dancing is a contact sport. Football is a *collision* sport."

12. A description of battle by one of its most distinguished chroniclers applies almost equally well to a football play: "close-range almost to the point of intimacy, noisy, physically fatiguing, nervously exhausting and, in consequence of that physical and nervous strain they imposed, narrowly compressed in time." John Keegan, *The Mask of Command*, (London: Penguin Books, 1988), pp. 115–116.

13. The comparable custom in baseball, the spring training that precedes the season, is far less Spartan and much more relaxed.

14. The episode became the subject of a book by Jim Dent, *The Junction Boys: How Ten Days in Hell with Bear Bryant Forged a Championship Team* (New York: St. Martin's Press, 1999), which was the basis of a made-for-television film broadcast in 2002.

15. In 2002 there were 290 professional players at 300 pounds or more. Ten years before there had been only eighty-three. Tim Keown, "Heavy Burden," *ESPN The Magazine*, October 29, 2002, p. 62. In 1972 the starting offensive linemen in the Super Bowl game weighed an average of 248 pounds. In the same game ten years later the average was 262 pounds. Ten years after that it was 281 pounds and in 2002 the number was 304 pounds. Gregg Easterbrook, "There's nowhere to run to, baby!" ESPN.com, October 22, 2002.

16. "From the end of last February to the end of June [New York Giants player Dan] Campbell and three offensive linemen—Mike Rosenthal, Jason Whittle and Chris Bober—spent two and a half to three hours a day, five days a week, lifting weights and running at Giants Stadium." Frank Litsky, "Campbell Plays Here and There for Giants," *The New York Times*, October 11, 2002, p. C18.

17. The overall commander, the coach, operates from outside the playing field, on the sidelines, just as generals since the nineteenth century have commanded from beyond the battlefield.

18. Helmets became mandatory in college football only in 1939 and it was also only at about that time that plastic began to replace leather as the material from which they are fashioned. Watterson, op. cit., p. 137.

19. According to a study done of former professional football players over a fifty-year span, "Among 870 former players responding … 65% had suffered a 'major injury' while playing—that is, an injury that either required surgery or forced them to miss at least eight games. The study also reported that the percentage of players incurring such injuries had increased alarmingly: from 42% before 1959 to 72% in the 1980s…." William Nack, "The Reckoning," *Sports Illustrated*, May 7, 2001, p. 62.

20. The increase in the size of players increases the risks of chronic injury. According to the former team physician for a professional football team, "We are creating a generation of super football players who will be crippled for the remainder of their life with arthritis.... Their joints are not built to withstand the extra strain." Mike Freeman and Linda Villarosa, "The Perils of Pro Football Follow Some Into Retirement," *The New York Times*, September 25, 2002, p. C16.

21. "[Former lineman] Mike Webster, whose Hall of Fame pro career was followed by more than a decade of physical and psychological turmoil apparently brought on by repeated blows to the head on the field, died yesterday in a Pittsburgh hospital. He was 50." "Mike Webster, 50, Dies: Troubled Football Hall of Famer," *The New York Times*, September 25, 2002, p. C19.

22. According to one eminently successful coach, "my job is to get men to do what they don't want to do—punish themselves." Thomas Boswell, "The Coach-GM Equation: When There's An Addition, Watch the Problems Multiply," *The Washington Post*, January 6, 2002, p. D5.

23. This is a principal theme of Victor Davis Hanson, *Carnage and Culture: Landmark Battles in the Rise of Western Culture* (New York: Doubleday, 2001).

24. "One reason I do what I do is that I'm willing to sacrifice and work when things are hard—whether I'm hot, hurt, or fatigued. I take pride in my ability to plow through discomfort; that's what makes me a football player." Professional football player Grant Wistrom, quoted in "Take It to the Limit," *Sports Illustrated*, August 13, 2001, p. 31.

25. On drill in the armed forces see Hanson, op. cit., pp. 329–330, and William H. McNeill, *Keeping Together in Time* (Cambridge, Massachusetts: Harvard University Press, 1995), p. 132.

26. Drill is also a method of developing group cohesion. McNeill, op. cit., p. 132.

27. Hanson, op. cit., p. 327.

28. Thomas E. Ricks, *Making The Corps* (New York: Scribner's, 1997), p. 289.

29. "Here's the deal with football players: To be a good one, you've got to force your body to perform actions that your mind is dead-set against. For a player to accept that bargain on a consistent basis, he'd better have a sense of something greater than individual gain, be it faith in a god or a coach, *a bond with his teammates*, or a profound fear of failure." Michael Silver, "American Beauty," *Sports Illustrated*, September 16, 2002, p. 45, quoting a former player. (Italics added.)

30. He was perhaps overstating the case. It was also he, after all, who said that in war, God is on the side of the bigger battalions.

31. The Arizona professional football team is also known as the Cardinals.

But when the team was founded, in Chicago at the outset of the twentieth century, the name came from the color, not the bird. Jim J. Campbell, "Team Histories," in Bob Carroll, Michael Gershman, David Neft, John Thorn, *Total Football: The Official Encyclopedia of the National Football League* (New York: HarperCollins, 1999), p. 39. The raven, the symbol of the Baltimore football team, is not dangerous but can be annoying.

32. Football fields are not completely neutral in their effects. Turf fields favor teams with speed more than grass fields do. And teams located in the northern parts of the United States often play better in cold weather than teams whose home cities never see snow, or that play their home games indoors, in domed stadiums.

33. Wittingham, op. cit., p. 93.

34. Roosevelt's great political antagonist Woodrow Wilson, a man more closely associated historically with the cause of peace than with a zest for war, was also, and for similar reasons, a football enthusiast. Watterson, op. cit., p. 26.

35. Ibid., pp. 58, 65. "All the great masterful races," Roosevelt once said, "have been fighting races, and the minute that a race loses the hard fighting virtues, then, no matter what else it may retain, no matter how skilled in commerce and finance, in science or art, it has lost its right to stand as the equal of the best." Quoted in H. W. Brands, *T.R.: The Last Romantic* (New York, Basic Books, 1997), p. 317. His friend and fellow imperialist Senator Henry Cabot Lodge of Massachusetts expressed similar sentiments: "The time given to athletic contests and the injuries incurred on the playing-field are part of the price which the English-speaking race has paid for being world-conquerors." Quoted in Warren Zimmerman, *First Great Triumph: How Five Americans Made Their Country a World Power* (New York: Farrar, Straus and Giroux, 2002), p. 163.

36. Brands, op. cit., p. 339.

37. The English folk-custom-turned-organized-sport divided into two distinct branches in 1823 when, according to tradition, a contestant in a game at the Rugby School was inspired to pick up the ball and carry it forward rather than propelling it by kicking. A meeting held in 1863 to try to reconcile the two divergent branches failed to do so and from that time onward the English, and ultimately other peoples, played two different games. One was called rugby football, in which carrying the ball is permitted. The other was called in England association football, in which carrying the ball is prohibited.

38. Play also stops when the ball carrier steps outside the boundary of the field ("out of bounds") and when a forward pass touches the ground rather than being caught.

39. Notre Dame's passer was Gus Dorais. Many of his passes were caught by a teammate whose association with Notre Dame football was just beginning: Knute Rockne.

40. "It's the single greatest indicator of power in pro football. The team that averages a higher yards-per-throw average in a game will win more than 80% of the time." Allen Barra, "Rating the Quarterbacks," *The Wall Street Journal*, November 23, 2001, p. W4.

41. Watterson, op. cit., p. 54.

42. Ibid., p. 25.

43. The penalties usually involved reducing the number of athletic scholarships the school could give or barring its team from postseason play for several years.

44. Between 1980 and 1989 by one estimate fully half of the Division I schools suffered NCAA-imposed penalties of one kind or another. Watterson, op. cit., pp. 353–354.

45. The incompatibility between the values of the academy and the norms of big-time sports were not the cause of deemphasis in every case, as evidenced by the fact that some of the schools that discontinued or downgraded football continued to maintain high-profile basketball programs, in which the status of the players was the same as in football but for which, because there were fewer players, less money for scholarships was required.

46. One devoted graduate of the University of Southern California managed to attend 797 consecutive games, spanning seventy-two years, that his team played. Wittingham, op. cit., p. 142.

47. "If you want to know why football is king, you have to remember how poor the South was made as a result of the War Between the States.... This was a way we got our pride back. When Georgia's team would go and beat schools from other states, well, darn if it didn't make you feel good and proud." Dan Magill, former tennis coach at the University of Georgia, quoted in L. Jon Wertheim, "Dawg Days," *Sports Illustrated*, December 23, 2002, pp. 57–58.

48. Wittingham, op. cit., p. 2.

49. Traditional rivals also typically field teams of roughly comparable skill. By this measure Kansas and Nebraska do not qualify because, although they fit the other criteria, the Nebraska team has consistently been far superior to the one fielded by Kansas. (The reverse has been true of the two schools' rivalry in basketball.)

50. Wittingham, op. cit., p. 87.

51. Ibid., pp. 92–93.

52. Interregional football games did take place before World War II and were somewhat more feasible to arrange than major league baseball games matching teams located at great distances from each other

would have been because football, unlike baseball, is played only once a week, allowing more time for travel.

53. The association between automobiles and professional football proved to be an enduring one. Car companies became major sponsors of the game on television because the audience for football is composed disproportionately of young men, who are major purchasers of cars.

54. In 1954, 93,000 people attended a game there involving the team from San Francisco, the 49ers. The other NFL games played that day drew crowds ranging from 17,000 to 27,000. David Maraniss, *When Pride Still Mattered: A Life of Vince Lombardi* (New York: Simon and Schuster, 1999), p. 159.

55. The trophy was first awarded in 1935, and named for Heisman the following year.

56. Unitas holds the record for passing for at least one touchdown in forty-seven consecutive games. (The next longest streak is thirty.) Although not as purely individual an achievement as Joe DiMaggio's fifty-six-game hitting streak, to which it is sometimes compared, this is a particularly impressive accomplishment because in the four decades after it was set, touchdown passes became more common, yet the record stood. Steve Hirdt, "U is for Unique," *ESPN The Magazine*, May 20, 2002, p. 22.

57. On rating quarterbacks see Zimmerman, op. cit. Both Unitas and Montana came originally from western Pennsylvania, the home of a large number of distinguished professional quarterbacks, including George Blanda, the longest-playing of them; Dan Marino, the most prolific passer; and Joe Namath, the most flamboyant.

58. Steve Spurrier of the Washington Redskins signed a contract in 2002 calling for him to be paid $5 million per year over four years. He resigned in 2004 and his successor, Joe Gibbs, who had previously coached the team with great success, received the same salary.

59. "More than a dozen football coaches, and a slightly smaller number of basketball coaches, now earn at least $1 million a year, in many cases making them their states' highest-paid public employee." Jodi Wilgoren, "Spiraling Sports Budgets Draw Fire From Faculties," *The New York Times*, July 29, 2001, p. 10. In 1982 Texas A&M University hired Jackie Sherrill, then head coach at the University of Pittsburgh, to lead its football team. His salary was $1.72 million over six years, plus benefits, the sum to be contributed by booster groups. This made him "not only the highest paid coach but also the highest paid university employee in the country." Watterson, op. cit., p. 351.

60. Baseball managers do not give such speeches because the spirit in

which baseball is effectively played is different. Adrenaline is not necessarily helpful on the baseball diamond. George Will, *Men at Work: The Craft of Baseball* (New York: Macmillan, 1990), p. 256.

61. Act 4, Scene 3, Lines 64–67.

62. In his coaching manual *Finding the Winning Edge*, (Champaign, Illinois: Sports Publishing Inc., 1998), Bill Walsh, who achieved great success as the coach of the San Francisco 49ers, includes quotes from generals George S. Patton, Dwight D. Eisenhower, and Omar Bradley and the Chinese military sage Sun Tzu. "[Washington Redskins' coach Steve] Spurrier's distaste for conservative play-calling was cemented during the summer of 1997 after his well-documented reading of 'The Art of War' by Sun Tzu. One of Spurrier's favorite books, it espouses the philosophy that opponents should be soundly defeated." Nunyo Demasio, "A Bountiful Mind," *The Washington Post*, September 4, 2002, p. H4.

63. The first incumbent of the Woody Hayes Chair was an eminent scholar named John Mueller whose best-known book, ironically, argued that the wars Hayes had believed had much to teach football coaches were becoming obsolete. Mueller, *Retreat from Doomsday: The Obsolescence of Modern War* (New York: Basic Books, 1989).

64. Quoted in Maraniss, op. cit., p. 103.

65. Walsh wrote a series of articles for *Forbes* magazine, which are listed in Walsh, op. cit., p. 407. See also Murray Sperber, *Shake Down the Thunder: The Creation of Notre Dame Football*, (New York: Henry Holt, 1993) p. 238. Generals also study business, and managers evoke the laws of war. Eliot Cohen, *Supreme Command* (New York: The Free Press, 2002), pp. 1–2.

66. The most compelling nonfiction studies of football concern the high school game. H. G. Bissinger's *Friday Night Lights*, Willie Morris's *The Courting of Marcus Dupree*, and Richard Rubin's *Confederacy of Silence* each explores the mores of a community, the first in West Texas, the other two in Mississippi, using high school football, which is important in each, as the vehicle.

67. Although exercising enormous influence over the Yale football team, Walter Camp never received a salary for his work. For one year, in 1881, Lucius N. Littauer coached the Harvard team, but the next year the Harvard captain regained that responsibility. Wittingham, op. cit., p. 50.

68. Eligibility rules, which today confine a college player to four years of eligibility, were looser in the nineteenth century. Lax rules for student participation lived on in the twenty-first century in one particular intercollegiate sport: chess. One of the members of the University of

Maryland Baltimore County (UMBC) team remained on scholarship and competed for the school for eight years. UMBC was one of two institutions of higher education—the University of Texas at Dallas was the other—that offered scholarships to chess players. Anne Zimmerman, "For Aging Knights Of College Chess, Endgame Is Near," *The Wall Street Journal*, July 10, 2003, p. A1.

69. Watterson, op. cit., p. 40.
70. That total placed him, when he retired, second only to Glenn "Pop" Warner, the inventor of the single wing, who had 319.
71. Wittingham, op. cit., p.53.
72. Idid., p. 100.
73. Studebaker paid him more to promote its cars than the president of the company earned. Sperber, *Shake Down the Thunder*, p. 238.
74. Quoted in Maraniss, op. cit., pp. 35–36.
75. Quoted in Wittingham, op. cit., p. 61.
76. Ibid., p. 15.
77. Paul Gallico, quoted in ibid.
78. He was flying to Los Angeles to discuss appearing in a musical film about college life.
79. The list includes Woody Hayes of Ohio State; Sid Gillman, an innovator of offensive tactics with several professional teams; Ara Parseghian, a successful coach at Notre Dame in the 1960s and 1970s; Weeb Ewbank, who won several professional championships; and Glenn "Bo" Schembechler, for many years the head coach at the University of Michigan. All were elected to the college or professional football Halls of Fame. Notable Ohio-born coaches are the subject of Sally Pont, *Fields of Honor: The Golden Age of College Football and the Men Who Created It* (New York: Harcourt, 2000).
80. Although it is widely believed that the team was named for the coach, it is not clear that this was so. "A contest was held through a local newspaper and 'Browns' emerged as the leading choice [of a name for the team] but whether that referred to the team's coach, to Joe Louis—the heavyweight boxing champion nicknamed 'The Brown Bomber'—or simply to a color preference never was made clear." Ed Gruver, "Team Histories: AFC Teams," in Carroll, et al., op. cit., p. 72.
81. Ibid., pp. 465, 497.
82. "Paul Brown brought organization into pro football. He brought a practice routine. I always felt before Paul Brown, coaches just rolled the ball onto the field." Sid Gillman, quoted in Kevin Lamb, "The Evolution of Strategy," in Carroll, et al., op. cit., p. 463.
83. Maraniss, op. cit., p. 446.

84. Ibid., p. 14.
85. Lombardi's undergraduate career connected him both to football's past and his own future. His coach at Fordham was Jim Crowley, one of Notre Dame's Four Horsemen. Crowley came originally from Green Bay, Wisconsin, where his high school coach had been Earl "Curley" Lambeau, who later became one of Lombardi's predecessors as coach of that city's professional team, the home stadium of which is named Lambeau Field. Maraniss, op. cit., p. 34.
86. Jack Clary, "The History of the National Football League," in Carroll, et al., op. cit., p. 25.
87. Maraniss, op.cit., p. 189.
88. The attendance was 61,946 in a stadium that could seat 100,000 people. Arguably the most famous Super Bowl is the third, in which the representative of the upstart AFL, the New York Jets, upset the mighty Baltimore Colts, the NFL champions, 16–7.
89. "Ask anyone to name the most memorable professional football championship and nearly everyone will cite the 'Ice Bowl,' the 1967 game between the Green Bay Packers and the Dallas Cowboys." Stephen Hayes, "Weather or Not: The Super Bowl, Outside, in the Cold," *The Wall Street Journal*, November 20, 2002, p. D8.
90. Maraniss, op. cit., p. 417.
91. Ibid., pp. 419, 420.
92. Television is superior to radio in conveying football, as is not the case for baseball. The reason is that in football many things happen at once and must be apprehended visually, whereas in baseball one thing happens at a time and so the action can be conveyed orally.
93. Tom Barnidge, "The NFL on TV," in Carroll, et al., op. cit., p. 511.
94. Phil Barber, "Super Bowl Commercials," in Carroll, et al., op. cit., p. 515.
95. The leader was the CBS news magazine *60 Minutes*, which began in 1968.
96. "It was up to us to create 'The Gods of Autumn,'" recalled Steve Sabol, who with his father produced the reels. "We made it a larger-than-life contest, with the fate of the universe at stake." John Helyar, *Lords of the Realm: The Real History of Baseball* (New York: Villard Books, 1994), p. 65.
97. "Unable to conjure up a good reason to root for or against Elvis Grbac, the pitiful [Kansas City] Chiefs quarterback, I had an inspiration: I could put money on the game! ... So, I went online, found an offshore bookie, and bet $350.... I watched every second of that game, screaming insanely every time Grbac was thrown to the turf. I can safely say I have never enjoyed a sporting event so thoroughly before or since."

Hugo Lindgren, "Handicap and Gown: What's wrong with betting on college sports?" Slate.com, June 28, 2001.

98. Basketball games, like football games, have point spreads. But because scoring is more difficult and rarer in football than in basketball, and scores are usually worth more, a single play can have a larger impact on whether or not the point spread is covered in football than in basketball. This makes gambling on football more suspenseful and exciting.

99. Robert Lipsyte, "As Gambling Is Sweeter, The N.C.A.A. Goes Soft," *The New York Times*, March 31, 2002, "Sports," p. 7.

100. An estimated $80 million was wagered legally on the 2003 Super Bowl. The amount wagered illegally, although impossible to estimate accurately, was surely far greater. "As many as $4 billion may be bet illegally on this Sunday's game in San Diego in wagers placed with local bookies or offshore betting parlors that operate Web sites." Christina Binkley, "Gentlemen, Place Your Side Bets," *The Wall Street Journal*, January 23, 2003, pp. D1, D34. Gambling is scarcely unknown in the other two team sports. It was a source of baseball's initial popularity in the nineteenth century. *Baseball As America: Seeing Ourselves Through Our National Game* (Washington, D.C.: National Geographic, 2002), p. 178. The nation's biggest sports gambling scandal occurred in baseball, with the fixing of the 1919 World Series, and basketball was plagued by similar scandals in the 1950s, when gamblers fixed college games.

101. Geoffrey Ward and Ken Burns, *Baseball: An Illustrated History* (New York: Knopf, 1994), p. 401.

102. Phil Barber, "Super Bowl Commercials," in Carroll, et al., op. cit., p. 515.

103. Stefan Fatsis, "NBC Sports Maps A Future Without The Big Leagues," *The Wall Street Journal*, January 31, 2003, p. A1.

104. Stuart Elliott, "A Super Sunday for Football and for Madison Avenue," *The New York Times*, January 24, 2003, p. C4. According to one survey, 14 percent of the viewers watch the Super Bowl only in order to see the commercials. Bruce Horovitz, "Smile! You're the stars of the Super ad Bowl," *USA Today*, January 24, 2003, p. B1.

105. Richard Reeves, *President Nixon: Alone in the White House* (New York: Simon and Schuster, 2001), pp. 292, 405.

106. Ken Denlinger, "George Allen Special Shows No Regular Guy," *The Washington Post*, October 23, 2001, p. D7.

107. Arnold J. Mandell, *The Nightmare Season* (New York: Random House, 1976), p. 17.

108. The story is told in Dent, op. cit.

109. In 2003 John Gagliardi, coach of St. John's College in Minnesota, surpassed Robinson's victory total.

110. The one-time holder of the NFL record for most yards gained over the course of a career, Walter Payton, played at Jackson State College in Mississippi. And the player who came to hold virtually all the professional records for pass receiving, Jerry Rice, arrived in the professional league from another historically black school, Mississippi Valley State.

111. Unlike the new ballparks for baseball, which were designed to evoke the past, several of the new football stadiums, such as the reconstructed Soldier Field in Chicago and the new home of the Arizona Cardinals in Phoenix, were emphatically modern in design.

112. Yet another sign of the higher status of the professional game was the decision to discontinue, after 1976, the annual preseason game between the professional champion of the previous year and a team composed of the best players to graduate from college in that same year. The game was first organized in 1934 by the sportswriter Arch Ward, the originator of the baseball all-star game, and in its early years provided a publicity bonanza for the then-obscure NFL. By the mid-1970s, however, the game had ceased to be competitive—the collegians had no chance of winning—and the professional teams did not wish to risk injuries to players who would join their ranks after the game. Carroll, et al., op. cit., p. 18.

113. After taking the snap from center, the quarterback could hand it to one running back, pitch it to another, or carry it himself. The inventor of the wishbone, the Texas coach Darrell Royal, once said that "when you pass, three things can happen and two of them [an incompletion and an interception] are bad." Wittingham, op. cit., p. 73.

114. The two features of the NFL aimed at this outcome were the college draft and the salary cap.

115. At the levels of college football competition below Division I, playoff systems similar to the one the NFL used were in effect.

116. In 2003, 20 million people watched. Steven Rushin, "Dog Day Afternoon," *Sports Illustrated*, May 5, 2003, p. 19.

117. This phenomenon is described and explained in Michael Mandelbaum, *The Ideas That Conquered the World: Peace, Democracy and Free Markets in the Twenty-first Century* (New York: PublicAffairs, 2002), pp. 121–128.

118. These trends led to a cultural gap between the American military and the rest of society, which is a theme of Ricks, op. cit., pp. 139, 167.

119. "It seems doubtful that Lombardi would have been malleable enough to confront the modern athlete, a challenge that ultimately proved too

daunting for a legendary contemporary, Tom Landry." Michael Farber, "Overrated and Underrated: Vince Lombardi," *Sports Illustrated*, August 27, 2001, p. 75. See also Maraniss, op. cit., p. 445.

120. He wrote a series of articles on this subject for *Forbes* magazine, which are listed in Walsh, op. cit., p. 408.

121. Bill Walsh with Glenn Dickey, *Building a Champion* (New York: St. Martin's Press, 1990), p. 153.

122. Ted Brock, "The West Coast Offense," in Carroll et al., op. cit., p. 493.

123. Choice of this kind did not originate with Walsh. Lombardi built into the rushing plays he designed a series of options for the ballcarrier.

CHAPTER 4

Basketball: The Chemistry of Teamwork

1. Red Auerbach with Joe Fitzgerald, *On and Off the Court* (New York: Bantam Books, 1986), p. 57.

2. This point, a staple of late-twentieth-century social commentary, is central, for example, to Daniel Bell, *The Coming of Post-Industrial Society* (New York: Basic Books, 1976) and Peter Drucker, *On the Profession of Management* (Cambridge, Massachusetts: The Harvard Business Review Press, 1998).

3. Bell, op cit., pp. 196, 198, 345; Drucker, op. cit., pp. 115, 326.

4. As armed forces incorporate post-industrial technology the chain of command tends to become "flatter"—that is, less hierarchical. Admiral Bill Owens, *Lifting the Fog of War* (New York: Farrar, Straus and Giroux, 2000), p. 204.

5. Like football and basketball coaches, baseball managers may have considerable authority over who is on the team and who plays when.

6. Coordination is easier to achieve in basketball than in football because there are fewer players to coordinate, five instead of eleven.

7. On the importance of teamwork in basketball see, for example, Bill Russell and Taylor Branch, *Second Wind: The Memoirs of an Opinionated Man* (New York: Random House, 1979), pp. 121, 126.

8. The University of Kentucky facility is called Rupp Arena, after longtime basketball coach Adolph Rupp. The University of North Carolina basketball team plays in the Dean Smith Center, also named for a coach.

9. Pat Riley, *The Winner Within: A Life Plan for Team Players* (New York: G. P. Putnam's Sons, 1993); Mike Krzyzewski with Donald T. Phillips, *Leading with the Heart: Coach K's Successful Strategies for Basketball, Busi-*

ness, and Life (New York: Warner Books, 2000); Rick Pitino with Bill Reynolds, *Success Is a Choice: Ten Steps to Overachieving in Business and Life* (New York: Bantam Books, 1997).

10. "As more and more institutions become information based, they are transforming themselves ... into responsibility-based organizations in which every member must act as a responsible decision-maker." Drucker, op. cit., p. 126.

11. Women in significant numbers do play softball, a form of baseball that uses a larger ball. And in 2000 a women's football league was founded, but it was more a curiosity than a national institution. See Brandon Lilly, "With Few Fans and No Pay, Women's Football Plays On," *The New York Times*, July 14, 2003, p. D5.

12. Peter C. Bjarkman, *The Biographical History of Basketball* (Lincolnwood, Illinois: Master's Press, 2000), p. 185–186; Alexander Wolff, *Big Game, Small World: A Basketball Adventure* (New York: Warner Books, 2002), p. 163.

13. The first part of the title distinguishes it from rugby football.

14. Dribbling in basketball refers to bouncing the ball on the playing surface, in soccer, to moving the ball ahead by kicking it. In fact, the principal method of propulsion in each is illegal in the other. In maneuvering to score, soccer players may not touch the ball with their hands, while basketball players are forbidden to touch it with their feet.

The goalkeeper in soccer may and does handle the ball. In basketball footwork is important, although not primarily for advancing the ball. Of the talented scorer and rebounder Moses Malone another player remarked: "Most basketball fans see Moses and they all think, look how tall he is. What they don't see is the quickness. How can a man that big have feet like that? No one watching that game sees his feet. They're amazing." David Halberstam, *The Breaks of the Game* (New York: Ballantine Books, 1981), p. 220.

15. In the 2002 World Cup, teams were tied or separated by a single goal 85 percent of the time. Steve Hirdt, "World Supremacy," *ESPN The Magazine*, July 22, 2002, p. 5.

16. Ian Cobain, "We sang, screamed, sighed, then we celebrated as one," *The Times of London*, June 8, 2002, p. 5. Of the same game an English novelist wrote: "Hard to calm down after the game. In fact I have to have a nap in mid-afternoon to decompress. Partly I suspect because I watched it on my own. When you do that you concentrate harder and it takes more out of you, as Ian Hamilton said: 'I don't play football any more, but you should see me watch it.' Underlying this is the point that a football match isn't a spectacle but an experience: you

don't look at it, you live through it." John Lanchester, "A Month on the Sofa," *London Review of Books*, July 11, 2002, p. 29.

17. In the world beyond the United States and Canada soccer is, of course, called football. It failed to establish itself as the equal of the three major team sports in the United States because the other three occupied the available cultural space—each dominates roughly four months of the year—because the game was seen as foreign rather than indigenous, and because the promoters of soccer were not particularly skillful. The question of why soccer lacks the status in North America that it enjoys elsewhere is the subject of Andrei S. Markovits and Steven L. Hellerman, *Offside: Soccer and American Exceptionalism* (Princeton, New Jersey: Princeton University Press, 2001).

18. In 1998 the total viewership for all the games (with many people watching several) by one estimate reached 33.4 billion people, more than five times the population of the planet. "Passion, pride and profit: A survey of football," *The Economist*, June 1, 2002, p.3. The audience for the championship game between France and Brazil was put at two billion. Eduardo Porter, "World Cup 2002: Si, Si," *The Wall Street Journal*, May 6, 2002, p. B1. In the 2002 competition the prestigious and widely read London-based newspaper the *Financial Times*, which ordinarily does not offer daily sports coverage, featured a daily page chronicling and analyzing the games.

19. Topaz Amoore, "A career of two halves," *The Sunday Telegraph* (London), June 9, 2002, "Review," p. 3.

20. "World Cup Diary," *The Independent*, June 12, 2002, World Cup section, p. 4.

21. See, for example, Nick Hornby, *Fever Pitch* (London: Gollancz, 1992), and Colin Shindler, *Fathers, Sons and Football* (London: Headline, 2002).

22. Tim Parks, *A Season With Verona: Travels around Italy in search of illusion, national character, and goals* (London: Secker and Warburg, 2002); Simon Kuper, *Ajax, the Dutch, the War: Football in Europe during the Second World War* (London: Orion, 2002); Alex Bellos, *Futebol: Soccer the Brazilian Way* (London: Bloomsbury, 2002).

23. In 2003 the most popular English soccer team, Manchester United, had the highest estimated value of any professional team in any sport anywhere, and the biggest estimated fan base worldwide. Thomas Heath, "Man U's Perfect Pitch," *The Washington Post*, May 1, 2003, p. D1.

24. Op. cit., Wolff, p. 7.

25. Almost as important is stamina. Soccer and basketball players run great distances during the course of a game. A top-class soccer player

may run as many as seven miles in a single match. Simon Kuper, "Why the boys from Brazil have the world at their feet," *Financial Times*, June 29/30, 2002, Weekend Section, p. XXII.

26. The basketball term for this is "hang time."

27. The inspiration for this central feature of basketball came from a childhood game Naismith had played in Almonte, Ontario, called "duck on a rock." It involved trying to knock a stone off a boulder with a smaller rock without tossing the rock very far beyond the boulder. This called for touch, and finding the optimal arc, in hurling the thrown rock, which are precisely the skills that shooting a basketball involves. Alexander Wolff, "The Olden Rules," *Sports Illustrated*, November 25, 2002.

28. Philip M. Hoose, *Hoosiers: The Fabulous Basketball Life of Indiana*, Second Edition (Indianapolis, Indiana: Guild Press of Indiana, 1995), p. 88. Until 1921 the game's name was written as two words: basket ball.

29. The link between them finds expression in the common term for a basketball arena—*gymnasium*—an ancient Greek word for a place of exercise but also the modern German word for a secondary school.

30. Alexander Wolff, *Big Game, Small World: A Basketball Adventure*, p. 7.

31. Bjarkman, op. cit., p. 186. In twelve years his teams won fifty-five games and lost sixty.

32. The nickname came from his voice, which boomed like a foghorn.

33. One of the most influential coaches, Pete Newell, who began his career in the 1940s, observed in the 1970s that "when I was young, college basketball was an extension of the college itself. Now it is a piece of some television network." Halberstam, op. cit., p. 286.

34. Although almost all had attended college, by one estimate at the end of the 1970s 80 percent of the players in the professional ranks had failed to earn a college degree. Halberstam, op. cit., p. 290. The proportion did not increase in the ensuing two decades. At the outset of the twenty-first century, the majority of players on successful college teams did not graduate. Stefan Fatsis, "Another March, the Usual Madness," *The Wall Street Journal*, March 22, 2002, p. W6.

35. Wolff, "The Olden Rules."

36. According to Pete Newell "[Luisetti] was closer to dominating the game than anyone other than Michael Jordan." "For the Record," *Sports Illustrated*, December 30, 2002, p. 28.

37. The New York schools were City College of New York, New York University, Long Island University, and Manhattan College. Also implicated were players from the University of Kentucky, the University of Toledo, and Bradley University in Peoria, Illinois. Together they were accused of rigging approximately 100 games over four years.

38. The initial title game was staged in Evanston, Illinois, and was won by the University of Oregon, whose leading player boasted a name that could have come from a Thomas Pynchon novel, Urgel "Slim" Wintermute.

39. For a while a team could enter both tournaments, and in 1950 a team representing the City College of New York won both. But by the last decade of the twentieth century the NIT had become a tournament for teams that had not won enough games during the regular season to qualify for the far more prestigious NCAA championship.

40. The first professional game on record took place in 1896. Todd Gould, *Pioneers of the Hardwood* (Bloomington, Indiana: Indiana University Press, 1998), pp. 5–6. Among the notable barnstorming teams were the original Celtics, a team based in New York City, and the Harlem Rens (for Renaissance), also from New York. The earliest league was formed in 1897. Bjarkman, op. cit., p. 542.

41. The marquee at Madison Square Garden when the Lakers were visiting announced: "Tonight: George Mikan vs. the Knicks."

42. The league also adjusted the rule governing the number of free throws awarded to the team being fouled. After a team had accumulated a certain number of fouls, two free throws were automatically awarded to the other team when one of its players was fouled, in order to make the tactic of deliberate fouling at the end of the game a less effective one.

43. Another distinguished African-American alumnus of UCLA was Ralph Bunche, the under-secretary-general of the United Nations and winner of the Nobel Prize for peace, who commended the school to Alcindor.

44. Halberstam, op. cit., pp. 315–316. "According to N.C.A.A. investigations and published reports, [Sam] Gilbert, a multimillionaire contractor and adviser to U.C.L.A. athletes, arranged and paid for abortions for players' friends and helped athletes get discounts on cars, stereos, and airline tickets." William C. Rhoden, "The Ghosts and Goblins of Westwood," *The New York Times*, March 14, 2003, p. C14.

45. He was prone to "stomping the sidelines, baiting of officials, and mocking of patrons behind the team bench. He even spit demonstratively on the floor to rile up opposition hometown crowds." Bjarkman, op. cit., p. 60.

46. Dan Shaughnessy, *Ever Green: The Boston Celtics* (New York: St. Martin's Press, 1990), p. 22.

47. Auerbach, op. cit., pp. 18–19.

48. For this reason basketball is sometimes divided into three parts: offense, defense, and "transition," with the fast break belonging to the third category.

49. From 1959 to 1966, when the Celtics won eight consecutive championships, their average home attendance for regular season games was 7,803, less than half the seating capacity of their arena. Shaughnessy, op. cit., p. 116.

50. Russell, op. cit., pp. 196–200.

51. A fellow player called him "an eagle with a beard," evoking his style of guarding the area near the Celtics' goal vigilantly and occasionally swooping to deflect a shot.

52. "You don't try to block every shot. What you try to do is to intimidate your opponent with the idea that you *might* block any shot." Russell, op. cit., pp. 123–124.

53. "You know what playing against Wilt was like?" an opponent once said. "It was like going back to biblical times and playing Samson." Steve Wulf, "Hershey's Kiss," *ESPN The Magazine*, March 18, 2002, p. 100.

54. From *The Indianapolis Recorder*, March 19, 1955, quoted in Hoose, op.cit., p. 143.

55. Ibid., p. xiv.

56. Knight was noted for his outbursts of bad temper, which ultimately led to his dismissal. He then took a position as head basketball coach at Texas Tech University in Lubbock. The all-sports television channel ESPN made a movie based on a book about him by John Feinstein titled *A Season on the Brink: A Year With Bob Knight and the Indiana Hoosiers* (New York: Macmillan, 1986), a companion film to the one ESPN made and showed about the equally successful and almost equally controversial Alabama football coach Paul "Bear" Bryant.

57. Among the best of them, who went on to stellar careers in college basketball although they did not shine in the professional ranks, were Rick Mount of Lebanon, Kyle Macy of Peru, and Steve Alford of New Castle.

58. Hoose, op. cit., pp. ix-x.

59. The structure of the tournament was partly responsible for the building of large gymnasiums. The tournament games took place in the largest arena in the part of the state the particular round encompassed. A team playing in its home arena, in familiar surroundings and before enthusiastic supporters (although the opposing team's supporters invariably traveled to the games wherever they were held: the state is compact enough to permit this), have a competitive advantage. By building a venue large enough to play host to tournament games, therefore, a community was helping its team to do well in the tournament itself.

60. Hoose, op. cit., pp. 122–123, 134. In the 1997–1998 season Indiana

abandoned the single, all-inclusive high school tournament in favor of the system prevailing almost everywhere else, in which the high schools are divided into several classes according to enrollment and each class stages its own tournament. In the wake of this change, overall interest in high school basketball, and attendance at tournament games, decreased sharply. Alexander Wolff, "Class Struggle," *Sports Illustrated*, December 2, 2003.

61. Hoose, op. cit., p. 103.

62. Wooden was actually raised on a farm near Centerton, Indiana, the population of which was fifty.

63. Auerbach, op. cit., p. 2.

64. Bjarkman, op.cit., pp. 2, 8.

65. Ibid., op.cit., p. 290.

66. Walter LaFeber, *Michael Jordan and the New Global Capitalism* (New York: W. W. Norton, 2002), p. 46. Through the 1980s an estimated 90 percent of all professional players came from the urban parts of the United States, and fully one-third of them were originally New Yorkers. Ibid., p. 41.

67. "Basketball is so inextricably woven into the fabric of Coney Island life that almost everyone in this neighborhood has grown up playing the game or following the fortunes of those who do. Huge crowds show up to watch the summer tournament games at the Garden, and almost everyone can recite a complete oral history of the neighborhood's great players—a remarkable number, too, considering the actual size of Coney Island." Darcy Frey, *The Last Shot: City Streets, Basketball Dreams* (Boston: Houghton Mifflin, 1994), pp. 104–105.

68. "I worked at basketball up to eight hours a day for twenty years—straining, learning, sweating, studying...." Russell, op. cit., p. 175. A study of professional players found that blacks were more dedicated to the game than were whites. Halberstam, op. cit., p. 34.

69. This is true as well, of course, of the other major American team sports, and indeed of the non-American varieties: soccer in Brazil, for example, and cricket in India and Pakistan.

70. *The Random House Dictionary of the English Language*, Second Edition Unabridged (New York: Random House, 1987), p. 606.

71. The first of these was Pete Axthelm, *The City Game: Basketball from the Garden to the Playgrounds* (New York: Penguin Books, 1982; first published, 1970). It was followed by Rick Telander, *Heaven Is a Playground* (New York: St. Martin's Press, 1976); Darcy Frey, *The Last Shot*, and Ben Joravsky, *Hoop Dreams: A True Story of Hardship and Triumph* (New York: Turner Books, 1995), on which a documentary film was based.

72. "Basketball is the great criterion in the ghetto, and the man who excels

at it gains a better sense of his own worth, even if he doesn't benefit in schools and jobs." "It's much more important than money to know that you are good at something. If you know that you can go out and play fairly and win, because of your own determination and abilities, you make people appreciate and respect you, and you appreciate and respect yourself." Quoted in Axthelm, op. cit., p. 150. "You learn quickly that you're all alone. And when you play basketball, the same independent attitude that you're forced to develop just carries over onto the court. As you grow up, you also realize it's going to be almost impossible for you to be a doctor or a lawyer. . . . There are very few professional black people in the neighborhood for you to identify with. . . . So you go with what you do best, what you enjoy best, and what you see black men succeeding at best—basketball." Quoted in Charles Rosen, *God, Man and Basketball Jones: The Thinking Fan's Guide to Professional Basketball* (New York: Holt, Rinehart and Winston, 1979), p. 58.

73. Axthelm, op. cit., p. ix.

74. LaFeber, op. cit., p.92.

75. The phenomenon is described in Robert H. Frank and Philip J. Cook, *The Winner-Take-All Society: Why the Few at the Top Get So Much More Than the Rest of Us* (New York: Penguin Books, 1996).

76. Ibid., p. 101.

77. Ibid., pp. 103–104.

78. At the time it attracted the largest total television audience of any such game. Championship games played in subsequent years had more viewers but never as high a proportion of the total possible television audience. Bjarkman, op. cit., p. 53; Markovits and Hellerman, op. cit., p. 149.

79. In the Russell era, however, the two teams met for the NBA championship six times and the Celtics won all six.

80. The first title came in the National Basketball League, before the Lakers joined the rival Basketball Association of America that became the National Basketball Association.

81. The Celtics won three times in five attempts, losing the other two to the Lakers. Johnson's Lakers, over the course of his career, won five of the nine championship rounds in which they participated, losing once to the Celtics.

82. "One preseason toward the ends of their careers, an interviewer approached Magic and Larry separately with the same questions. 'How do you motivate yourself after all these years? How do you get yourself ready for one more season?'

'I think of Magic,' Larry replied. 'Wherever he is, I know how hard he's working.'

'It's Larry,' said Magic. 'Larry Legend. I'd *better* be working hard, 'cause I sure know he is.'" Wolff, *Small World, Big Game*, p. xvi.

83. All the games that Bird played in Boston were sold out, beginning with the first one. In Russell's thirteen seasons the Celtics almost never sold all available tickets for regular season games. Auerbach, op. cit., p. 50.

84. At the end of that decade ten teams were for sale or on the verge of bankruptcy and only six were profitable. LaFeber, op. cit., p. 48.

85. Halberstam, op. cit., pp. 237–238.

86. At the end of the 1970s the audience rating for the National Football League was 16.9, for major league baseball 13.5, for college football 12.8, and for the NBA 5.6. Even auto racing and golf, not to mention college basketball, had more viewers than professional basketball. Bjarkman, op. cit., p. 105.

87. The first championship series in which they opposed each other earned a television rating of 7.6. Three years later, the rating for the series matching the same two teams was 16. David Halberstam, *Playing for Keeps: Michael Jordan and the World He Made* (New York: Random House, 1999), p. 133.

88. Duke did so in 1991 and 1992.

89. The NBA also had a three-point line, which was located twenty-two feet from the basket on the sides of the court and twenty-three feet, nine inches around the rest of the perimeter of the basket.

90. In the first year of the three-point rule, one out of every 6.4 field goal attempts came from three-point range. Fifteen years later the ratio was one in every 3.1 shots. Grant Wahl, "The 3 is the Key," *Sports Illustrated*, March 18, 2002, p. 42.

91. Vitale differed in appearance from most other sportscasters in one striking way: He was bald. Cosell had worn a hairpiece. Vitale disdained wearing one.

92. The number was subsequently increased to sixty-five and the last two teams met in a "play-in" game to determine which one would gain entry to the actual tournament.

93. "Madness" here connoted excitement, not insanity.

94. The same theme is found in English soccer in the Football Association Cup competition, which any team can enter and that, at the outset of the twenty-first century, more than six hundred teams did enter. In one match in January 2003, one of the mightiest English teams, Arsenal, played against semi-professional Farnborough. At the beginning of the competition bookmakers gave odds on Arsenal's winning as 11 to 4, and on Farnborough as 10,000 to 1. Arsenal won the game, 5 to 1. George Vecsey, "Democracy in Action in England's F.A. Cup," *The New York Times*, January 26, 2003, Sports Section, p. 5.

95. LaFeber, op. cit., pp. 131, 169.

96. Michael Hiestand, "Spanning the Globe," *USA Today*, April 30, 2002, p. 2C.

97. Ibid.

98. The next season began with more non-American players—seventy-three—from fewer countries outside the United States—thirty-four. Simon Kuper, "Courting warmer international relations," *Financial Times*, December 20/21, 2003, p. W20. College teams also imported players from abroad. For the 2001–2002 season, for example, of the ten scholarship players on the University of Hawaii team, eight came from outside the United States. Kelli Anderson, "Rainbow Coalition," *Sports Illustrated*, January 28, 2002, p. 82.

99. Steve Hirdt, "Foreign Legions," *ESPN The Magazine*, February 17, 2003, p. 16.

100. LaFeber, op. cit., p. 101.

101. Halberstam, *Playing for Keeps*, p. 132.

102. Jordan's collegiate career gave him a direct connection to the origins of the game. His coach at North Carolina, Dean Smith, had played at Kansas for Phog Allen, the colleague of and successor in that position to James Naismith.

103. He launched a second comeback in 2001 with a team of which he had become part owner, the Washington Wizards. He played well for two seasons but could not lift the team to success. In both years the Wizards failed even to qualify for the postseason playoffs, let alone win the championship.

104. In 2003, when the English soccer star David Beckham joined the Spanish team Real Madrid, he chose to wear number 23 in honor of Michael Jordan. "Bedlam Greets Beckham in Madrid," *The New York Times*, July 3, 2003, p. C11.

105. LaFeber's book, *Michael Jordan and the New Global Capitalism*, has as its wider subject the economic globalization of the latter part of the twentieth century. Halberstam's *Playing for Keeps: Michael Jordan and the World He Made* is a history of the NBA in the 1980s and 1990s, seen as both a commercial entity and one of the many mini-societies embedded in the larger society of the United States. That book, together with Halberstam's predecessor volume on the same subject, *The Breaks of the Game*, give the best available overview of professional basketball in the years after the reign of Bill Russell's Boston Celtics, the last three decades of the twentieth century, as well as an excellent appreciation of the major personalities in that period and the texture of the society that they, the coaches, and the owners formed. Halberstam also wrote notable books on major league baseball: *The Summer of '49* (New York: Morrow and Company, 1989), and *The Teammates: Portrait of Friendship* (New York: Hyperion, 2003).

106. Halberstam, *Playing for Keeps*, pp. 6, 8, 334.

107. LaFeber, op. cit., p. 133. Jordan's popularity carried over to his second comeback, with the Washington Wizards. In his first year with the team it experienced the greatest increase in average attendance of any of the twenty-nine NBA franchises. Marty Burns, "In terms of dollars, Jordan was NBA's real MVP," CNNSI.com, May 7, 2002, p. 1. Jordan's absence from the championship series coincided with declining television ratings. In 2003 the games attracted the smallest viewership in twenty years. Rachel Nichols, "NBA Finals Ratings Lowest Since 1981," *The Washington Post*, June 17, 2003, p. D4.

108. LaFeber, op. cit., p. 134.

109. The company whose shoes he endorsed, Nike, also prospered. In 1984 its net worth was $919 million and its revenues $40 million. By 1997 those figures were $9 billion and $800 million. Halberstam, *Playing for Keeps*, p. 413.

110. Ibid., p. 417.

111. Ibid., p. 4.

112. LaFeber, op. cit., p. 14. In Mandarin Chinese Jordan's name was composed of two characters. "*Qiao* means 'skillful,' 'ingenious,' and 'clever.' It has connotations of honor and honesty. *Dan* is a term from medicine suggesting miraculous power. But *dan* also indicates the verb 'to shoulder or carry'—to take upon oneself. And *dan* signifies the color red, with its associations of action, celebration, and authority, in addition to the esteemed Oxen [Bulls] for which Qiao Dan played. Thus the Chinese could essentially sound out Jordan's English surname while conveying in their own tongue the attributes they associated with him." Wolff, *Big Game, Small World*, pp. 246–247.

113. Halberstam, *Playing for Keeps*, p. 397.

114. Ibid., p. 402.

115. Ibid., p. 10.

116. The former Celtic player and coach Tom Heinsohn once asserted that "anybody who averages 30 points is hurting his team." Rosen, op. cit., p. 119. Jordan averaged more than thirty points per game over the course of his career.

117. As the emphasis on acrobatic, Jordan-like "moves" increased, shooting skills also declined in both the college and professional games. See Alexander Wolff, "Just Do It Right," *Sports Illustrated*, November 25, 2002, and Dan Ackman, "Nothing But Air? Shooting Skills Waning in NBA," *The Wall Street Journal*, June 3, 2003, p. D5.

118. The league itself reinforced the point by organizing its slam-dunk competition, with the winner the player judged to have performed the most difficult and acrobatic maneuver.

119. It was not only players whose salaries soared. When Phil Jackson entered the league as a player for the New York Knickerbockers in 1967, his annual salary was $30,000. Three decades later, as the Chicago Bulls coach, he received twice that amount for each game. Halberstam, *Playing for Keeps*, p. 54.

120. The shoes could be expensive, with some selling for upwards of $200 per pair. They were highly prized, so much so that instances were reported of youngsters being murdered for their shoes.

121. Halberstam, *Playing for Keeps*, p. 132.

Conclusion: The Future of Sports

1. Leonard Shapiro, "Series' Ratings Hit All-Time Low," *The Washington Post*, October 29, 2002, p. D1. The ratings for the 2003 World Series were also low, lower in fact than those for any championship other than those of 2000 and 2002.

2. Andrew Zimbalist, *May The Best Team Win: Baseball Economics and Public Policy* (Washington, D.C.: Brookings Institution Press, 2003), pp. 42–53.

3. Ibid., p. xiii.

4. Ibid., pp. 5, 55–74.

5. The second half of the twentieth century also saw the decline of boxing, the most warlike, because the most explicitly violent, of individual sports.

6. Some misconduct involved taking advantage of opportunities available only to athletes. "Forty-four former [Philadelphia] Eagles cheerleaders added six more NFL teams to their suit claiming players watched them through peepholes from the visiting team's locker room as they showered and changed." *The Washington Post*, January 10, 2002, p. D5. Not only athletes but coaches as well turned out to behave badly. In May 2003, the head coaches of the University of Alabama football team and the Iowa State University men's basketball team were dismissed from their positions for improper conduct, under the influence of alcohol, with young women to whom they were not married.

7. O. J. Simpson was the most celebrated athlete charged with murder but not the only one. Another professional football player, Rae Carruth, was tried and convicted of paying someone to kill his pregnant girl friend. In 2003 Kobe Bryant, as famous for his exploits in basketball as Simpson had been for his football career, was charged with rape. Like Simpson's murder trial, the Bryant case attracted enormous attention from the media.

8. The subtitle was *My Life and Hard Times Throwing the Knuckleball in the Big Leagues* (New York: World Publications, 1970).

9. Geoffrey Ward and Ken Burns, *Baseball: An Illustrated History* (New York: Alfred A. Knopf, 1994), p. 421.

10. Shaun Powell, "Take It From 'Ball Four' Author: Wells' Book Strikes Out," *Newsday*, March 6, 2003, pp. A66–67.

11. Selena Roberts, "Blazers Gain Reputation for Misbehavior," *The New York Times*, December 11, 2002, p. C 20.

12. This was so even though the sympathy the public might have felt for young men in trouble was undoubtedly reduced by the fact that these particular young men were, as a result of the astronomical increases in players' salaries, far wealthier than the members of the public whose patronage supported them. In the European context, soccer became, in the words of one French observer, "twenty-two of the newly rich playing for millions of the newly poor." Xavier Rivoire, "Les mots et les shows," *Le Figaro*, May 29, 2002, p. 13.

13. Some athletes did not even suffer in this way for their misconduct, even when it involved a brush with the law. "After being in a murder trial, Ray Lewis is more popular than ever. He has got national endorsements, including one for EA Sports. . . . Latrell Sprewell choked his coach, went to the biggest media market in America, then rehabilitated his image in less than 24 months to become something of a media darling." Michael Wilbon, "The 'Unseemly' Reality of Celebrity Notoriety," *The Washington Post*, August 7, 2003, p. D1. See also Frank Deford, "A sorry trend," CNNSI.com, July 23, 2003.

14. These drugs are particularly useful to, and so particularly widely used by, athletes in individual sports, which led the way in banning them. The most notorious violation of their prohibitions involved Ben Johnson, a Canadian sprinter who was stripped of the gold medal he had been awarded for winning the 100-meter dash in the 1988 Olympic Games when his use of a proscribed compound was discovered.

15. During his record-setting 1998 season McGwire was found to be taking androstenedione, a steriod-like substance that was not prohibited by baseball's rules.

16. In 2003 Amerians spent more money on video games than on movie tickets. David Kushner, "Be A Virtual Superstar Athlete," *Parade*, November 23, 2003, p. 12.

17. Quoted in Virginia Postrel, "Economic Scene," *The New York Times*, April 25, 2002, p. C2.

Epilogue

1. "There have been about 200 times when I've said to myself, 'Holy crap, I can't believe that happened.' I have the same giddy conversations with the same giddy people. Every Red Sox fan is the same—we can't believe what happened, we can't get over what happened, we don't want to get over what happened." Bill Simmons, "Red Sox Nation," *ESPN The Magazine*, December 20, 2004, p. 81.

2. On the devotion of Red Sox fans see Leigh Montville, *Why Not Us? The 86-Year Journey of the Boston Red Sox Fans from Unparalleled Suffering to the Promised Land of the 2004 World Series* (New York: PublicAffairs, 2004). Some college football teams compare with the Red Sox in the intensity of their supporters' attachment to them. See, for example, Warren St. John, *Rammer, Jammer, Yellow Hammer* (New York: Crown Books, 2004).

3. "... pilgrimages to the deceased ... were repeated throughout the graveyards of New England. The totems changed, but the sentiments remained the same. At Mount Auburn Cemetery in Cambridge, for instance, gravestones were decorated with Red Sox pennants, hats, jerseys, baseballs, license plates and a hand-painted pumpkin." Tom Verducci, "Sportsmen of the Year," *Sports Illustrated*, December 6, 2004, p. 61.

4. See above, p. 59.

5. See above, p. 77.

6. "Curt Schilling, the All-Star pitcher, memorably told *Sports Illustrated* in 2002, 'Guys out there look like Mr. Potato Head, with a head and arms and six or seven body parts that just don't look right.'" Michael Sokolove, "The Lab Animal," *The New York Times Magazine*, January 18, 2004, p. 33.

7. See above, pp. 10–11.

8. In fact the use of steroids was not the only difference between the conditions in which Babe Ruth played and the era of McGwire and Bonds, and some of those differences actually made hitting easier for Ruth than it was for them. Ruth traveled shorter distances, had fewer night games, played in a park more favorable for hitting home runs, and did not compete with African-Americans or Latin Americans, whom Major League Baseball did not accept in his day.

On the other hand, Aaron played in an era in which, because of a larger strike zone and higher pitchers' mounds, home runs were *more* difficult to hit than was the case in the 1990s. In the competition for the career home run record, the metaphorical playing field was tilted against him and in favor of Bonds.

9. "In fact, baseball's record book never listed Maris's total with an asterisk—it received a separate line alongside Ruth's for 30 years..." Alan Schwarz, "Finding a Power Stroke When Most Hitters Start to Fade," *The New York Times Sports Sunday*, December 12, 2004, p. 4.

10. Tom Verducci, "The Asterisk Era?," *Sports Illustrated*, March 15, 2004, p. 39.

11. See above, pp. 66–7.

12. This was the second year in a row with such a result. The year before Oklahoma and Louisiana State University had played in the championship game while USC, which, like the two of them, had lost only once, was omitted.

13. There are also two additional divisions—II and III—in college football.

14. Ray Glier, "Division I-AA Has Game Plan for Division I-A Playoff," *The New York Times*, "Sports Sunday," December 19, 2004, p. 6.

15. See above, pp. 143–4.

16. See above, pp. 155–7.

17. "Among those who made the last-minute switch: writers in Austin, Dallas, and Fort Worth, Texas." Stewart Mandel, "Intrigue and Injustice," *si.com*, December 6, 2004.

    "Helping push Texas past California into the Rose Bowl at the last minute, four voting coaches placed Cal at a curiously low No. 7, two placed Cal at a farcically low No. 8, two placed Texas at a comically high No. 3, and one placed Texas at a farcically high No. 2." Chuck Culpepper, "Chuck Culpepper's Top 25," *Newsday*, December 10, 2004, p. A98.

18. Jack McCallum, "The Ugliest Game," *Sports Illustrated*, November 29, 2004, pp. 44–5.

19. Red Auerbach and John Feinstein, *Let Me Tell You a Story: A Lifetime in the Game* (New York: Little Brown, 2004), p. 285. In St. Louis one night "some guy comes out of the stands, walks up to like three feet away from me, and throws an egg in my face. Got me right in the forehead." *Ibid.*, p. 284.

20. McCallum, *op. cit.*, p. 46.

21. See above, pp. 263–71.

INDEX

ABOUT THE AUTHOR

Anne Mandelbaum

Michael Mandelbaum, the Christian A. Herter Professor of American Foreign Policy at The Johns Hopkins University School of Advanced International Studies in Washington, D.C., is a life-long sports fan, as well as one of the nation's leading authorities on American foreign policy and international relations. He is the author or co-author of eight other books, including *The Ideas That Conquered the World: Peace, Democracy, and Free Markets in the Twenty-first Century*.

PublicAffairs is a publishing house founded in 1997. It is a tribute to the standards, values, and flair of three persons who have served as mentors to countless reporters, writers, editors, and book people of all kinds, including me.

I.F. STONE, proprietor of *I. F. Stone's Weekly*, combined a commitment to the First Amendment with entrepreneurial zeal and reporting skill and became one of the great independent journalists in American history. At the age of eighty, Izzy published *The Trial of Socrates*, which was a national bestseller. He wrote the book after he taught himself ancient Greek.

BENJAMIN C. BRADLEE was for nearly thirty years the charismatic editorial leader of *The Washington Post*. It was Ben who gave the *Post* the range and courage to pursue such historic issues as Watergate. He supported his reporters with a tenacity that made them fearless and it is no accident that so many became authors of influential, best-selling books.

ROBERT L. BERNSTEIN, the chief executive of Random House for more than a quarter century, guided one of the nation's premier publishing houses. Bob was personally responsible for many books of political dissent and argument that challenged tyranny around the globe. He is also the founder and longtime chair of Human Rights Watch, one of the most respected human rights organizations in the world.

For fifty years, the banner of Public Affairs Press was carried by its owner Morris B. Schnapper, who published Gandhi, Nasser, Toynbee, Truman, and about 1,500 other authors. In 1983, Schnapper was described by *The Washington Post* as "a redoubtable gadfly." His legacy will endure in the books to come.

Peter Osnos, *Founder and Editor-at-Large*

Made in the USA
Lexington, KY
26 September 2011